GANGSTER
GOVERNMENT

GANGSTER GOVERNMENT

BARACK OBAMA AND THE NEW WASHINGTON THUGOCRACY

DAVID FREDDOSO

Since 1947
REGNERY
PUBLISHING, INC.
An Eagle Publishing Company • Washington, DC

Library of Congress Cataloging-in-Publication Data

    Freddoso, David.
      Gangster government / by David Freddoso.
        p. cm.
      Includes bibliographical references and index.
      ISBN 978-1-59698-648-0
      1. United States--Politics and government--2009- 2. Obama,
Barack. I. Title.
      E907.F74 2011
      973.932--dc22

                                  2011006594

Published in the United States by
Regnery Publishing, Inc.
One Massachusetts Avenue, NW
Washington, DC 20001
www.regnery.com

Manufactured in the United States of America

10 9 8 7 6 5 4 3 2 1

Books are available in quantity for promotional or premium use. Write to Director of Special Sales, Regnery Publishing, Inc., One Massachusetts Avenue NW, Washington, DC 20001, for information on discounts and terms or call (202) 216-0600.

Distributed to the trade by:
Perseus Distribution
387 Park Avenue South
New York, NY 10016

Nire hartzatxuentzat:
"Ez nekeak, ez da bide txarra."

CONTENTS

	Foreword by Michael Barone	ix
Chapter One	"Gangster Government"	1
Chapter Two	Stop Us If You Can: Saving the UAW	17
Chapter Three	On the Precipice: Obamacare	53
Chapter Four	The Most Expensive Story Ever Told	81
Chapter Five	We're Gonna Help Our Friends: Big Labor	117
Chapter Six	We're Gonna Help Our Friends: The Trial Lawyers	141
Chapter Seven	"We're Gonna Punish Our Enemies"	157
Chapter Eight	Recovering from Gangster Government	189
	Acknowledgments	207
	Notes	209
	Index	249

FOREWORD

BY MICHAEL BARONE

"We have just seen an episode," I wrote in a May 5, 2009, column in the *Washington Examiner*, "of Gangster Government." The subject of the column was the Chrysler bankruptcy package that was being hammered out by White House advisers Steven Rattner and Ron Bloom. Ordinarily in bankruptcy secured creditors—those who lent money only on the contractual promise that if the debt was unpaid they'd get specific property back—are paid off in full before any payment goes to unsecured creditors.

But in the case of Chrysler, the Obama administration insisted that Chrysler's bondholders, who were secured creditors, would get only about 29 cents on the dollar, while United Auto Workers retirees, who were unsecured creditors, would get about 50 cents on the dollar. More than that, Barack Obama made a point of referring to the bondholders as "speculators." And one of the bondholders' lawyers claimed that his client "was directly threatened by the White House in essence compelled to withdraw its opposition to the deal under threat that the full force of the White House press corps would destroy its reputation if it continued to fight." An odd threat—except that Rattner is widely known to be one of the best friends of the publisher of the *New York Times*.

This was a case of the White House transferring the property of one group of people to another group to which it owed political debts. The UAW has long been one of the Democratic party's strongest supporters, and labor unions contributed $400 million to Democratic campaigns in the 2008 cycle. Those contributions apparently paid off.

Some may consider this an isolated episode. Others may point out that it's possible to identify episodes of gangster government in previous administrations of both political parties. But, as I predicted at the end of my May 2009 column, this was part of a continuing series, for two reasons.

First, under the Obama administration, the federal government became intertwined with the private sector in unprecedented ways. It owns large shares of two large auto companies and what was one of the nation's largest insurance companies. It extended enormous loans to the nation's largest banks. The administration's defenders can point out, accurately, that some of these measures were initially taken in circumstances of financial emergency during the Bush administration. But that administration was not responsible for actions taken after January 20, 2009.

The second reason that this administration seems unusually inclined toward gangster government is the philosophy of its leader. When asked what he looked for when choosing a nominee for the Supreme Court, Barack Obama said he wanted "someone who understands justice is not just about some abstract legal theory," but someone who has "empathy." In other words, judges should decide cases so that the right people win, not according to the rule of law. The president himself taught law at the University of Chicago. But his principles seem to be conducive to the kind of gangster government the city of Chicago has from time to time experienced.

But let the facts speak for themselves, as assembled and presented by my *Washington Examiner* colleague David Freddoso. As in his 2008 book, *The Case Against Barack Obama: The Unlikely Rise and Unexamined Agenda of the Media's Favorite Candidate*, Freddoso is self-confessedly not a partisan of the president. But he is also a fine reporter who respects the facts and refuses to draw unwarranted conclusions. He understands that people sometimes have good motives to do bad things.

Gangster government is always a danger, whoever is in power. It is a greater danger the more government is deeply enmeshed with the private sector and when its leaders believe that rules should be bent or ignored in order to benefit favored constituencies. So thanks to David Freddoso for providing a report that enables citizens to decide just how far gangster government has gone in this administration.

> ***Michael Barone** is senior political analyst for the **Washington Examiner**, resident fellow at the American Enterprise Institute, and co-author of* **The Almanac of American Politics**.

CHAPTER ONE

"GANGSTER GOVERNMENT"

"Were these acts committed on a petty scale and detected, they would be severely punished—the perpetrator suffering great disgrace. Those who commit such petty crimes are called temple robbers, kidnappers, burglars, con-men and thieves. But if only a man will go to the additional trouble of relieving his victims of their freedom, along with the contents of their pocketbooks—if only he turns them from citizens into slaves—why, then, instead of suffering insults and accusations, he is deemed happy and blessed, not only by his victims, but by all who hear that he has ascended to the very pinnacle of perfect injustice."

—*Thrasymachus in Plato's* **Republic.**[1]

To his admirers, President Barack Obama is a philosopher king—or a philosopher president—as this snippet from the *New York Times* suggests:

In New York City last week to give a standing-room-only lecture about his forthcoming intellectual biography, "Reading Obama: Dreams, Hopes, and the American Political Tradition," [Harvard historian James T. Kloppenberg] explained that he sees Mr. Obama as a kind of philosopher president, a rare breed that can be found only a handful of times in American history.

"There's John Adams, Thomas Jefferson, James Madison and John Quincy Adams, then Abraham Lincoln and in the 20th century just Woodrow Wilson," he said.[2]

His vice president, Joseph Biden, informs us that Obama only comes off as aloof because "he's *so* brilliant. He *is* an intellectual."[3]

His longtime friend and White House advisor, Valerie Jarrett, reminds us, through author David Remnick, that Obama is like no ordinary man:

I think Barack knew that he had God-given talents that were extraordinary. He knows exactly how smart he is….He knows how perceptive he is. He knows what a good reader of people he is. And he knows that he has the ability—the extraordinary, uncanny ability—to take a thousand different perspectives, digest them and make sense out of them, and I think that he has never really been challenged intellectually….So, what I sensed in him was not just a restless spirit but somebody with such extraordinary talents that had to be really taxed in order for him to be happy…. He's been bored to death his whole life. He's just too talented to do what ordinary people do.[4]

Newsweek's Evan Thomas says Obama's greater than any small idea like America. He compares him to another recent president—and to the Almighty:

Reagan was all about America…. Obama is "We are above that now." We're not just parochial, we're not just chauvinistic, we're not just provincial. We stand for something—I mean in a way Obama's standing above the country, above—above the world, he's sort of God….[5]

Sort of God. The One. The Light-Worker. The Philosopher President.

Descriptions like these abound in our mainstream media, where our president's fan club never loses its zeal. But they do not apply so well to the real Barack Obama—the one who comes from the murky politics of Chicago and

Springfield, Illinois. The one who won his first election for state Senate by throwing all of his opponents off the ballot.[6] The reputedly arrogant and prickly state senator who nearly got into a fist fight with one of his state Senate colleagues in 1997, declaring to him on the Senate floor, "I'm going to kick your ass!"[7]

The Obama of media myth also bears no resemblance to the president of the United States whom we've seen over the last two years—the one who refers to his political adversaries as "teabaggers" (which as liberals snickeringly know refers to an obscene sexual practice), and talks about "punishing" his enemies.

Obama didn't come to Washington from Mount Olympus. He came from the corrupt and dirty politics of Chicago. "Philosopher" seems like the wrong word for anyone who got ahead by forging so many unsavory but expedient political alliances with Chicago politicians. Rod Blagojevich and Tony Rezko do not strike one as types who "pal around" with philosophers.

Neither does Mayor Richard M. Daley, an Obama political ally whose brother William now serves as Obama's chief of staff. Daley's ways are captured well within Obama's 2008 campaign boast: "If they bring a knife to the fight, we bring a gun."[8]

It's the Chicago way.

That's what Mayor Daley was doing at 1:30 on the morning of March 31, 2003. Instead of guns, he brought bulldozers. They suddenly appeared along the lakefront at Merrill C. Meigs Field, a small airstrip built in 1948 on a man-made island in Lake Michigan. Its runways, used mainly by small private planes, were just a few hundred yards from the city's vibrant downtown. The airport was valued for its convenience to downtown, and had reportedly been a favorite landing point for Republican Governor Jim Edgar. Meigs was also the site where a non-profit organization that honors the Tuskegee Airmen gave free monthly flights to introduce inner-city children to air travel in its Young Eagles program.[9]

The Chicago Park District owned the land on which the airfield operated. Daley had been trying to close Meigs for years and turn it into a park. He tried to shut it down in 1996 by refusing to renew its lease. The state legislature had responded by threatening to take it over.

Daley backed down—for a time. And in December 2001, it appeared the matter had been settled for good. Daley struck an agreement with the legislature and Republican Governor George Ryan to keep Meigs open until 2026 in exchange for a bill in Congress to guarantee federal approval of the expansion of O'Hare International Airport on the outskirts of town.

But when Daley did not immediately get his end of the deal—Illinois Republican Senator Pete Fitzgerald, a longtime opponent of O'Hare's expansion, filibustered the bill—the mayor exacted his revenge with bulldozers. He was sending a clear message to anyone who might think of crossing him in the future. Their engines roaring, the city's bulldozers gouged gigantic X-marks in the 3,900-foot runway, rendering it useless.

The destruction came as a complete surprise to the airport staff in the tower, federal authorities, pilots, Democrat Governor Rod Blagojevich, all fifty of the city's Aldermen, members of Congress who had been working on the O'Hare deal, and even the Department of Homeland Security.[10]

Mayor Daley had also not bothered to inform the Federal Aviation Administration—whose regulations require at least a month's notice before an airport can be shut down—until the moment the demolition began, with a letter to the FAA dated March 31. The mayor's office also claimed that someone informed the FAA "orally." Perhaps this was a phone call, shouted over the roar of the bulldozers. In the aftermath, Daley's lawyers argued the city had no choice but to redirect federal funds intended for Chicago's other two airports to demolish this busy little airfield, because it had been "abandoned." No one had told that to the owners of the sixteen small planes that were left stranded on the field.

The feds didn't buy any of this, and the city ultimately paid the maximum fine the FAA could charge them under the law for destroying the airfield. Unfortunately, that came to a pathetic $33,100.[11] But Chicago at least evaded justice on the count that it had illegally diverted federal money from its other airports to destroy Meigs. The city was fortunate enough to settle the case with the FAA for just $1 million. It could have been fined as much as $9 million. Daley spent at least $200,000 on outside lawyers to defend his overreach.[12]

But if you're the mayor of Chicago, it's better to ask forgiveness than it is to lose the initiative and become just one more little person who lives under and not above the law.

Years later, a similar line of thinking helped President Obama squeeze his health care reform bill through Congress by one vote, despite overwhelming public opposition. To tamp down discontent over this unconstitutional manifestation of Hope and Change, congressional leaders offered as reassurance, "We have to pass the bill so you can find out what is in it."[13]

At first, Daley claimed that the destruction of Meigs had been a homeland security matter: "Those airplanes appear to be going to Meigs, but with a sudden turn they could cause a terrible tragedy downtown or in our crowded parks. That scares me."[14]

It was a naked lie that he never really tried to back up. When asked, Homeland Security Secretary Tom Ridge said that no one had consulted him or his department about the matter at all. Ridge said the fate of the airport was none of his business, but he also pointed out that the plans to close Meigs predated 9/11 by many years.[15]

Not that it mattered. Nobody believed Daley's cover story, and he probably didn't care if they did. As for the security implications, the airport's closure, and the eventual elimination of its airspace classification meant that there would be less, not more, control over planes flying through downtown Chicago's lower altitudes.

After Ridge's comments, Daley offered instead an explanation of how wonderful it would be to have a park in the airfield's place, on Northerly Island: "That's what makes Chicago unique from the rest of the world," he said. "That we have protected this wonderful lakefront."

Actually, what makes Chicago unique, or at least noteworthy, is that it is a municipal dictatorship. Its politics are both crooked and brutal. Its elected officials believe, almost to a man, that they are above the law. The story of Meigs is a typical story of "gangster government," of ends justifying the means, of government power being abused to reward friends and punish enemies.

That's how things work in Chicago. Daley got his park, and for decades hence, Chicagoans and visitors will be able to visit it and view a monument to what a civic leader can accomplish by ignoring the law and acting unilaterally. Daley eventually got his O'Hare expansion, too. With Barack Obama in the White House, it would become the most heavily federally subsidized airport renovation project in the history of the United States.[16]

ABOVE THE LAW

The professorial columnist Michael Barone, whose *Almanac of American Politics* is the essential reference on every Washington journalist's shelf, was the first to use the words "gangster government" to describe the Obama administration. He coined the phrase in May 2009 while describing how the Obama administration intervened in Chrysler's bankruptcy to make sure that the autoworker's union was protected at the expense of the firm's senior creditors:

> Think carefully about what's happening here. The White House, presumably car czar Steven Rattner and deputy Ron Bloom, is seeking to transfer the property of one group of people to another group that is politically favored. In the process, it is setting aside basic property rights in favor of rewarding the United Auto Workers for the support the union has given the Democratic Party.... We have just seen an episode of Gangster Government. It is likely to be part of a continuing series.[17]

Barone had sounded an alarm, but this was not alarmism. No one was suggesting that Barack Obama was a government version of Tony Soprano, who sends "Sicilian messages" or sells drugs or moonshine or untaxed cigarettes out of the White House basement. Gangster government is about something else: about governing without recognizing the legitimate limits of one's power. It's about officials who use public office to make winners into losers and losers into winners; who bend, break and make the law to help their friends and punish their enemies.

If you want to understand "gangster government," there's no better place to start than Chicago, the place where Barack Obama learned the art of politics from some of its most notorious figures. Obama has brought Chicago to Washington, not just in the sense that some of his most trusted aides and advisors hail from there—Mayor Daley's brother, Rahm Emanuel, David Axelrod, Valerie Jarrett—but also because the city has left a mark on him and his political methods.

In Chicago, politically connected contractors think it's safe to defraud the public. Political appointees run bribery and extortion rackets from their positions of power. City lots are sold to politically important pastors for a dollar in exchange for their support.[18] It's a place were city Aldermen fix tickets and firefighters' exams for friends and family, and extort business owners who need permits.[19] It's a place where the lowliest Alderman and the mightiest governor take kickbacks, put friends and relatives on the government payroll, and use their clout to get family members admitted to the state's prestigious flagship university in Urbana-Champaign.[20]

Not everyone in Chicago politics is on the make. Sitting at the top of Chicago's corrupt politics is Mayor Daley, who has never been credibly accused of pocketing a dime that wasn't his own. But as the Meigs case demonstrates, he has his own ways of showing that he believes he's above the law. And his dictatorial power has brought manna from heaven for many of those closest to him. *Chicago Tribune* columnist John Kass summed up what was wrong with the mayor's rule when he cited the "obscene amounts of taxpayer dollars that go to his pals. In deal after deal after deal, the attitude is that his guys can take what they want, and the people in the neighborhoods better shut up about it, while higher taxes put more and more pressure on families to pay for the deals."[21]

Daley survived almost unscathed through several major corruption scandals in his administration. In the Hired Truck program, taxpayers handed over $42 million a year to what was essentially a crime ring run by city employees. They fixed trucking contracts in exchange for bribes and contributions to Mayor Daley's campaign and his political organizations. It was all made possible by top Daley aides who manipulated the hiring process. One of them, Robert Sorich, just got out of prison in November 2010.[22]

Daley's longtime friends and supporters, the Duff family, milked the city for $100 million using bogus front-companies to win minority set-aside contracts.[23] James Duff, convicted in 2005, is scheduled for release in 2014.

In recent years, Daley's family has gotten into the act as well, demonstrating that political smarts don't necessarily run in the family. His son Patrick and his nephew, Robert Vanecko, bought into a sewer contractor at the right moment—just before it won $4 million in no-bid city work. They then cashed out, without ever revealing their involvement as the law required.[24] Their stake in the company had been deliberately concealed in the company's documents filed at City Hall.[25] The company has since folded, and its former president has been indicted for mail fraud.[26]

Vanecko went deeper into the swamp after this, teaming up with another Daley crony—President Obama's former law firm boss, Allison Davis—in a real estate investment venture called DV Urban Realty. Davis and Vanecko won a contract to invest $68 million in real estate from five Chicago city pension funds. Their management fee was a guaranteed $3 million, with the possibility of making nearly three times that amount by 2014.[27] In spring 2009, it was discovered that the city had paid $500,000 to lease one of the warehouses DV Urban had purchased. The lease was on a month-to-month basis—a temporary arrangement, apparently designed specifically in order to avoid getting approval from the City Council.[28] Vanecko quit DV Urban around the same time, two weeks after a federal grand jury began investigating the pension funds' decision to invest in the company.[29]

Daley and his cronies are hardly alone. This is the way important politicians in Chicago and Illinois operate—like they own the place.

Emil Jones, Jr., the former state Senate president, was Obama's political mentor from the moment Obama got to Springfield. For Jones, politics is a family affair. In 2008, he ensured his son, Emil Jones III, inherited his state Senate seat by waiting until after the primary election to announce his retirement. The younger Jones had begun public service by taking an unadvertised, $57,000-a-year job in state government—not bad for a 28-year-old without a college degree. The elder Jones had loyally sided with Democrat Governor Rod Blagojevich in every major intra-party fight in the legislature, and Blagojevich looked out for his friends.

In late 2005, the elder Jones married a Ph.D. psychologist who worked as a deputy director in the state Department of Human Services. At just the same time, she received a promotion and a $70,000 raise (to $186,000 a year), so that she was actually making more than the governor. As the AP noted: "[T]he agency proposed a special job category that applied only to her. The administration asked the Civil Service Commission to approve the new classification, arguing that it was necessary to attract high-quality candidates for a demanding job. But [Lorrie] Jones was already in the job."[30]

The *Chicago Sun-Times* reported in 2007 that Jones's stepson, tech contractor John Sterling, was doing more than $100 million in work for twelve different government agencies.[31] It's nice work if you can get it—and you probably can if you're related to Emil Jones. Wrote the *Sun-Times'* Carol Marin: "Illinois, after all, is not only the Land of Lincoln, it's also the Land of Coincidence."[32]

In terms of notoriety, former Governor Rod Blagojevich is now the top Chicago politician. His career serves as proof that everything in Illinois is for sale. Blagojevich's comical lack of restraint appears to be the only thing that kept him from a long, healthy life of corruption. As of this writing, he still stands accused of trying to sell President Obama's old Senate seat. But that high-profile scandal has perhaps overshadowed other important charges against him, which—like the scandals in Daley's office—help illustrate how the world of Illinois politics really works.

In 2002, Obama and Rahm Emanuel had been top advisors to Blagojevich's campaign.[33] But, the more interesting connection between Obama and Blagojevich is their mutual friend, the slumlord and political fixer Tony Rezko.

Prosecutors allege that Rezko, now a convicted felon (whom President Obama was forced to disown during his 2008 campaign), hired Blagojevich's wife to a no-show, no-work job at his real estate development company. According to court documents, this allowed Rezko to write her at least $150,000 in checks between 2003 and 2004.[34] Coincidentally, Rezko was very influential in getting Blagojevich to appoint his friends (including Obama's law firm boss Allison Davis) to important state boards.[35] Rezko even managed, with Blagojevich's direct intervention, to get one of his relatives into the University of Illinois at Urbana-Champaign, despite low ACT scores.[36]

According to prosecutors' evidentiary documents in Blagojevich's trial, Rezko was also paying regular cash bribes of $10,000 a pop to Blagojevich's chief of staff, Lon Monk. Those documents detail Monk's hilarious struggle to get Mrs. Blagojevich to do a better job pretending she actually worked in Rezko's office:

> Monk had conversations with Blagojevich and his wife about the need for her to actually go into the office to work on a regular basis. The problem with that approach, however, was that Blagojevich's wife was taking care of their infant daughter.

Monk talked with Rezko about the issue of Blagojevich's wife going to the office. Rezko was willing to do whatever it took to get her money, whether it was from a monthly retainer or through hiring her to work on his development....Rezko did not seem to care if she actually did anything to earn the money.[37]

This means of funneling money to Blagojevich is separate from Rezko's 2008 criminal conviction. That revolved around his conspiracy to shake down firms that sought to do business with state pension funds and make them give money to Blagojevich's campaign.[38]

So here's a question: Do you think that Rezko befriended Obama and gave and raised $168,000 for his campaigns, for different reasons than the ones behind his friendship with Rod Blagojevich? Do you think that Obama reciprocated his friendship because the two shared an interest in Kantian metaphysics?

Bearing in mind the more robust picture we have today of the Blagojevich-Rezko relationship, consider once more a question largely forgotten since Obama's election as president. In 2005, Rezko and Obama purchased adjoining pieces of land, from a seller who had insisted that both parcels—one with a house, and one an empty lot—sell at the same time. Without Rezko's purchase of the empty lot, Obama's purchase of the adjoining house would have at least been more complicated. And that is to say nothing of Obama's subsequent, unusual transaction in which he bought a ten-foot strip of land from Rezko later in the same year.

Why did Tony Rezko help Obama in this way? Obama is a very smart man. If he didn't think at all about Rezko's motives, perhaps he thought they didn't matter. In a city where every Alderman and state representative thinks he's above the law, they *usually don't matter*.

Barack Obama was not responsible for creating Chicago's seedy political scene. He was not one of its major players. But this is the milieu from which he emerged. And his own choices show he is not some demi-god immune to its ways.

To have Emil Jones as one's political godfather is a genuinely dubious distinction. Obama famously asked Jones to make him into the next

U.S. senator from Illinois. Jones did what he could, first by giving Obama other senators' popular bills to sponsor—including a deliberately toothless ethics bill designed to allow Jones to keep his $570,000 campaign war chest for himself.[39] While still in office, Jones was using the money to make interest-free loans to himself—which was legal under this ethics law—and he continues to loan himself the money today, in his retirement.[40] (The law does not require him to repay it, either.)

Jones also gave Obama a choice committee assignment, from which he could ingratiate himself with the SEIU, a labor union that would prove essential to his victory in the 2004 Senate primary.[41] Obama didn't forget. At the Democrats' 2008 nominating convention, he gave his patron a place on the dais, even though Jones had caused a stir by calling a black Hillary Clinton supporter an "Uncle Tom."[42]

In September 2008, as his campaign came under growing pressure to address his political godfather's behavior back in Illinois, Obama finally challenged Jones for what might have been the first time. He asked his political godfather to stop single-handedly blocking a modest ethics reform bill in the Illinois Senate.[43] Jones backed down. This, Obama's only significant contribution to the cause of reform in Illinois, came just as Obama ended his representation of the state permanently.

When it came to Mayor Daley, Obama always walked on eggshells. In August 2005, at the height of the scandals in Daley's office, a reporter from the *Sun-Times* asked Obama whether he would endorse Daley for re-election. At first, Obama blurted out that the corruption reports had given him "huge pause." Minutes later, he called back to walk back this unduly harsh comment and praise Daley, stating that Chicago has "never looked better."[44] That "huge pause" never returned. That was the most critical thing Obama ever said about Daley.

Like other Chicago politicians, Obama believes the end justifies the means. He has a Chicago politician's sense of entitlement. He shares with the others the notion that politics is about looking out for your friends. And yes, the philosopher president looks out for himself, too.

Upon his election to the Senate, his wife received a promotion and an almost 200 percent pay raise at the University of Chicago Hospital. Obama later requested a $1 million earmark for her generous employer.[45] When Mrs. Obama left her position job to become First Lady, the position was eliminated in a reorganization. Such things happen in the Land of Coincidence.

In *The Audacity of Hope*, Obama tells a story about how his credit card was declined by a rental car company at the 2000 Democratic Convention in Los Angeles.[46] Obama was then working as both a state senator (annual salary: $58,000) and a private attorney, but he had been neglecting his private law practice and it was a "very dry period" at his law firm.[47] Faced with difficult financial circumstances, Obama did what any American would have done under the circumstances: he got a wealthy political donor named Robert Blackwell to pay him $112,000 in legal retainers over a 14-month period. Meanwhile, Obama and one of his state Senate aides (who was moonlighting for Blackwell, which is somehow legal in Illinois) helped Blackwell's ping-pong company get $320,000 in state tourism grants.[48]

For a philosopher president, Obama knows his way around the system pretty well.

EXPANDING POWER

As president, Obama shows a healthy appetite for expanding government power and the federal government's indirect, subsidy-driven patronage, on a scale that makes Mayor Daley look like an apostle of Adam Smith. Gangster government on the federal level creates new, trillion-dollar opportunities. Our current president is not letting them go to waste.

- Obama has reached well beyond the federal government's constitutional powers. Our Founding Fathers could not have imagined a day when the nation's executive branch would guarantee the warranty on your car, fire business executives, or require Americans to purchase a commercial product, like health insurance, as a legal condition of living in the United States.
- Obama has dramatically intervened in the private sector, not just bailing out selected industries, but dictating how they will do business from now on.

- Obama has politicized the Department of Justice, endangering government's most important domestic function.
- Obama has appointed nominees to powerful positions who are unworthy of the public trust. Among his choices are people who have lied to Congress, cheated on their taxes, abused previous positions of authority, and received massive, hard-to-justify payoffs prior to entering public service. When their extremism or shady business dealings have been too ludicrous for Congress to overlook, Obama has simply bypassed the Senate with recess appointments, despite having a Democratic majority that could approve any reasonably acceptable liberal.
- Behind a thin veneer of concern about average Americans, Obama has displayed aggressive favoritism to the groups that got him elected. This favortism comes at average Americans' expense, and at the expense of government integrity and effectiveness.
- Obama has used the appearance of "transparency" to mollify those overseeing his administration, all the while concealing the business-as-usual nature of its affairs. Even as his administration was revealing the names of White House visitors in a laudable and unprecedented fashion, his aides were concealing countless meetings with lobbyists by holding them in locations outside the White House grounds.[49]

The automotive bailout, finalized in the opening days of Obama's presidency, provided an early taste of things to come. In order to save a politically important union—a cash-rich but member-poor stronghold in the dying world of organized labor—Obama bailed out GM and Chrysler with tens of billions of dollars in taxpayers' cash. He hired a team of bureaucrats to run the two automakers and to manipulate the bankruptcy and tax codes to the United Auto Workers' advantage.

Obama was not content to turn the federal government into the world's largest automotive investor. He went on with a stimulus package that turned the federal government into what the *Wall Street Journal* called the world's largest private equity firm.[50] With the health care bill, he effectively made Uncle Sam the world's largest human resources firm, insurance claims adjuster, hospital administrator, and even primary care provider.

Gangster government views the private sector sometimes as its handmaiden, and other times as its adversary. Obama's administration speaks of American business with casual comments like this one: "You don't want to kill the golden goose, but you don't want it to crap all over you either."[51] His officials have deprived lenders of their money, telling them, "I don't need lenders."[52]

Gangster government is arrogantly confident that its business-novice officials know more about creating prosperity than businessmen do. It knows more about health care than the nation's doctors. Witness Obama's famous comments:

> If there's a blue pill and a red pill, and the blue pill is half the price of the red pill and works just as well, why not pay half price for the thing that's going to make you well? ...
>
> [Y]ou come in and you've got a bad sore throat, or your child has a bad sore throat or has repeated sore throats, the doctor may look at the reimbursement system and say to himself, you know what, I make a lot more money if I take this kid's tonsils out.[53]

Gangster government is also politically reckless, arrogant, and tone-deaf. When Congressman Marion Berry of Arkansas, a five-term moderate Democrat, expressed his concern that the health care law would cause a repeat of the Republican victories of 1994, Obama replied, "Well, the big difference here and in '94 was you've got me.'"[54]

For all the high-minded reform rhetoric of his 2008 campaign, all the talk of a "new politics," all the passages in his books about respecting others' points of view, Obama's response to people who objected to his administration's massive expansion of federal power was to deride and insult them. He didn't merely criticize his political opponents or conservative talk radio hosts, he disparaged and belittled *the voters* who disagreed with him as irrational or "teabaggers."[55] Of Republicans, as noted, he said, "They can come for the ride, but they have to sit in back."[56] As for listening to other points of view, he said, "I don't want the folks who created the mess to do a lot of talking."[57]

Accordingly, his White House has sought out new bogeymen to attack nearly every month—both high-profile targets, like FOX News, and obscure ones, like the Koch family. It is a pattern of behavior to which his predecessor, for all his faults, never descended. If it resembled the behavior of another president, it was Richard Nixon with his enemies list.

The philosopher Plato wrote thousands of pages of dialogues on what makes for good government, good law, and good leadership. At one point in *The Republic*, a character named Polemarchus offered this notion:

> [J]ustice is that craft which provides good to friends and evil to enemies.[58]

It has been more than 2,300 years since this proposition was refuted in Socratic dialogue, but it lives on in modern times. In the heat of the moment, on the campaign trail and fearful of a huge congressional election loss in 2010, President Obama offered this:

> We're gonna punish our enemies and we're gonna reward our friends who stand with us on issues that are important to us.[59]

This book will take a sober look at the momentous first two years of a presidential administration that lives by this rule. It will examine Obama's subversion of our Constitution and laws and cast a hard look at a president whose training on Chicago's political playground shines through with every bent law and every broken promise.

CHAPTER TWO

STOP US IF YOU CAN: SAVING THE UAW

The Tea Party and its predecessors, who eschewed federal loans to GM, simply got it wrong, failing to perceive that a "bailout"can just as easily be called an "investment."[1]

That was *Newsweek*'s reaction to the successful initial public offering (IPO) of General Motors common stock in November 2010. Taxpayers were supposed to be impressed that the new GM did not immediately lose half of its value. Swept aside were the fact that the company had just been relieved of $65 billion in liabilities through a kangaroo bankruptcy proceeding, infused with $50 billion from taxpayers, given an additional $14 billion toward future federal taxes (in spite of tax laws to the contrary), and even exempted during its IPO from anti-fraud statutes.[2]

With those advantages, nearly any bad company could have put on a successful IPO. But only GM and Chrysler got it, when in fact both companies probably deserved to be liquidated, and to have the grounds of their head-quarters salted for good measure.

GM's demise in late 2008 was the culmination of decades of poorly designed automobiles, reckless cannibalization of the company by its union, and a corporate culture that both tolerated and fostered terrible business practices.

We don't need to view the bailout from the outside. We have as our guide the Obama administration's former car czar, Steve Rattner. In his book on the bailout, *Overhaul*, Rattner is clearly proud of what he and his team accomplished. Yet he also unwittingly provides as strong an argument against the bailout as any conservative writer could serve up.

Overhaul offers the reader as many details as any taxpayer can reasonably stomach about GM's hapless management and its CEO, Rick Wagoner. For as White House aides and bureaucrats scrambled to find a way to save the company, GM's directors and managers fiddled. Asked to save themselves, they drew up unrealistic "viability plans" which simply assumed the company's way back to prosperity and growing market share.

From the very beginning, when they were still dealing with officials from the exiting Bush administration, GM's top brass exuded supreme confidence that the government would not fail to rescue a company as important as theirs. Bush and Obama—but especially Obama—proved them right.

The following excerpts from Rattner's book tell the story in brief:

- "'No one had a list of all the GM bank accounts worldwide,' a GM adviser told us."[3]
- "The GM team seemed placidly to take for granted that somehow, some way, the government would agree to its requests."[4]
- "The overall concept seemed to be to trim only what was easily achieved and absolutely necessary, and use taxpayer dollars to ride out the recession."[5]
- "GM seemed to be living in a fantasy that, despite the evidence of decades of decline, it was still the greatest carmaker on earth, in a class by itself."[6]
- "Laid-off workers received 95 percent of their normal pay."[7]
- "Under the UAW contract, auto-workers got paid nearly the same whether they built cars or not. [GM, Ford, and Chrysler] actually maintained 'rubber rooms' where idled workers could job-hunt, watch TV, and work crossword puzzles while they collected pay."[8]
- "[Nissan CEO Carlos Ghosn] had approached Rick Wagoner as early as June 2006 about taking a 20 percent stake in GM,

but Wagoner persuaded his board to rebuff the deal, in part to save his own job as CEO."[9]

- "The 'viability plan' delivered by GM in February had proven management incapable of dispassionately and analytically creating an achievable business plan."[10]
- "From 1995 through 2008, GM had lost a third of its U.S. market share. There was absolutely no justification for the increase in market share that GM had assumed as part of its viability report...."[11]
- "Our task force would later learn that, on Wagoner's instructions, GM was making no contingency plans, no preparations whatsoever for a possible bankruptcy filing....This attitude would add materially to the cost of the eventual rescue."[12]

After reading about "rubber-rooms" and laid-off workers who make 95 percent of their salaries, it probably won't surprise you that with its extremely generous worker and retiree health plan, General Motors had become the world's largest purchaser of Viagra,[13] or that generous retiree benefits were adding $1,500 to the cost of each car.

Nor should it be a shock that GM had let itself become so utterly dependent on one supplier, Delphi, that it had no choice but to pump hundreds of millions of dollars into the bankrupt company with no hope of return. "Incredibly," Rattner writes, "GM had never tried to stockpile critical components in the event of a Delphi shutdown, nor had it done any meaningful work to create alternative sources of supply."[14] As a result, a single supplier was able to hold a gun to GM's head and extort cash at any time—and it did so, even in the midst of the bailout.

Rattner's view of GM is dim indeed. As you read his comments, bear in mind that this is the man who saved the company with your money. The miracle is not that this company was saved, but that anyone was dumb enough to save it.

For that, President Obama can be thanked. He chose to throw good money after bad because the money was not his own. It was yours. And the money involved in the GM and Chrysler bailouts—about $80.1 billion from taxpayers—saved the United Auto Workers[15] from the total irrelevance that would have resulted from its having no autoworkers to represent.

It is unconscionable that billions of dollars of taxpayer money were flushed to save GM, Chrysler, and especially the UAW. But far worse is the Obama administration's blithe disregard for the Constitution in bailing out the automakers and rewarding its friends at the UAW. The bailout was run essentially without congressional oversight or approval. It set new precedents for government interference in business. It required the stretching of tax and bankruptcy laws to the breaking point. And it undermined investors' and creditors' faith in America's free-market system, just when that faith was most important.

This is a story of a presidential administration helping its friends at the expense of everyone else, simply because it could. It is a story of gangster government.

DETROIT'S FORTUNATE SONS

If anyone wonders whether the automotive bailout was all about saving a union, the answer is yes. There is no other reason why two domestic automotive manufacturers—both historically significant, but neither remotely indispensible to the economy—would get the bailout they did when nearly 90,000 businesses failed in the financial crisis and received no government help.[16]

As recently as 2007, the UAW had gone on strike against both Chrysler and GM, demanding higher wages, more benefits, and more favorable work rules—the kind of rules that had GM paying 7,500 workers to sit in "Rubber Rooms" and do nothing while it was losing $10 billion a year.[17] By mid-2009, both GM and Chrysler were teetering. Chrysler was so close to liquidation that Obama's task force seriously debated killing it off and rolling its good assets into GM—White House economic advisor Austan Goolsbee was especially fond of this plan, which he argued would have strengthened the other automakers. In the end, Rattner writes, "The case for saving Chrysler was based more on political and social reality" than on any business reality.[18]

As president-elect, Barack Obama embraced President Bush's first steps toward the bailout—the lending of a combined $17.4 billion to the two automakers. But as president, Obama went much further than a few loans. His team essentially ran the companies for months, transformed their operations, replaced their senior managers, and set the terms for their future. They also manipulated the bankruptcy process to steer a significant amount of the companies' equity to the UAW, and used the stimulus package and some creative regulation to alter the tax code to give the automakers advantages that reorganized companies do not normally enjoy.

The UAW had everything at stake in the automakers' survival. It made some relatively minor concessions, such as making access to "Rubber Rooms" a temporary benefit rather than a permanent one and agreeing to lower wages for *new hires*—all the way down to $14 per hour—so that its current members could continue to collect base pay greater than twice that amount.[19] But the UAW was allowed to continue to exist. Since 2001, it had already lost half its membership (falling from 702,000 to 355,000 active members).[20] By the time of their bankruptcies, GM and Chrysler together employed some 77,600 UAW members.[21] Tens of thousands more worked for various auto parts suppliers that depended on the companies' survival, including 17,000 members at Delphi alone.[22] With so many union jobs at stake, the government rigged the companies' bankruptcies so that the UAW would emerge stronger than any of the other stakeholders, including taxpayers.

If GM and Chrysler had not been bailed out, the UAW could have lost about a third of its active membership. UAW would have easily lost the majority of its autoworkers—as of 2007, before the economy's swoon, Ford employed only 72,000 UAW workers.[23] What would have remained was the union's growing share of lower-wage workers that it has recruited only recently, including 40,000 graduate students, janitors, clerical workers, and adjunct faculty on college campuses.[24]

By 2000, the UAW had already amassed over $1 billion in investment assets, most of it the union's much-vaunted strike fund. It was still sitting on this mountain of cash in 2009. If it was willing to empty out the strike fund, the union could have continued to exist without GM and Chrysler—but why?

Without a bailout, the UAW was just a full vault with no autoworkers left to represent.

The UAW has 518 officers and employees in its national headquarters who draw six-figure salaries, according to its 2010 filings with the Labor Department.[25] How long could they justify this arrangement without members?

Unionism is on the decline. Import car brands are gaining market share. Manufacturing is moving increasingly to right-to-work states in the South. New UAW hires are paid significantly less than their older colleagues. All of these trends suggest that the union's membership will not be rebounding any time soon. And so even the union's massive strike fund can only last so long. In the long run, someone has to pay all of those big salaries at headquarters, fund the union's $10 million annual lobbying and political activity expenditures, and maintain its money-losing $7.5 million golf course in northern Michigan.

Rattner goes on for pages describing the hemming and hawing of then-UAW President Ron Gettelfinger over the terms of the GM bankruptcy. Gettelfinger wanted corporate bonds, not GM stock, in exchange for the union's unsecured claims against the old GM.[26] He did not want the union's benefits to be subjected to the whims of the market or to depend on the health of the company. But on the inside, Gettelfinger had to be laughing during the negotiations. His union's benefits fund was getting something more valuable than the debt-ridden GM's promises; it was getting a bailout from the more reliable Uncle Sam. It was getting the common stock of a company whose good assets were intact, and which would be nearly debt-free after a kangaroo bankruptcy. Judge Robert Gerber made GM's bondholders—unsecured creditors like the UAW—take a backseat, in order to "prevent the death of the patient on the operating table."[27]

Unspoken were the facts that this patient was only being kept alive at the federal government's insistence, and that the UAW would be the chief beneficiary of its survival.

The UAW sold one-third of its GM stock in November 2010, and was on pace to collect 100 percent of what GM had owed it, if it could just sell the rest for an average of $36 per share—just above the IPO price.[28] (The stock was already trading above that level as of this writing.) The taxpayers did not do nearly as well. A January 2011 report from the Congressional Oversight Panel explained that taxpayers are certain to lose billions on the deal:

> [I]t is important to note that Treasury received a price of $33.00 per share—well below the $44.59 needed to be on track to recover fully taxpayers' money. By selling stock for less than this break-even price, Treasury essentially "locked in" a loss of billions of dollars and thus greatly reduced the likelihood that taxpayers will ever be repaid in full.[29]

The UAW's 55 percent stake in the post-bankruptcy Chrysler was also a lot more than they would have received, but for the intervention of Gangster Government. Both bailouts were pretty sweet deals for the UAW.

Yet the union deserved a major part of the blame for dragging down the automakers. In 2006, the cost of each UAW union man-hour at GM—including wages, employers' payroll taxes, unemployment and disability insurance, pension and health benefits—stood at $73, far exceeding the labor costs of Toyota's U.S. operations (estimated at $48 per hour in 2005) or Honda's ($43 per hour in 2005).[30] Chrysler's figure was even worse—it cost them nearly $76 per hour worked by a UAW employee.

Thanks to the UAW, GM and Chrysler could not reduce these costs through layoffs (they would only be filling up "Rubber Rooms"), and so GM resorted to buy-outs. In order to bring labor costs down closer to $60 per hour, the company spent $3.8 billion in 2006 buying out 34,000 of its higher-paid veterans. Over the next two years, the company bought out 32,000 more workers and shifted billions of dollars—and responsibility for health benefits—to a new UAW benefits fund.

This is the fund into which the bankruptcy put 17.5 percent of GM's common stock and 55 percent of Chrysler's—the one the taxpayers have bailed out. Also among the beneficiaries of this bailout were the UAW workers at Delphi, the poorly run GM supplier that had been spun off from the poorly run GM. Delphi had been running on fumes since its own prolonged bankruptcy process began in 2005.

The government's pension insurance agency, the Pension Benefit Guaranty Corporation, was taking over employee pensions at Delphi, meaning 20 to 40 percent cuts in pensions and a complete loss of retirees' health and life insurance benefits. The Obama administration, however, decided to funnel money through the new GM to sweeten this sour deal, but *only for the company's UAW employees.* The bailed-out GM would not be honoring pension commitments to Delphi's salaried, non-union employees.[31] The overt favoritism of this deal prompted the *Washington Post* to ask one of the most important questions about the auto bailout: "The Obama administration's auto task force... concluded that GM's commitment to the UAW was legally binding on a taxpayer-owned post-bankruptcy GM.... But why did the administration make pension obligations to the UAW sacrosanct in the first place?"[32] (To rephrase the question, do you think President Obama cares about winning Michigan in 2012?)

Rattner admits that he failed to use a "once-in-a-lifetime opportunity" to curb the over-generous work-rules, pay, and pension benefits the UAW had negotiated with the complacent management of the automakers.[33] When it came to pensions, his team reasoned that "attacking the union's sacred cow after virtually every other issue had been resolved could jeopardize the whole agreement."[34] This only raises the question of whose interest they were acting in: The union's? Obama's? Their own, given that "success" for them meant simply getting a deal done and avoiding the automakers' liquidation? It seems unlikely that they were working in the taxpayers' interests.

But the Obama administration certainly had a profound interest in the UAW. As *Washington Examiner* reporter Tim Carney noted, "The autoworker union's political action committee spent $13.1 million on the 2008 election. If you take the PACs [political action committees] of Exxon, Halliburton, Peabody Coal, and Lockheed Martin, combine their 2008-cycle political spending, *and multiply by four,* you get just over $13.1 million."[35]

Five million of those dollars went directly to help Obama. But that's just the union's PAC. Its other political activities are rolled into its annual figure of $9.5 to $10.5 million in lobbying and political expenditures; and as a member-union of the AFL-CIO, the UAW is an important part of a much larger political operation.

The bailout saved the UAW and satisfied an important rule of Gangster Government: you help your friends—especially the ones who help you most.

RUNNING AMERICA LIKE HE OWNS IT

Try to imagine any other situation in which a team of consultants comes into a failing company and oversees a complete turnaround. They replace its hapless management with competent stewards, change the ownership, improve its business strategy, and overhaul its archaic accounting practices. They push the company through bankruptcy in an incredibly short time—a mere matter of months—and then bring about a successful IPO just as the company posts a profitable quarter.

Viewed in those terms, it's not hard to see why Steve Rattner is so proud of what he did as Obama's car czar. If you think of this as a pure business transaction, the GM bailout would be a great American business success story.

But there's one detail in the story that changes everything: the entire process was directed by the heavy hand of government. All of the money that made the bailout possible came from taxpayers. And without the irresistible weight of the U.S. Treasury Department behind every step of the transaction, there is no way it could have occurred. We know what was gained: two automotive giants were propped up, at least for a while, and a politically powerful union was protected and even rewarded. But what was lost?

The first casualty was the free-market system that supposedly defines America's economy. However over-regulated that system is, however much it is distorted by lobbyists who secure corporate welfare subsidies, most Americans still believe that America has a vibrant and dynamic economy in which good businesses can thrive. An entrepreneur with a good idea can still find investors, make a fortune, employ his fellow Americans, and pass something along to his children. A bad business will go under, and the capital and labor wasted there will find new, more profitable uses in the hands of others.

Government's role is supposed to be that of a fair broker. Government enforces contracts. It makes laws and ensures that all parties obey them. It prevents and punishes fraud against consumers and harm to innocent bystanders. It treats all parties on an equal footing.

But gangster government doesn't do any of these things—and it was gangster government that took over the economic management of two failing corporations in order to reward its friends in the UAW at the expense of taxpayers, Chrysler's secured creditors, Delphi's non-union retirees, and the bailed out automakers' competitors.

Rattner writes that the bailout was necessary because "GM embodied the intimate connection between the free capital markets and the social and political contract on which they depend. It could not be allowed to disappear."[36] In other words, Uncle Sam should bail out any company, no matter how bad, if the president deems it sufficiently iconic (that is, if it has enough potential votes attached to it). To Rattner, some businesses are indeed "too big to fail," and we can expect future bailouts. WalMart, General Electric, IBM, and UPS all have more U.S. employees than the pre-bailout GM. If they ever fall prey to bad management, there is now a precedent for saving them at taxpayers' expense. Some future government functionary in Rattner's former position will be telling us why it's all necessary, and government bureaucrats will take over and run these businesses until they conform to whatever model the government deems best.

Another casualty of the bailout was respect for the Constitution and the rule of law. In school we're taught that the founders instituted checks and balances so that no one branch of government could become too powerful and steamroll the others. Compare your civics lessons with Rattner's striking reflection on the automotive bailout and the state of American politics today:

> The auto rescue succeeded in no small part because we did not
> have to deal with Congress … I was stunned to realize that if the
> task force had not been able to operate under the aegis of TARP,
> we would have been subject to endless congressional posturing,
> deliberating, bickering, and micromanagement, in the midst of
> which one or more of the troubled companies under our care
> would have gone bankrupt.[37]

That does not sound like a civics lesson. But it gets worse:

> Either Congress needs to get its act together or we should explore
> alternatives....If our country wants to do a better job of solving
> its problems, it needs to find a way to let talented government
> officials operate more like they do in the private sector.

In short, Rattner believes "talented government officials" should do what they like with taxpayers' money, unhindered by Congress. Presumably, the "talented government officials" he has in mind are Democrats. Rattner has donated some $800,000 to the Democratic Party, and his wife, Maureen White, is a Democratic National Committee finance chair.

But Rattner is also a creature of Wall Street. His previous career involved cajoling public officials into paying him and his Quadrangle investment group millions of dollars to manage their billions of dollars worth of pension funds.

Even as Rattner was taking the job as auto czar, federal authorities suspected that some of Rattner's methods of "persuasion" of New York State pension officials were really just illegal kickback schemes. He allegedly won business with the state by trading favors with the staff of disgraced former Comptroller Alan Hevesi and funneling money to his campaign.

After leaving the White House, Rattner was forced to settle a Securities and Exchange Commission action against him related to this issue for $6.2 million.[38] The settlement includes a two-year ban on associating with investment professionals. After that settlement, then-New York Attorney General Andrew Cuomo sued Rattner to recover alleged ill-gotten gains. Rattner settled again, this time for $10 million, and agreed to a five-year ban on dealings with New York's pension funds.[39]

Neither of Rattner's settlements involved any admission of wrongdoing. For $16.2 million, you can pretty much avoid admitting anything.

But Rattner's idea, that a small group of well-insulated executives should run things in America without oversight, is an interesting one that says a lot about gangster government. He couches it in terms of making government look more like the private sector. But our Founding Founders understood that there was a difference between public and private. The private sector is and should be driven by self-interest and the profit motive. Government, on the other hand, should be disinterested in outcomes and safeguard the rights of all.

The founders would have been horrified at the Rattner model—at someone governing America *as if he owned it.* They consciously strove to frustrate people like Rattner and President Obama, who will pay any price in liberty to see government *get things done.* For such accomplishment usually comes at the expense of freedom, fairness, and property rights.

BLANK CHECK

But as Rattner's comments suggest, the *get-things-done* crowd outsmarted the founders and the safeguards of our constitutional system during the automotive bailout. When President Bush threw GM and Chrysler their first lifelines (with President-elect Obama's assent), he did so without congressional approval. After Congress voted specifically to prevent an auto bailout, Bush turned to the overly broad and hastily written TARP statute, which Congress had passed under extreme duress and threats from Treasury Secretary Hank Paulson that their failure to act would cause financial Armageddon.

When TARP was under consideration, I spoke to Republican Congressman John Shadegg of Arizona, who told me that Paulson "was attempting to use fear…in an effort to stampede the Congress." Paulson tricked the Congress into giving a blank check to Presidents Bush and Obama.

President Obama took full advantage of this unlimited political line of credit, using TARP as a justification for limitless executive meddling in economic decisions best left to private stakeholders. He has acted in keeping with the famous strategy that his chief of staff, Rahm Emanuel, shared with the *Wall Street Journal*: "You never want a serious crisis to go to waste…. This crisis provides the opportunity for us to do things that you could not do before."[40]

And Obama certainly did do things that "you could not do before," like making the United States government the majority shareholder in an automaker without congressional approval. As Rattner observed, it was the only way to make the deal work.[41] President Obama saw no need to involve Congress in such decisions. So he certainly wasn't going to consult them on such minor matters as whether Uncle Sam should be backing warrantees on new cars. (Rattner's estimate of the cost of that decision alone is $600 million.)[42]

All of this "accomplishment" stands in rather stark contrast with the plain language of the TARP statute. It permitted the Secretary of the Treasury to purchase "troubled assets" from "financial institutions," which are defined thus:

> The term "financial institution" means any institution, including, but not limited to, any bank, savings association, credit union, security broker or dealer, or insurance company, established and regulated under the laws of the United States or any State, territory, or possession of the United States, the District of Columbia, Commonwealth of Puerto Rico, Commonwealth of Northern Mariana Islands, Guam, American Samoa, or the United States Virgin Islands, and having significant operations in the United States, but excluding any central bank of, or institution owned by, a foreign government.[43]

It is no small feat to make this definition apply to GM or Chrysler, yet apply it they did. That's what the words "included, but not limited to" are for. So if you find yourself in financial trouble, consider writing the Secretary of the Treasury. Under TARP, he could probably even deem your family a financial institution.

President Bush erred when he said he had "abandoned free market principles to save the free market system."[44] What he had really done was write his successor a blank check.

Consider the irony: Chrysler, where Rattner writes that a worker "could not so much as tighten a screw if it was not in his job description,"[45] was now being run by government officials who certainly did not have "running a car company" in their constitutional or statutory job descriptions. Obama's automotive task force made nearly every important decision about the automakers' operations and future in 2009.

Rattner fired GM's hapless CEO Rick Wagoner, something he had no legal right to do (even if it was a good idea from a business perspective). He later forced out GM's acting chairman and recruited its new chairman, Ed Whitacre. Rattner's task force hand-picked staff, micromanaged GM's relationships with its suppliers and foreign subsidiaries, chose the facilities it would close, chose the brands it would kill, set the pace at which it would shed dealerships, and even at one point considered forcing GM to move from its iconic Detroit headquarters.[46]

Rattner writes that he and his team did what they could to make it look like GM and Chrysler were making the decisions themselves, but this was only for show. "As we drafted press statements and fact sheets, I would constantly force myself to write that 'GM' had done such and such," Rattner writes. "Just once I would have liked to write 'we' instead."[47]

And Rattner's reflections are borne out by the public record. It was obvious who was pulling the strings at Chrysler, but it became a lot more obvious when the once-secret emails between Treasury and Chrysler officials saw the light of day in bankruptcy court. *The Wall Street Journal* reported on one string of emails, which included then-CEO Bob Nardelli and other Chrysler officials, as well as Rattner's deputy, Ron Bloom:

> Chrysler quickly learned to defer to the Treasury team. In one email chain, Ron Bloom of the Treasury chastised a Chrysler official for trying to hammer out some lingering issues with Daimler, Chrysler's former partner, without looping in the Treasury.
>
> "I am more than a little surprised," Mr. Bloom wrote, that Chrysler was proceeding "without our approval."
>
> Mr. Nardelli jumped in: "Ron, thought we were helping, how would you like to handle!"
>
> Later, the Chrysler executives deleted Mr. Bloom from the address line, and continued talking. "I guess the UST is running it!" said Mr. Nardelli, referring to the Treasury.

In one of the emails, a Chrysler official even referred to the Treasury Department as "God."[48]

Aside from the government's highly irregular decision to take a 60 percent ownership stake in GM, there were several other irregularities in the bailout. For example, the IRS bars companies from carrying their operating losses through major changes in ownership. Congress did this deliberately in 1986. The idea was to prevent large, profitable companies from buying up cheap losers at tax time, so that they could avoid taxes by applying bad companies' losses against their own profits.

But buried just over halfway through President Obama's 400-page stimulus law is a carefully written provision allowing such tax write-offs, and it applies only to companies that emerge from bankruptcy under majority ownership of a union benefits fund.[49] How many of those do you suppose there are?

Majority union ownership had been the plan for both automakers as early as February 12, 2009, when this provision was first added to the bill. In Chrysler's case, that's how it worked out—the UAW benefits fund became the majority owner. But late in the game, in May 2009, it became clear that the government would have to take majority ownership of GM if the deal was to work.[50] So in order to give GM the same special tax break, the IRS had to create an exception to tax law for bailed-out companies.[51]

This means that the first $45 billion that the new GM makes over the next twenty years will be tax-free. In effect, the owners of the new GM will get all the benefits of GM's losses while suffering none of their negative consequences. Taxpayers have been put on the hook not only for GM's $50 billion bailout, but for an additional effective tax credit estimated at $14 billion to $16 billion.[52] GM would pay no taxes at all in liquidation, so this is not a total loss. But if the company had been liquidated, some company or combination of companies would have acquired GM's good assets and likely made a taxable profit from them. (A good use would likely have been found for many of the company's skilled workers, too, but this possibility seems never to have occurred to the Obama administration's central planners.)

It is difficult to imagine any company not controlled by the president of the United States receiving this kind of treatment.

In addition to the tax bailout, GM's turnaround was made possible by the White House's deft manipulation of the bankruptcy code. In an attempt to hasten the process, Rattner's team employed the same tactics against the judiciary as Secretary Paulson had used on Congress to get TARP passed:

> In the fine print of the $33.3 billion of debtor-in-possession financing that we'd extended to the company, [the team] set a deadline of July 10. At the end of that time—a scant 40 days!—either the Treasury would have to extend its financing or GM would be forced to liquidate. This was the financial equivalent of putting a gun to the heads of the bankruptcy judge, GM's stakeholders, and of course Team Auto itself.[53]

A gun to the head. That's gangster government, when at every turn the government manipulates law and process to achieve its aims.

"I DON'T NEED LENDERS"

More than 160 years ago, the witty French economist Frédéric Bastiat wrote a famous essay, "That Which Is Seen and That Which Is Not Seen."[54] He identified what we call the "broken window fallacy," which wrongly holds that if a boy breaks a window, he's actually stimulating the economy because he's created business for the glazier. Bastiat notes that this is wrong because it neglects the hidden costs to people who might have otherwise received the money spent on fixing the window, like the baker or the cobbler. Their loss is *unseen* because it represents something that never happened—sales that never materialized, improvements that could not be made because a window had to be purchased.

Bastiat would have laughed at President Obama's "Cash for Clunkers" program, which Rattner's team had conjured up during the bailout. "Cash for Clunkers" effectively gave out taxpayers' money in exchange for destroying useful capital—automobiles that were, by the law's requirements, drivable, and, in many cases, perfectly good. Car owners and dealers were given government handouts of up to $4,000 in trade toward new, fuel-efficient cars. Nice for them, but not so nice for the taxpayers who got stuck with the bill for each act of economic sabotage.

Bastiat's insights are useful, too, for recalling the many *unseen* costs of the automotive bailout, as Dan Ikenson of *Forbes* noted:

> Had GM been forced to severely atrophy or liquidate, the other automakers would have had greater revenues, more market share, and probably higher profits. They would have been able to attract GM's best engineers and line workers. They would have more money to invest in R&D and to lead the industry into the future. Instead, by keeping GM in the mix, some of those industry resources remain misallocated in a company that the evolutionary market process would have made smaller or extinct....
>
> By rescuing GM, the government overrode market forces, and there are significant costs to assign for that. Witness the stagnant economy with 9.6 percent unemployment. Is it not plausible that businesses are sitting on their cash and not investing or hiring because of the fear inspired by the government interventions starting with the bank and auto bailouts? It's more than plausible. The regime uncertainty that persists to this day was spawned by the GM bailout and other interventions.[55]

We will never know how many workers *would have been hired* had the market been given the proper opportunity to reallocate the capital misused by bad businesses like GM and Chrysler. Nor will we ever know how many entrepreneurs lost opportunities to take the ashes of GM's and Chrysler's failure and turn them into a new and profitable phoenix.

In the case of the Chrysler bailout, there were many hidden victims, but there were also very visible ones: particularly the company's secured creditors. The theft they suffered was the most egregious irregularity in the automotive bailout, and it gave rise to the cry of "Gangster Government" in the first place.[56] Secured creditors, whose rights in bankruptcy the law considers sacred, were manhandled by the Obama administration so that a UAW benefits fund could take 55 percent of the new Chrysler's equity.

Chrysler's assets were sold to a newly created shell company, which assumed the identity of New Chrysler. Mark Roe of Harvard Law and David Skeel of the University of Pennsylvania Law School, writing in the *Michigan Law Review*, described the transaction thus:

> [T]he totality is that Old Chrysler was reorganized in Chapter 11 via a pseudo-sale to a shell company controlled by those who controlled Old Chrysler. It's no more a sale than if you move your wallet from your coat pocket to another pocket and drop a few dollars along the way; you haven't sold or bought anything. *Chrysler* was a de facto reorganization, not an arm's-length sale.[57]

The underlying legal fiction of the transaction effectively allowed Chrysler to reap the benefits of a Chapter 11 bankruptcy while shirking its obligations to the company's secured creditors, who were owed $6.9 billion in all.

Secured creditors are entitled to full repayment before unsecured creditors are entitled to anything. In situations like the one at Chrysler, where the company was worth little in liquidation but the business still had value as a going concern, they would normally be offered equity in the new firm in exchange for their cooperation, because the law gives them so much leverage.[58] But that wasn't going to happen in the restructuring of Chrysler, because the equity had already been committed to the UAW.

"We have other plans for [the equity]," Rattner told the representative of Chrysler's secured creditors. And Rattner's Obama-appointed deputy, Ron Bloom, chimed in with a perfect gangster government quip: "I need workers to make cars, but I don't need lenders."[59]

Of course, the American economy does need lenders, something Obama kept reminding everyone as he funneled taxpayer money to shore up Wall Street and the banks with TARP, the AIG bailout, and a bevy of big government projects, including parts of the stimulus package. Yet here he was, undermining the confidence of all lenders that their obligations would be honored. Given this manipulation by gangster government, why would wise investors ever lend to any large American business again? At any moment, a presidential appointee can step in, say, "I don't need you," and steer your money to a labor union.

Ironically, with Citigroup, JP Morgan, and Goldman Sachs, Obama was bailing them out through TARP even as he was stiffing them in the Chrysler deal. It's no wonder the larger secured creditors went along even as the smaller ones resisted.

When President Obama vilified Chrysler's small creditors—the ones who had not taken any TARP money and were therefore not beholden to his administration—Rattner suddenly realized there might be a problem. "For my part, I hadn't adequately anticipated the extent to which the President's statement, together with our disparate treatment of the various stakeholders, would constitute another frightening message to a Wall Street already shaken by repeated attacks from Washington."[60]

Obama's denunciation of the creditors was harsh. It also left no room for misunderstanding about who was pulling the strings:

> While many stakeholders made sacrifices and worked construc- tively, I have to tell you some did not. In particular, a group of investment firms and hedge funds decided to hold out for the prospect of an unjustified taxpayer-funded bailout. They were hoping that everybody else would make sacrifices, and they would have to make none. Some demanded twice the return that other lenders were getting. I don't stand with them. I stand with Chrys- ler's employees and their families and communities. I stand with Chrysler's management, its dealers, and its suppliers. I stand with the millions of Americans who own and want to buy Chrysler cars. I don't stand with those who held out when everybody else is making sacrifices. And that's why I'm supporting Chrysler's plans to use our bankruptcy laws to clear away its remaining obligations so the company can get back on its feet and onto a path of success.
>
> Because of the fact that the UAW and many of the banks, the biggest stakeholders in this whole process have already aligned,

have already agreed, this process will be quick. It will be efficient. It's designed to deal with those last few holdouts, and it will be controlled.... [I]t was unacceptable to let a small group of speculators endanger Chrysler's future by refusing to sacrifice like everyone else. So I recognize that the path we're taking is hard. But as is often the case, the hard path is the right one.[61]

Those are the words of a man who *doesn't need lenders.*

The stakeholders repudiated by Obama were simply creditors trying to preserve their legal claim to a slightly larger portion of the money they were owed. With his statement, the president showed how much he respected property rights.

Obama and the man he hired as Rattner's deputy—Ron Bloom, a former investment banker and consigliere for the president of the Steelworkers' Union—share a view of how business should be subordinated to the power and will of government. In 2006, the newsletter *Democratic Left* reproduced one of Bloom's more revealing speeches in op-ed form:

In today's world the blather about free trade, free-markets and the joys of competition is nothing but pablum for the suckers. The guys making the real money know that outsized returns are available to those who find the industries that get the system to work for them and the companies within those industries that dominate them.

Does anyone seriously think that the free-marketeers at Goldman Sachs have such staggering returns on equity because all they know is what everyone else knows? Did Bill Gates accumulate a net worth larger than the entire bottom third of our nation because he kept the playing field level? In the real world, he who makes the rules of the game, rules the game.[62]

How true. And how fitting that such a crony capitalist and manipulator of the rules would lead the Obama administration's charge over the mangled bodies of Chrysler's secured creditors.

Sponge off taxpayers. Loot creditors. He who makes the rules of the game, rules the game.

And the non-rulemakers? They're roadkill. Like the non-union retirees of Delphi and Chrysler's secured creditors. Like the taxpayers. They get nothing except the distinction of being gangster government's victims.

ROADKILL

Chrysler wanted a special favor from the bankruptcy courts—an opportunity to shed its obligations to its secured creditors, yet keep all of its good assets. This was to be done through what is known as a Section 363 asset sale. This provision of the law existed in order to save value where it would literally disappear in a short time—for example, if an orchard goes into bankruptcy and its fruit is on the verge of going bad unless it is sold right away.

Chrysler's team rushed to the bankruptcy court in New York City at the moment of Obama's April 30 speech, Rattner writes, because they wanted to make sure their case was heard in the most favorable venue possible.[63] They feared that Tom Lauria, who was representing some of Chrysler's secured creditors, would initiate a case by suing somewhere else to stop them. For as one bankruptcy attorney explained to *Michigan Business Review*, "This jurisdiction, the Second Circuit, New York in particular, has done this frequently.... In other circuits it wouldn't be allowed."[64]

The reason it wouldn't be allowed is that the current bankruptcy code was created in part to prevent abuses precisely like the one that occurred in the Chrysler case. Roe and Skeel, the Ivy League law professors, described how insiders used to loot broke companies and preserve what value they could for friends, while shutting out other creditors:

> In the receiverships of the late nineteenth and early twentieth century, insiders would set up a dummy corporation to buy the failed company's assets. Some old creditors—the insiders—would come over to the new entity. Other, outsider creditors would be left behind, to claim against something less valuable, often an empty shell.[65]

This is exactly what happened in the Chrysler bankruptcy. Roe and Skeel argue that this case effectively reversed a 1913 Supreme Court decision which had pushed back strongly against such abusive practices and required that creditors' rights be respected.[66] "Change" was taking us back to the late nineteenth century.

Robert Manzo, Chrysler's financial advisor, submitted his estimated valuation of Chrysler to the court, asserting that in liquidation, Chrysler would be worth between $2.6 billion and $654 million to the secured creditors.[67] The higher estimate would have meant 38 cents on the dollar for secured creditors, a better deal than they were getting. The lower end estimate represented a 9 percent recovery.

No one had the opportunity to contradict these estimates in the hasty trial that followed, and this low estimate of value certainly served the interests of those seeking to make the deal go through. But more importantly, everyone acknowledged that as a going concern, Old Chrysler was worth far more than the $2 billion that the New Chrysler (a shell company being funded and directed by the government) was paying old Chrysler. Remember that Chrysler, even as it filed for bankruptcy and claimed assets of just $2.6 billion, was promising $4.6 billion in stock to the UAW.

The company's value as a running business was as high as $25 billion. It was effectively transferring itself *to itself* for a mere fraction of this, with government pulling the strings on both ends of the sale. The purpose of the transaction was to leave less for the secured creditors, so that more spoils from the new company could be divided between the UAW, the Italian carmaker Fiat (which was being cut in on the deal), and the government.

What if someone else had wanted to bid? Gangster government had that possibility covered, as Skeel and Roe explain:

> With the Treasury and the UAW as parties who would evaluate the bids under the court-approved procedures, the court signaled that there would not be a substantial, serious bidding process, thereby chilling whatever outside interest existed in alternative configurations.[68]

Lauria and Indiana State Treasurer Richard Mourdock stood opposite the Obama administration at trial. Mourdock was representing the interests of his state pension and highway funds, which owned $42 million in secured Chrysler debt and wanted to see the law upheld. Mourdock's funds hadn't paid full price for it, but they were legally entitled to full price.

The first trial did not go well for him. This was mostly because of the gun that Rattner was putting to the judge's head. In order to meet the June 15 deadline that Obama's Treasury had set for restructuring Chrysler—an impossibly short window for such a complex case—the bankruptcy court had given the creditors' legal team just hours to depose dozens of people and compile its own comprehensive audit of Chrysler's assets.

The rush had to do with Fiat, the partner that the Treasury Department had hand-picked for Chrysler's arranged post-bankruptcy marriage. Perhaps the UAW needed this deal most, but Fiat probably got the best deal out of it. On the back of Indiana's pensioners and all of the other secured creditors, the Italian automaker was to get 20 percent of Chrysler's equity for…nothing. That's right, for free. The purported reason for the rushed sale was that Sergio Marchionne, Fiat's CEO, was threatening to back out of the deal otherwise—something Marchionne later denied.[69]

(After winning Chrysler's assets, Fiat announced that it will begin selling its own automobiles in America again—to be manufactured at a Chrysler plant in Mexico.[70] As Mourdock told me, bitterly, "We have a government that says it's okay to rip off our retirees and use the money to subsidize foreign companies.")

In his court briefs on behalf of the secured creditors, Lauria argued that the sale of Chrysler from one government-controlled company to another "constitutes an impermissible sub rosa plan of reorganization that strips the Chrysler Senior Lenders of the protections"—in other words, that it was a sham designed by government officials to cheat Lauria's clients out of their money. He argued that the sale price was less than the amount of the secured debt and therefore failed a condition of a 363 sale. And he also referred to President Obama as he pointed out the involvement of gangster government:

The sale of assets by the Debtors to New Chrysler is not a sale that was negotiated by independent parties at arm's length. Rather, it is a sale that was orchestrated entirely by the Treasury and foisted upon the Debtors without regard to corporate formalities, the fiduciary duties of the Debtors' officers and directors or the other important checks and balances typically found in good faith sales. Indeed, well before the filing, the Debtors had ceased to function as an independent company and had become an instrumentality of the government. President Obama, in his public statements, made it clear that the Debtors would be required to pursue the sale transaction with Fiat and ordered the Debtors to cease all efforts to pursue any other transaction. Both actions are clearly inconsistent with the requirements of a good faith sale. And, the government exerted extreme pressure to coerce all of the Debtors' constituencies into accepting a deal which is being done largely for the benefit of unsecured creditors at the expense of senior creditors.

Lauria also tried to separate out the simple matter of law before the court, versus irrelevant concerns about the survival of the domestic automotive industry:

The Debtors bear the burden to prove that the proposed sale is fair, equitable, in the interest of *the estate*, and not unfair to the creditors. The proposed sale fails each of these requirements. Recognizing this failure, the Sale Motion focuses largely on the interests of the United States economy, the automotive industry and other interests. But the focus of the inquiry has to be on the Debtors' creditors. The proposed sale is clearly unfair to them...[71]

The bankruptcy court ruled in favor of Obama's team anyway. Chrysler's internal email communications, which were filed in the district court just as the case ended, detail the inner workings of how the government was laboring to ensure as bad a deal for these creditors as possible. One particularly damning exchange came between Robert Manzo, Chrysler's financial advisor, and Obama Team Auto member Matt Feldman.

In the late evening of April 29, 2009, just hours before the bankruptcy papers were to be filed, Manzo wrote Feldman at his government email address to tell him it would not be hard to find a bit more money for the secured creditors who were holding out. Their demands, Manzo wrote, were not excessive, and the deal was "too close to not exhaust every avenue to get this done....We can easily find $250 million of savings to help fund this last piece. We have other ideas as well."

Feldman's thuggish, two-sentence reply came back two minutes later: "I'm now not talking to you. You went where you shouldn't."

Manzo, apparently in a panic, shot back this obsequious reply just five minutes later:

> Sorry. I didn't mean to say the wrong thing, but I obviously did. I was just trying to make sure that if we had to contribute to the solution you knew we had some room. Sorry I didn't realize it was a mistake!! Bob.

Feldman's response, which could have been lifted from the script of a mobster movie, came at 4:00 a.m.:

> It's over. The President doesn't negotiate second rounds. We've given and lent billions of dollars so your team could manage this properly. I've protected your management and Board and now your [sic] telling me you're going to put me in a position to have to bend to a terrorist like Lauria. That's BS.

So it's not that the secured creditors could not have gotten more of their money. It's just that they didn't, because gangster government didn't want them to.

"This wasn't about 'Hope and Change,'" Mourdock told me in an interview. "This was about 'Stop us if you can.'"

Mourdock finally got the decision he wanted—sort of—from the Supreme Court, on December 14, 2009. It was still a defeat for his pensioners, who would not get their money back, but it was also a partial vindication of the position he had taken in pursuing the case—a position that his Democratic opponent for re-election would use against him (to little effect) in 2010.

The Supreme Court remanded the Chrysler case to a lower court for dismissal on grounds that it was moot—for by that time, Fiat, the UAW, and the governments of the United States and Canada had all of Chrysler's equity. The high court, however, also vacated the appeals court decision that had approved gangster government's plan for the automakers. The Supreme Court effectively expunged from the books, and from the realm of precedent, the lower courts' rubber-stamping of the bankruptcy. No one would be able to cite the Chrysler case in a courtroom in an attempt to swindle secured creditors in the future.

"What we will never know," Mourdock said, "is how many billions of dollars in that critical period left this country to be invested overseas. If the words 'secured creditor' don't mean what they've always meant in our courts, then that money is going overseas, where they haven't changed the rules."

CAPTIVE INDUSTRY

"He who eats my bread sings my song."[72]

This is what auto czar Rattner remembers his father saying. It's another version of the admonition we probably all got from our parents—"As long as you're under my roof, you'll do as I say." Except in this case, the children were American industries co-opted by the Obama administration.

Mourdock and Chrysler's other small secured creditors had been holding out in negotiations for about 37 cents on each dollar they were owed, instead of the 29 cents they were being offered. This handful of hedge funds, representing in many cases university endowments and public pension funds for workers less influential than the UAW, stood to lose their shirts on this deal either way. They were just hoping to keep a few buttons.

But their biggest problem was that the larger secured creditors, who accounted for most of Chrysler's $6.9 billion in secured debt, *were* taking

TARP money, and were therefore looking out for Barack Obama's interests ahead of their investors. As the *New York Times* reported, the administration did not let this crisis go to waste:

> [T]his is no ordinary bankruptcy. JP Morgan Chase and other large banks involved in the negotiations are, to greater and lesser degrees, beholden to Washington. Many have received billions of taxpayer dollars, as well as other generous subsidies. For the banks, defying the administration was never a serious option, according to people close to the talks with lenders, who asked not to be identified because they had signed confidentiality agreements.[73]

TARP was bad enough. A president willing to use it to increase his power and leverage in corporate bankruptcy proceedings was even worse.

Lauria, the bankruptcy attorney who represented Mourdock and several of the non-TARP creditors, was certainly not an anti-Obama partisan. His political contribution history shows that he had given $10,000 to the Democratic Senatorial Campaign Committee in 2008, and also $1,000 to Hillary Clinton's 2006 Senate campaign. That was before he and his clients, who had purchased $295 million in Chrysler debt in the mistaken belief that their secured debt was actually "secured," became Obama's targets.

In a May 2009 radio interview on WJR 760 in Detroit, Lauria described his clients: "They bought a contract that said that they get paid before anyone else does from Chrysler. And they have been told by the government, who is in complete control of Chrysler, oddly enough, that despite their contractual right, they do not get paid before everybody else."

He then described the method by which the Obama White House had just caused one of his clients, the investment firm Perella Weinberg, to back down and accept the government's gun-to-your head deal:

> It's no fun standing on this side of the fence, opposing the President of the United States....I can tell you for sure that I represent

one less investor today than I represented yesterday. One of my clients was directly threatened by the White House and in essence compelled to withdraw its opposition to the deal under threat that the full force of the White House press corps would destroy its reputation if it continued to fight....That was Perella Weinberg.[74]

In fact, the Obama's threats had prompted Lauria to request permission to redact his clients' names from their court filings, to prevent retaliation.[75]

Lauria was clear that he did not oppose the government bailout, or the funding of the UAW's pension. "I actually think that in the troubled economic time we're in, that is an appropriate role for the government to perform," he said. "What we do oppose, however, is the abuse of the bankruptcy laws to coerce first-lien lenders to subsidize the rehabilitation of Chrysler."

Bill Frezza, a partner at the venture capital firm Adams Capital Management, echoed Michael Barone's sentiments on "Gangster Government" when he described the pall that this sad episode cast over Wall Street, the engine of American capital investment:

> Why would anyone buy the shares of TARP-backed banks or invest alongside them knowing that their executives have proven their willingness to sacrifice shareholders' interests and throw co-investors under the bus any time the president snaps his fingers?
>
> Why would foreigners buy the distressed debt of American companies knowing that this debt cannot be secured by law but only by political clout?[76]

That's one way Gangster Government worsens an economy. Here's another. Because it was mostly hedge funds that tried to act in their investors' best interests during the Chrysler bankruptcy, hedge funds were now threatened with new regulations. As Zachery Kouwe reported in the *New York Times*:

> [N]ow that Chrysler has tipped into bankruptcy, some industry executives worry the administration will try to turn this episode

to its political advantage. Washington, these people contend, needed some political cover for the mess in Detroit—and Wall Street provided a handy scapegoat. A move is already afoot to tighten oversight of hedge funds and end certain tax benefits for private investments funds. The Chrysler bankruptcy, and Wall Street's role in it, will make resisting those efforts more difficult.[77]

Of course, the hedge funds that had the misfortune of being steamrolled by Gangster Government had nothing to do with the failure of Chrysler or GM. But note that by nationalizing automakers, Obama had given himself leverage to extend his power into an entirely new area. Gangster government begets more gangster government.

President Obama was pulling the strings on Wall Street, and he was pulling them in Detroit as well. He had given this assurance: "Let me be clear. The United States government has no interest in running GM. We have no intention of running GM."[78] But having taken ownership of GM, and having taken control of its day-to-day operations, this was, at least in the short run, not true; Rattner, the architect of Obama's bailout, tells us so. He recounts signing off on every major expenditure and deal by the pre-bankruptcy General Motors, something he and the government had no legal authority to do.

As he did so, Rattner was thinking about the *Washington Post*. He writes in *Overhaul* that whenever he had a big decision to make about GM's operations, he first subjected it to what he called "the *Washington Post* test." He tried to imagine the public reaction to the story on that newspaper's front-page about his decision, and what the political implications would be for Obama.[79] Rattner writes that he refused to sign off on several GM deals that involved the company's foreign subsidiaries—some of which "may have represented good business decisions"—simply because they failed this test. That's how government officials make decisions (by covering their rears), but it's no way to run a business.

And the Democratic Congress, despite its voluntary lack of oversight or initiative in the bailout, did not want to be left out entirely. Rattner writes that as his team combed over GM's assets and made decisions about which plants would close, congressmen and senators began inundating his office with calls trying to save facilities in their own district. Some were hostile, some seemed resigned to failure, and "sometimes the monologue droned on so long that I could get a number of emails answered."[80]

Congress, so long ignored, at least attempted to insert itself into the automakers' business operations, where it had no business interfering—the question of which dealerships would have their franchises revoked.

Rattner insists that he stayed out of decisions about which dealers to close. That would have been a waste of his time. His focus was forcing GM to close more dealerships, and faster. But it was ironic that even as the Obama administration rushed to subsidize make-work jobs that served no economic purpose through the stimulus, it was pushing Chrysler and GM to kill off tens of thousands of private sector jobs at car dealers.

The dealers' existence didn't directly cost the auto companies anything; they were forced to close because they were supposedly causing an image problem for Chrysler and GM in comparison to other automakers like Toyota: "GM and Chrysler dealers were generally dramatically less profitable, had less cash to invest in their stores, and projected a substantially less attractive retail experience to customers. For the many Americans who thought the automakers owned the dealers, this affected the brand perception and ultimately hurt sales."[81]

Naturally, the administration was accused of shutting down dealers for political reasons.[82] This is another danger of political control of business. Business decisions like these are second-guessed by voters who naturally assume that every dealer and plant closing, every hiring and compensation decision made by government officials, and every new rule created for the automotive industry is driven by politics (and often it is). Andrew Grossman of the Heritage Foundation made this point while testifying before Congress about the bailout:

> Unfortunately, such pressure and such doubt, will accompany every decision made by General Motors and Chrysler in the months ahead. Some, for example, speculate that General Motors and Chrysler threw their support behind President Obama's new emissions and fuel efficiency standards at the

behest of his Administration. No doubt politics played some role in transforming the automakers' former intransigence on the issue.[83]

Speaking of which, we have no precise record of what brought GM and Chrysler to support the new Obama fuel efficiency standards. But these standards threaten to undo the entire bailout, or even force another one.

All three Detroit companies—GM, Chrysler, and Ford, as well as the UAW—had long opposed tightening of these standards. Rattner writes that he applied no pressure at all—that in fact he heard nothing on the subject whatsoever from Obama's climate czar, Carol Browner.[84] But Jonathan Alter, a sympathetic Obama biographer who was granted access to White House sources, described the regulatory change thus:

> While he had his foot on their necks, Obama moved aggressively in late spring to force the auto companies to adopt fuel economy standards (35.5 miles per gallon by 2016, up from 27.5) that they had loudly resisted for decades (the auto task force said it has nothing to do with this White House policy, which is a little like investment bankers who say they never talk to traders working for the same bank). Because he considered reducing dependence on foreign oil to be a national security issue, Obama made an exception to his promise not to use his leverage to tell Detroit how to build cars. The CEOs came to the White House and acted as if they loved the idea.[85]

Pulitzer Prize-winning cartoonist Mike Lukovich of the *Atlanta Journal-Constitution* depicted the event thus: A reporter in one frame asks a GM executive hidden in the frame how he, as the head of GM, feels about the new fuel efficiency rules. The second frame reveals that the executive is, in fact, President Obama, who says he is pleased with his own decision.

GM and Chrysler had every reason to oppose the new rules. When originally put in place in the 1970s, the CAFE (Corporate Average Fuel Economy) program was a classic case of liberal overreach that forced the automakers to upend their entire business model. CAFE's arbitrary legal classification scheme caused them to abandon the most practical passenger cars then in existence for big families—station wagons. These large vehicles dragged down the average fuel economy of the cars the automakers sold.

The automakers worked around the regulations and continued serving families by producing so-called "light trucks"—minivans and eventually SUVs. Because they were built on truck chassis, they were under different and less stringent fuel economy rules.[86] Japanese automakers had locked up the small-car market long ago, and still own it today. Even so, the demand for bigger cars is so great that even Toyota and Honda sell nearly as many light trucks as they do cars.

"Light trucks" are certainly Detroit's specialty. In 2010, Chrysler sold nearly three of them for every passenger car it sold. GM sold 1.4 million "light trucks" and only 800,000 cars.[87] Detroit's smallest cars were built and sold at a loss *solely* to offset the emissions of the automakers' profitable cars and satisfy government regulations. Consider this amazing fact: in October 2010, the *Detroit News* reported that GM was about to begin building the first-ever *profitable* UAW-made small compact in the history of the Big Three.[88]

Yet the automakers accepted this tightening of the screws without even a whimper. They had no choice, with gangster government's foot to their necks.

COLLUSION COLLISION

In 2010, GM's market share declined by nearly a full point from its weak 2009 performance. Even then, its sales were propped up by the federal government purchasing a quarter of its domestic hybrid vehicles.[89] Yet in 2010, the bailed-out company GM still reopened its political action committee (GMPAC) and started spreading the wealth on Capitol Hill.[90]

GMPAC gave in order to put weight behind the company's lobbying operation, which had never really stopped, not even in bankruptcy. Between late 2008 and its rebirth in July 2010, GM spent $11.3 million lobbying Congress. The conclusion that the lobbying was done with taxpayers' money is inescapable. The PAC money guaranteed that lawmakers would listen when GM needed a friend—or perhaps its next bailout.

The White House was so convinced of its mandate from heaven to help GM that, after the bailout, it colluded with the automaker to project the misleading impression that GM had paid back the government's money. In April 2010, GM rolled out new television spots, combined with a *Wall Street Journal* op-ed by Chairman and CEO Ed Whitacre, to convince Americans that GM had repaid the government's money. The op-ed's headline read, "The GM Bailout: Paid Back in Full," and it stated, "We're paying back—in full, with interest, years ahead of schedule—loans made to help fund the new GM. Our ability to pay back these loans less than a year after emerging from bankruptcy is a sign that our plan for building a new GM is working."[91]

The statement was strictly true, but intended solely to mislead. GM, the piece implied, was Government Motors no longer, and that just wasn't true, as *Reason*'s Shikha Dalmia pointed out in an article for *Forbes*. GM had received $50 billion in the bailout, and that certainly wasn't being paid back. The payback amount was $6.7 billion in government loans, which GM was paying back with money from another government grant—a $13.4 billion escrow account the government had set up for the new GM.

But even beyond that, GM was paying back one government loan even as it applied for a much bigger one:

> [T]he company has applied to the Department of Energy for $10 billion in low (5%) interest loans to retool its plants to meet the government's tougher new CAFE (Corporate Average Fuel Economy) standards. However, giving GM more taxpayer money on top of the existing bailout would have been a political disaster for the Obama administration and a PR debacle for the company. Paying back the small bailout loan makes the new—and bigger—DOE loan much more feasible. [92]

GM later had increased its loan request to $14.4 billion.[93]

Despite these facts, Obama's Treasury Department issued a misleading press release on April 21, 2010, that the average American could have easily mistaken as stating that GM had paid the government back in full. Its title: "GM Repays Treasury Loan in Full."[94]

As GM struggled with its image as Government Motors, and Chrysler simply struggled to survive, there was also the question of Ford. That automaker raised its own cash instead of becoming dependent on the taxpayer. It has received much praise and public good will for this. Rattner has relatively little to say about Ford in his book, except that it was a better-run company. He also mentions that its officers and directors were carefully watching the bailouts to make sure they were not placed at a competitive disadvantage.

In fact, we know they really weren't. If you wonder why Ford didn't complain more about the bailout of its competitors, consider the fact that Obama was giving Ford its own series of smaller bailouts under the radar. These included:

- $5.9 billion in low-interest (5 percent) loans from the Department of Energy's Advanced Technology Vehicles Manufacturing program. The loans, made in 2009, were to help the company meet new government fuel efficiency standards—something it would have to do anyway.[95] GM and Chrysler, in their poor financial condition, didn't qualify for this program.

- $93 million in direct Department of Energy stimulus funds for electric and hybrid vehicle development. (Ford's British partner, Smith Electric vehicles, received another $10 million.) In addition to the direct subsidy, hundreds of millions more went to university research into batteries that would help Ford and others in their costly attempts to build electric vehicles that remain stubbornly expensive and undesirable for consumers.[96]

- In August 2010, the Export-Import bank, a United States federal agency, gave the company a $250 million loan guarantee to finance 211,000 auto sales to customers in Canada and Mexico.[97] This does not mean that Ford will export any additional vehicles beyond what it already does, but it does mean that Ford is off the hook—and the taxpayers are on it—for bad loans to purchasers in those countries.

- In late November 2010, the Federal Reserve Bank was finally forced to reveal the full extent of its bailout activities at the height of the financial crisis. It disclosed that the Fed had bought $15.9 billion in auto loans from Ford Credit, the company's auto finance arm.[98] Chrysler Financial and GMAC got these secret, backdoor bailouts, too.

So Ford didn't receive a direct bailout. It did even better than that. It successfully avoided the double stigma of bankruptcy and government control, which probably helped its 1.2-percentage point gain in market share after the auto bailout. At the same time, it got to enjoy substantial benefits from the Obama administration's largesse. How could anyone in that position complain?

FAILURE IN SUCCESS

In one sense, the automotive bailout was a success. It came off in record time, despite many difficult circumstances. It saved many existing jobs.

But it is impossible to assess the bailout's net benefit, even in strictly financial terms. We do know that taxpayers appear set to lose a lot on the stock and a little from the tax breaks given to the automakers. Some additional value must be assigned to the $650,000 in risk that Obama's Treasury Department took for each of the 77,000 jobs supposedly saved at GM, and the $779,000 risk per job at Chrysler.[99] The companies could still fail and bring everything to naught. The economic benefit of the bailout could be zero or even negative. And as Bastiat would tell us, it might be zero or negative even if they succeed. We will never know how many new jobs the bailout prevented.

More important is the damage done to our rule of law and our Constitution by President Obama's incredible expansion of executive power. One hundred years of bankruptcy law were overturned, and Fifth Amendment protections of property rights were discarded in favor of politics. When White House chief of staff Rahm Emanuel suggested using crises to "do things you can't normally do," he really meant it.

CHAPTER THREE

ON THE PRECIPICE: OBAMACARE

"It will be of little avail to the people, that the laws are made by men of their own choice, if the laws be so voluminous that they cannot be read, or so incoherent that they cannot be understood ..."

—*James Madison, Federalist No. 62*

President Obama is a former law school lecturer, a talented writer, and a gifted public speaker. But sometimes even he chooses the wrong word. At the White House on December 15, 2009, immediately after a meeting with Senate Democrats to discuss their plans for passing health care reform, he said: "[F]rom the discussions we had it's clear that we are on the precipice of an achievement that's eluded Congresses and Presidents for generations—an achievement that will touch the lives of nearly every American."

"On the verge" carries a neutral connotation. "On the cusp" is usually positive. But "on the precipice"—that is always bad. It conveys the idea of an imminent fall from great height.

And it might be one of the most accurate statements Obama has made as president, even if it was unintentionally so.

Almost exactly one year after Obama declared the nation "on the precipice" of achievement, Obamacare—now a law and no longer just a bill—suffered its first great fall in federal court. On December 13, 2010, U.S. District Judge Henry Hudson ruled that law's requirement for all Americans to buy insurance was unconstitutional. He ruled that even if the Constitution permits the federal government to regulate interstate commerce, it cannot *force* Americans to engage in commerce by requiring their purchase of commercial health insurance.

Hudson agreed with the argument of Virginia's Republican Attorney General Ken Cuccinelli that if the federal government can require Americans to purchase health insurance, then there is no remaining logical limit to federal power. Otherwise, what is there to stop government from making all Americans buy newspapers, with the worthy goal of saving that troubled industry?[1] Or why not make us all buy GM and Chrysler automobiles?

As Judge Hudson put it: "On careful review, this court must conclude that Section 1501 of the Patient Protection and Affordable Care Act—specifically the Minimum Essential Coverage Provision—exceeds the constitutional boundaries of congressional power."[2]

Having struck down what the government had defended and characterized as the law's "linchpin," without which the bill would be impossible to implement, Judge Hudson had one further question to decide: how much of the law could be allowed to stand?

There was an interesting story behind this question. Although the policy debate over Obamacare had lasted several months, the legislation's final form had been reached quite haphazardly, considering its complexity and importance. The final changes had been penciled in immediately before the bill's passage on Christmas Eve 2009. Few senators understood the fine print, and several important things were left out, including what is known as a "severability clause"—the provision stating that even if a court strikes down part of the law, the rest must stand.

Without the severability clause, there was a real question about whether Judge Hudson would declare the entire thing null and void. He did not, but in preserving the law's remainders, he offered a rare treat for those bored by dull legal writing—a hysterical back-handed justification based on the very fact that Obamacare had been so shoddily crafted and hastily passed.

> Having found a portion of the Act to be invalid…the Court's next
> task is to determine whether this Section is severable from the

balance of the enactment. Predictably, the Secretary counsels severability, and the Commonwealth (Virginia) urges wholesale invalidation....However, the bill embraces far more than health care reform. It is laden with provisions and riders patently extraneous to health care—over 400 in all.

In other words, there was so much in the bill unrelated to the individual mandate—indeed, unrelated to health care altogether—that there was no need to strike down the whole law. Hudson also declined to consider whether Congress would have passed Obamacare without an individual mandate:

> The final element of the analysis is difficult to apply in this case given the haste with which the final version of the 2,700 page bill was rushed to the floor for a Christmas Eve vote. It would be virtually impossible within the present record to determine whether Congress would have passed this bill, encompassing a wide variety of topics related and unrelated to health care, without [the individual mandate]. Even then, the Court's conclusions would be speculative at best.

"Even King George could not compel the colonists to buy British goods, but we have a President and a Congress who believe that they can," Cuccinelli told me, hours after the ruling was handed down in his favor. "Neither the administration nor congressional Democrats took seriously the limits of the Constitution on anything they do," he went on. "If we lose this case [on appeal], and the federal government has power to force people to buy products, then federalism is dead, and there is no distinct sphere of authority for the states."

The court case had created an additional and unexpected casualty. President Obama had promised, repeatedly and unequivocally, that he would not raise "any" taxes on American families making less than $250,000 per year. He insisted that the penalty imposed on Americans failing to purchase qualified insurance plans was not a tax: "For us to say that you've got to take a responsibility to get health insurance is absolutely not a tax increase," he told George Stephanopoulos.[3]

But in court, the administration sang a different tune. In order to defend the provision's legitimacy under the Constitution, the Obama administration argued that the individual mandate *was* a tax, and that it was therefore constitutional under the federal government's taxation power.

The court didn't buy it—in fact, in four out of four courts to hear challenges to Obamacare, not one has bought it, not even the two courts that have upheld Obamacare. But this duplicitous argument did give the public one more glimpse of just how serious President Obama's promises are.

President Obama had exceeded his Constitutional authority, or so two courts have said as of this writing. Obamacare amounted to bad policy, bad process, and bad faith on the president's part. It was his most outrageous and public act of underhanded dealing, misleading rhetoric, and disdain for the Constitution. As such, it was an act of gangster government.

AN OFFER YOU CAN'T REFUSE

How do you sell a product that can only hurt most of its buyers? That was the task facing President Obama and his team. The only way is to lie, and that's what they did. In June 2009, just before the health care reform debate began, an ABC-*Washington Post* poll of 1,001 adults found that 84 percent of Americans had health coverage.[4] The poll also found that 81 percent of the insured were satisfied with their coverage, and 88 percent of them were satisfied with the care they received through it. Obama's goal, then, was to convince a goodly portion of these satisfied customers to support a massive expansion of federal power that was not only unlikely to help them, but would probably ruin something they already have and like.

Obama did not possess a miracle cure for anything. He did not have some great discovery of which the medical profession was unaware. All he had were a few well-packaged deceptions. The first was that the bill would not force Americans to change their coverage. President Obama repeated on many, many occasions what he told the American Medical Association in June 2009: "If you like your health care plan, you will be able to keep your health care plan. Period. No one will take it away. No matter what."[5]

The best refutation to this unequivocal statement came from Obama's own appointees, in June 2010. The Department of Health and Human Services revealed that the government's mid-range estimate was that "66% of small employer plans and 45% of large employer plans" would be voided under Obamacare's rules by 2013.[6] In other words, Obamacare would force literally millions of Americans to change their coverage within two years. Period. No matter what.[7]

The second lie was more outrageous, but harder to expose: namely, that Congress could magically improve the quality of health care. "Quality" became the most overused buzzword in the entire debate.

"People do what is necessary to pass a health care bill to improve quality, lower cost, and make America healthier," said Democrat Speaker of the House Nancy Pelosi.[8]

But just how did Congress plan to improve health care when 83 percent of Americans are happy with the quality of their care—including 88 percent of the insured? It *is* possible to imagine legislation that could improve America's health payment and insurance system, which leaves many Americans dependent on their employers and suffers from runaway costs. But advances in quality of care itself are different. Government agencies already spend billions improving our understanding of medicine and health care. Consider, for example, the Agency for Healthcare Research and Quality (AHRQ), and the National Institutes of Health (NIH), and the Centers for Disease Control (CDC), to name just a few; or the hundreds of university medical programs that the federal government subsidizes, both directly and indirectly. Before Obamacare had been written, the 2009 stimulus package dedicated $1.1 billion to medical "comparative effectiveness research." That's above and beyond regular appropriations.

If health care reform had simply been an exercise in throwing money at improvements to quality of care, it's hard to imagine vigorous opposition taking shape. But the real issue is not the quality of health care, but who *controls* health care. Obamacare promises to improve the quality of care while simultaneously reducing costs, and it proposes to do so through a virtual regulatory takeover of the entire health care system. It just doesn't add up.

UNCLE SAM: THE ENFORCER

If the unrealistic promises of Obamacare are troubling, its many requirements and punishments are more so. Right off the bat, it raises taxes by $770 billion in hard economic times, according to the Congressional Budget Office.[9] Obama and Congressional Democrats did this in order to pad the bill's bottom line and make it appear to reduce the deficit.

Pending federal appeals, the law will require every American to purchase insurance. And you can't just buy any insurance policy. It must be government-approved insurance, with a sufficiently low deductible and other high-end terms that the Congressional Budget Office says will make premiums higher for buyers in the individual market—a prediction that is already playing itself out.[10] And if you don't buy government-approved insurance, you must pay a penalty. The only ways to exempt yourself from this requirement are suicide, expatriation, and conversion to Christian Science.[11] In order to collect the fine, the Internal Revenue Service can take away your tax refund.[12]

Obamacare also places new burdens, and creates perverse incentives, for employers. By historical accident, our tax code already encourages every employer to act as a health insurer on the side. Obamacare takes this a step further, with an annual penalty for employers of $2,000 per uncovered employee. If, as an employer of at least fifty people, your company does not offer government-approved insurance, then depending on the precise circumstances, the hiring of your fifty-first employee (or your 101st employee, depending on your state) could cost you an immediate $42,000 (or $142,000) in fines to the government.[13]

If your business *does* offer health insurance, it can't be the more affordable kind that covers the basics—a so-called "mini-med" plan. These are forbidden, unless you can navigate the system and get a special exemption from the Obama administration—as 729 entities, including 165 labor unions, had done by the end of 2010.[14]

And the requirement for more expensive plans sets you up for another landmine. You'll want to avoid hiring people with big families, working spouses, or other sources of income, because there is a harsher penalty—$3,000 per employee—if your employee's share of the premium exceeds 9.8 percent of his monthly household income. In other words, it's best to avoid hiring those most in need of a job, because the high-premium plans required by Obamacare could put them over the limit. Your choices are to pay high penalties, pay more for your company's insurance, or hire fewer people.[15]

If you have fifty-five employees, Obamacare provides you with a tremendous incentive to let five of them go. And what employer would want to hire his fifty-first employee and submit himself to this nightmare of regulations and fines? Many American companies are already trying to cut costs by hiring overseas; Obamacare can only make this worse.[16]

Obamacare was not supposed to be all about penalties. It was also supposed to help small businesses. President Obama made much of its tax credit for small businesses that provide health insurance. He sold it as a boon for the smallest businesses— the ones with fewer than twenty-five employees making an average annual salary of $50,000 or less.

That was the promise, but it was a lie. The credit is almost worthless unless you have fewer than ten employees and you pay them practically nothing, as the Associated Press reported: "When the administration unveiled the small business tax credit earlier this week, officials touted its 'broad eligibility' for companies with fewer than 25 workers and average annual wages under $50,000 that provide health coverage….Lost in the fine print: The credit drops off sharply once a company gets above 10 workers and $25,000 average annual wages."[17]

The AP told the story of Zach Hoffman, a small business owner in Springfield, Illinois, who has twenty-four employees who make $35,000 on average. Hoffman pays about $80,000 a year to insure his employees, but he wasn't eligible for the credit at all under its complicated formula. The formula is spelled out in Obamacare in language about as clear as mud:

> The amount of the credit determined under subsection (b) without regard to this subsection shall be reduced (but not below zero) by the sum of the following amounts:
>
> (1) Such amount multiplied by a fraction the numerator of which is the total number of full-time equivalent employees of the employer in excess of 10 and the denominator of which is 15.

(2) Such amount multiplied by a fraction the numerator of which is the average annual wages of the employer in excess of the dollar amount in effect under subsection (d)(3)(B) and the denominator of which is such dollar amount.[18]

When you add up all of this legislative gobbledygook, the final answer is no tax credit for about 65 percent of small businesses, according to the National Federation of Independent Business.[19] (In retrospect, you can feel better about the fact that many members of Congress did not read this bill before voting for it. Most of them wouldn't have understood it anyway.)

Consider your employer's dilemma. If he has ten employees, the government might pay him to reduce their salaries. If he has fifty employees, the government might penalize him a full year's pay for hiring one more.

Larger firms are insulated from some, though not all, of these perverse incentives. But if you work for one, there is still a decent chance that Obamacare will prompt your employer to change your health coverage, or to send you out looking for your own policy. And if your coverage does not change, the law will still affect your benefits package in other ways. It makes Health Savings Accounts (HSAs) less valuable, and it makes employer-provided Flexible Savings Accounts (FSAs) almost useless. In an effort to further squeeze taxpayers and make it look like the bill doesn't add to the deficit, Democrats crafted Obamacare to forbid the use of either pre-tax account for spending on over-the-counter drugs. So if there is an over-the-counter drug that you need to take regularly, Obama has just raised its price for you. You can defeat this by getting your doctor to write you a prescription for it, but doctor visits aren't free, and doctors don't have unlimited time for stupid, unnecessary visits caused by ill-advised acts of Congress.

PUTTING THE SQUEEZE ON SENIORS

Senior citizens, whose medical need is greatest, come under the most pressure from Obamacare. Nearly all the talk of "cost-cutting" is directed toward them. In an April 2009 interview with *The New York Times Magazine*, President Obama was asked about cutting costs in health care. The example he gave was instructive:

THE PRESIDENT: When my grandmother got very ill during the campaign, she got cancer; it was determined to be terminal. And about two or three weeks after her diagnosis she fell, broke her hip. It was determined that she might have had a mild stroke, which is what had precipitated the fall.

So now she's in the hospital, and the doctor says, Look, you've got about—maybe you have three months, maybe you have six months, maybe you have nine months to live. Because of the weakness of your heart, if you have an operation on your hip there are certain risks that—you know, your heart can't take it. On the other hand, if you just sit there with your hip like this, you're just going to waste away and your quality of life will be terrible.

And she elected to get the hip replacement and was fine for about two weeks after the hip replacement, and then suddenly just—you know, things fell apart.

I don't know how much that hip replacement cost. I would have paid out of pocket for that hip replacement just because she's my grandmother. Whether, sort of in the aggregate, society making those decisions to give my grandmother, or everybody else's aging grandparents or parents, a hip replacement when they're terminally ill is a sustainable model, is a very difficult question. If somebody told me that my grandmother couldn't have a hip replacement and she had to lie there in misery in the waning days of her life—that would be pretty upsetting.

Leonhardt: And it's going to be hard for people who don't have the option of paying for it.

THE PRESIDENT: So that's where I think you just get into some very difficult moral issues. But that's also a huge driver of cost, right? I mean, the chronically ill and those toward the end of their lives are accounting for potentially 80 percent of the total health care bill out here.

Leonhardt: So how do you—how do we deal with it?

THE PRESIDENT: Well, I think that there is going to have to be a conversation that is guided by doctors, scientists, ethicists....[20]

The image Obama presents—of government panels of doctors, scientists, and ethicists searching for a politically palatable way to tell people the government won't pay for their grandmothers' hip replacements—helps explain why the health care reform debate generated such robust opposition among senior citizens. Seniors had a lot at stake in this debate. Unlike the younger patient, who relies on government to keep his insurer honest, Medicare patients are entirely at the government's mercy. That's what Obama calls "society making the decisions."

We've all heard the barely amusing joke about the Tea Party activist who demands that the government keep its hands off his Medicare. But the very creation of Medicare, even as it expanded health coverage for the old, also guaranteed that there is no viable, private alternative for those who cannot pay for their care out of pocket. The semi-alternative that does exist—the subsidized Medicare Advantage program, in which 11.1 million seniors had enrolled seeking better coverage—Obamacare was determined to destroy, in order to save about $136 billion over ten years.[21]

The law also contained something known as "productivity adjustments" in Medicare, which would cut Medicare payments for everything from ambulances to home health care to prosthetics, according to more or less arbitrary goals. Richard Foster, the actuary of Medicare, wrote in an April 2010 memo that Obamacare's long-term cuts to Medicare would make it even harder for the elderly to find doctors who would see them: "Simulations by the Office of the Actuary suggest that roughly 15 percent of [Medicare] Part A providers would become unprofitable within the 10-year projection period as a result of the productivity adjustments."[22]

The Congressional Budget Office, for its part, recognized the cuts as partially a budget fiction, whose purpose was to make it look like Obamacare would not add to the deficit. But just before the bill passed, CBO director Doug Elmendorf noted: "Adjusting for inflation, Medicare spending per beneficiary under the legislation would increase at an average annual rate of roughly 2 percent during the next two decades—well below the roughly 4 percent annual growth rate of the past two decades. It is unclear whether such a reduction in the growth rate could be achieved, and if so, whether it would be accomplished through greater efficiencies in the delivery of health care or would reduce access to care or diminish the quality of care."[23]

So according to the government's own estimates, Obamacare's spending cuts were either unrealistic, potentially catastrophic, or both. Unfortunately, this memo became public the month *after* Obamacare passed.

Medicare's physician and hospital underpayments for certain services are already chronic. The Mayo organization, which the president praised during his push for Obamacare, announced in January 2010 that its Glendale, Arizona, facility would no longer take Medicare patients. Mayo did not take this decision lightly—it had lost $840 million in the previous year treating Medicare patients. At the end of 2008, one-third of America's doctors would not see new Medicare patients, because they were losing money on them.[24] This is a lesson lost on the writers of Obamacare.

To save another $16 billion, Obamacare creates a government panel to determine cost-effective medical practices—the Independent Payment Advisory Board. This is the so-called "death panel." Whatever you think of this loaded term, consider how it applies to a similar government panel's decision that recommended fewer mammograms for women under age fifty.[25] That decision, announced in November 2009, was met with a vast public outcry—and it came at a very inconvenient moment for President Obama. It showed how government, with one-size-fits-all prescriptions, could cut costs by skimping on care.

Americans got a taste of what this might look like on December 16, 2010, when Obama's Food and Drug Administration revoked its approval of the drug Avastin for treating advanced breast cancer cases. The decision was difficult because the doses needed for breast cancer treatments for the average patient cost nearly $100,000 a year, and only half of the patients respond well. But among those, some patients' lives were extended for months or even years without further progression of their tumors.

As government unavoidably does, the FDA made a one-size-fits-all decision. Its commissioners are not supposed to consider costs, but the conclusion that they did is unavoidable. The FDA cited the drug's side-effects in its decision, but it did not ban the drug, which has other approved applications. Nor did it even ban the drug's use for breast cancer patients. Instead, it shifted late-stage breast cancer treatment to the category of "off-label." The only effect of this decision is to take the government off the hook for payment, and to give private insurers political and legal cover to do the same. The 17,500 women who are prescribed Avastin each year for breast cancer must now fend for themselves.

If you find decisions like this one disturbing, just bear in mind that there will be many, many more to come. As the Heritage Foundation's James Hoff noted, panels and agencies will be issuing rulings and decisions and regulations on Obamacare's implementation for years to come: "The link between Administration actions and changes in health care delivery will not always be apparent to patients and their providers: The government's actions will largely be hidden behind the screen provided by the various actors it controls—insurance companies, states, and the new purchasing exchanges. Behind that screen, officials of the federal government will be pulling these actors' strings."[26]

Gangster government prefers to operate from the shadows of bureaucracy.

THE RIGHT SIDE OF THE GUN

Along the stretch of Pennsylvania Avenue that runs between the White House and the Capitol Building, the top executives of America's largest drug companies gathered in the historic Willard Hotel on the morning of July 22, 2009. There were no signs in the lobby to indicate that such a meeting was taking place. There had been no public announcements. The concierge dutifully denied the meeting's existence when asked that morning by telephone.

But they were there, all right. The first clue was the number of well-dressed and important-looking people streaming into the lobby and heading for the stairs to the basement. The drug industry's powerful trade organization, PhRMA, had just negotiated a major deal with the Obama administration. The industry group was going to:

- Spend $150 million to $200 million on an advertising and grassroots campaign promoting Obamacare
- Give the government's medical programs up to $68 billion in savings over the next ten years

- Pay an excise tax of $2.3 billion per year, with each large drug company paying in proportion to its market share

In return for this, PhRMA was going to get the bill they wanted.[27]

- They would be protected from imported prescription drugs
- They would be protected from further "cost-savings" efforts beyond the $80 billion they had pledged
- Government agencies would not be able to negotiate lower prices for their drugs

This meeting was not open to the public—I was stopped at the door and asked to leave. But inside, they must have been smiling. The concessions offered by the White House were worth at least as much as the drug-makers had given up. House Democrats had been hoping to extract more than $150 billion in savings on drugs.[28]

Over the next few months, President Obama and his spokesman, Robert Gibbs, danced around the deal's exact terms. He didn't want to appear to have let big PhRMA off the hook.[29] But he had. The drug-makers released the details of the deal when they thought the White House was reneging on its terms. But in the end, there was honor among thieves.

We have seen how individuals, employers, senior citizens, and the very sick will be affected by Obamacare. But another interesting part of the story is to see who *wasn't* touched, and why.

"One of the reasons we made that agreement was to literally buy some certainty over the next ten years, to make the right research and development decisions for our companies," PhRMA spokesman Ken Johnson told me at the time. He maintained that it hadn't been such a great deal for the drug-makers—"It's a mistake to say that our companies are not going to feel some pain," he said.[30]

But the drug-makers were smarter than that. They knew that "Hope and Change" had come to Washington, and they understood gangster government. They had watched the automotive bailout, and they knew which side of the gun they wanted to be standing on when it went off.

PhRMA's leaders had made a better deal than anyone realized at the time. For one thing, it would cost them even less than it appeared. Two separate analyses—one by Credit Suisse and another by the AARP—found that despite non-existent inflation, the drug industry had raised prices by about 9 percent in 2009. The projected increase in profits from this one-year increase was $100 billion over ten years—more than enough to offset the $80 billion in savings it was giving the federal government.[31] PhRMA had seen Obamacare as a great opportunity from the beginning, which is why it spent $78 million lobbying before the deal was made. In a March 2009 interview on CNBC, PhRMA president and CEO Billy Tauzin, a former Republican member of Congress, had said that the bill would be good for pharmaceutical companies, because its subsidies for insurance would broaden the industry's customer base:

> By and large, think about what this plan does. This plan talks about providing comprehensive health insurance to people who don't have it—that means to patients who can't take our medicines because they can't afford it. $650 billion spent to better insure Americans for the products we make. That ought to be a very optimistic and positive message for everyone who is interested in our sector of the economy.... Think about this: Almost half of the prescriptions that are written today go unfilled. And they're unfilled primarily because people don't have adequate insurance—they have no insurance, or their insurance doesn't cover our products the way it covers hospitalizations.... We're going to quarrel over price controls... but we also believe more people ought to have good insurance.[32]

Tauzin had quit his congressional seat and the chair of the House Energy and Commerce Committee in 2004 to take his job with PhRMA. And Obama, during his 2008 presidential campaign, referred to Tauzin in a campaign ad, although he did not say his name:

> The pharmaceutical industry wrote into the prescription drug plan that Medicare could not negotiate with drug companies.

And you know what? The chairman of the committee who pushed the law through, went to work for the pharmaceutical industry making two million dollars a year. That's an example of the same old game-playing in Washington. Well, I don't want to learn to play the game better, I want to put an end to the game-playing.[33]

Now that Obama was "learning to play the game better," Tauzin didn't let any petty grudges stand in his way. The drug companies he represented were being given a license to print money, because they'd put themselves on the right side. No price controls, no vilification from the White House, no reimportation of prescription drugs.

During his 2008 campaign, Obama had gone so far as to promise, at least eight times, to conduct all of the negotiations on C-SPAN, and not behind closed doors.[34] Perhaps that was a bit too ambitious, but his behavior toward PhRMA put him as far away from that promise as he could have possibly gone. His conduct clearly and unmistakably violated both the letter and the spirit of his promise.

Now let's compare this to Obamacare's treatment of another industry vital to health care—the insurers, who resisted at least part of Obama's health care overhaul. Under Obamacare's "guaranteed issue" and "community rating" policies, insurers must essentially change their entire business model. They cannot deny individual applications for insurance for any reason, nor can they base their premiums on the actual medical risks that a patient poses (tobacco use is the sole exception).[35] They can only slightly vary premiums based on age, but not enough to reflect the fact that a 20-year-old is a lower risk than a 60-year-old. There are no explicit price-controls, but the Secretary of Health and Human Services is charged with forcing the companies to justify "unreasonable" increases.

The new law also requires insurers to spend at least 80 percent (in some cases 85 percent) of the premiums they collect within each state on health care within that state. The remaining 20 or 15 percent has to cover administrative expenses and profit. If the insurers don't spend the full amount on health care, they must refund the excess to consumers.

There are several drawbacks for consumers in these provisions. In Maine, "guaranteed issue" and "community rating" drove nearly every insurer from the state, and sent premiums for family policies in the individual insurance market skyrocketing above $1,500 per month.[36] The 80 or 85 percent rule will arbitrarily reduce what some insurers can spend on customer service, whose poor quality is already a perennial source of frustration. This rule will also reduce what companies can spend to investigate insurance fraud, and even remove incentives to prevent it—more fraud could actually allow for bigger profits.[37] Moreover, this provision will force millions of relatively healthy consumers out of inexpensive, high-deductible health plans that cannot meet the requirement and into more expensive coverage.[38]

But with these particular concerns in the background, think for a moment about what gangster government has done to the insurers. While the pharmaceutical firms remain free to run their businesses, the insurers have had their industry converted, essentially, into a public utility. In fact, the reason Obama chose the 85 percent number is that if he had gone up to 90 percent, the Congressional Budget Office literally threatened to count the insurers as government entities and put their finances into the scoring of the Obamacare bill. As CBO put it, "This further expansion of the federal government's role in the health insurance market would make such insurance an essentially governmental program."[39]

Insurers will now have profit-caps, strict and detailed government pricing guidelines, minimum coverage mandates, and a prohibition on measuring risks when issuing policies. They cannot write off more than $500,000 per year for any executive's pay. They barely qualify as private companies anymore. And beginning in 2014, the insurance industry gets slapped with an excise tax several times as great as the one applied to the pharmaceuticals—$8 billion in 2014, more than $11 billion in 2015, and $14 billion by 2018.[40]

They were also vilified by President Obama himself throughout the health care debate. He offered one fairly representative sample of his ire during a July 22, 2009, press conference: "There have been reports just over the last couple of days of insurance companies making record profits, right now. At a time when everybody's getting hammered, they're making record profits, and premiums are going up."[41]

Even Politifact, an outlet not exactly known for its fair-mindedness toward conservative viewpoints, rated Obama's claim as "false."[42] And the fact is, if you really wanted to wring inefficiencies out of the health care system, then the insurance industry is the wrong turnip to squeeze. The big money in health care is in the drug industry, whose profit margins are much larger.

Fortune's top ten drug-makers—including Merck, Bristol-Myers Squibb, and Johnson & Johnson—enjoyed a collective profit margin of 25 percent in 2009, with two of them approaching 50 percent.[43] *Fortune*'s top ten health insurers, on the other hand, had a collective profit margin of just 4.5 percent in 2009, with four of the top ten profiting by less than 3 percent.[44] The top ten insurers' total profit was about $12.7 billion. The top ten pharmaceutical firms, on the other hand, brought in a staggering $62.4 billion in 2009.

That's why Warren Buffett, asked in March 2010 about his view of the health insurance industry, remarked that it wasn't the real driver of costs, and even added that it wasn't nearly profitable enough for him to invest. "I'm in the property-casualty [insurance] business and I'm not in the health care business," he said. "Draw your own conclusion."[45]

Don't feel bad for the insurers. If Obamacare survives in court, every American will be forced to buy their product, under penalty of law. They will also collect billions in subsidies, and they're already raising their premiums to pay the costs of Obamacare and its new excise tax. They resisted Obamacare because they rightly wanted to avoid a government-run health insurance plan, but gangster government has given them a big enough cut of the taxpayer pie that they will get by.

The real losers are you and me, the consumers. All of the regulatory costs incurred by the insurers, drug-makers, and medical device makers (who get a $2 billion excise tax in Obamacare) will be passed on to us.

This episode illustrates the importance of making deals with and buying protection from gangster government. The bill President Obama signed into law didn't necessarily target the right people if the goal was to save money on health care. But it certainly did reward and punish the industries according to their relationships with the Obama White House.

DIRTY DEALS, DONE VERY EXPENSIVE

Many conservatives derided Obamacare as a government takeover of health care, which is true but can also be misleading. Obamacare did not establish a single-payer system or a health care system literally run by the federal government. Instead it heavily regulates what health insurers and providers can do. Government will pull the strings, call the shots, and pick the winners. Players that aligned themselves with the White House—the drug-makers, the labor unions, the trial lawyers, the congressional majority—were the major winners.

Trial lawyers, consistently among the Democratic Party's biggest donors and one of the most powerful lobbies inside the Obama White House, wanted to resist public pressure for reforms to the medical malpractice system. In the states where it had been tried—Texas and Mississippi, for example—simple medical malpractice reforms had cut costs and stemmed an exodus of doctors. But despite the fact that they could save far more than the $16 billion promised by Obama's rationing board, malpractice reforms were not included in Obamacare. Trial lawyers got their way, and can continue to pursue seven- and eight-figure windfalls.

For the AARP, a name trusted by millions of senior citizens, the choice to endorse and advertise on behalf of Obamacare was easy. For them, the bill was a goldmine. By cutting the Medicare Advantage program, which serves 10 million seniors, it would seriously damage or eliminate a major source of competition to AARP's Medigap insurance plans. A *Bloomberg News* study in 2008 found that AARP has essentially transformed itself into a business over the last decade.[46] Medigap supplemental insurance policies and other AARP-endorsed products made up only 11 percent of AARP's revenue in 1999. In 2008, these business activities made up 57 percent of the group's revenue, or $653 million.[47]

But AARP was getting an even better deal than that. In December 2010, the Obama administration gave the group an exemption from several of the harshest rules that govern other insurers. Its CEO can continue making more than a $1 million a year, as he did in 2008, according to the group's tax filings.[48] AARP won't have to pay the excise taxes that other insurers pay. It has also been exempted from the rule that requires insurers to spend 85 percent of the premiums it collects on customers' medical expenses.

The American Hospital Association and the Federation of American Hospitals also had interests at stake. For years, the for-profit and non-profit hospitals had been trying to get rid of the competition they receive from doctor-owned hospitals, whom they accuse of taking the best-paying patients. As early as 2007, they were promoting a bill which would have prohibited the expansion of existing doctor-owned hospitals and banned new ones.[49] With Obamacare they finally got their wish. At least one doctor-owned hospital chain was already selling off its facilities by the end of 2010.[50]

After Obama and congressional Democrats cut deals with industry, they had to cut deals with their fellow Democrats in Congress. This led to an avalanche of exemptions and amendments allowing favored states to get special treatment—everything from getting the federal government to cover the cost of Medicare expansion to exemptions from different provisions of the law:

- Vermont's senators, virtually unnoticed, managed to secure $600 million for their state to cover Medicaid expansion.
- A Nebraska deal promised to save one of the state's doctor-owned hospitals from the hospital lobby's provision, mentioned above.
- Another deal was struck to protect just two insurance companies—one in Nebraska, another in Michigan—from the new insurance excise tax.
- There was also a $300 million Medicaid provision to secure support from Democrat Senator Mary Landrieu of Louisiana. She later denied that it had been necessary to win her support.
- Fearing the fallout from Medicare Advantage cuts, Democrat Senator Bill Nelson of Florida slipped in an exemption for the residents of his state.
- Democrat Senator Chris Dodd of Connecticut tossed in a plain old earmark—a $100 million grant whose language was carefully written to apply only to a new hospital desired by the University of Connecticut.
- Another earmark came from Democrat Senator Max Baucus of Montana who secured Medicare coverage for Montana miners who had been exposed to asbestos.[51]

The bill, which passed on Christmas Eve, was becoming what Washington wags refer to as a "Christmas Tree"—covered with ornaments tagged on by every member of Congress with a special interest to serve. This wheeling-and-dealing drew a denunciation from no less staunch a supporter of Obamacare than Democrat Senator Russ Feingold of Wisconsin: "These 'sweeteners' are unjustifiable and only detract from our collective goal of putting America's health care system on a better and more sustainable path," Feingold wrote. "Several provisions were included in the health reform bill that create, rather than diminish, inequity.... Simply put, they are intended to provide an undeserved windfall to specific states."[52]

Obama later acted as if these special deals weren't his responsibility. As he told Diane Sawyer in an interview on ABC's *World News Tonight*:[53] "I didn't make a bunch of deals. There is a legislative process that is taking place in Congress and I am happy to own up to the fact that I have not changed Congress and how it operates the way I would have liked."

But he was not being truthful. His chief of staff, Rahm Emanuel, made it very clear in an interview just days later that he had been there directing Senate Democrats:[54]

> **EMANUEL:** Look, we were involved in the legislation all the way through.
> **COURIC:** Were you involved in that?
> **EMANUEL:** Yeah. I'm not gonna go through all of it... ·
> **COURIC:** But in the Ben Nelson deal?
> **EMANUEL:** We were helpful in getting the bill off the Senate floor. And in retrospect the things—as I said to you just earlier, things you would have done different.

The "Ben Nelson deal" that Couric referred to was the most notorious of all the backroom deals that made their way into the Obamacare bill. It became known as the "Cornhusker Kickback," which put the federal government on the hook for 100 percent of Nebraska's Medicaid expansion, estimated at $100 million. It wasn't the most expensive deal, but it was the most significant because it allowed Obamacare to become law.

Democrat Senator Ben Nelson of Nebraska had earlier sold his vote on the stimulus package.[55] On Obamacare, he was holding out for a statutory guarantee that Obamacare would not pay for abortion. He had originally campaigned for office as a pro-life Democrat, and he wanted a provision identical to what Democrat Congressman Bart Stupak of Michigan had inserted into the House version of Obamacare. But Nelson suddenly dropped his abortion concerns after winning the Cornhusker Kickback. He literally sold out his beliefs for a special interest favor.

Stupak appeared on the FOX Business Network and criticized Nelson: "I encouraged him just to hold tough," he told FOX Business in a lengthy interview. "He should have held onto that principle."

Stupak also took a shot at the Democratic leaders, House Speaker Nancy Pelosi and Senate Majority Leader Harry Reid, in that same interview: "I think for the party, it's hopefully a wake-up call to leadership that the agenda you set and the pace you're going...you have to be more inclusive of all members."

But only sixty days later, Stupak himself succumbed to party pressure. In exchange for a meaningless executive order from President Obama asserting that the health bill maintained existing restrictions on federal funding for abortion, Stupak announced that he would vote for the Senate-passed bill. Stupak even delivered an angry speech on the House floor, attacking Republicans for trying to add his own pro-life provision back into the bill.

"IT GETS BETTER"

A month after House Republicans gained sixty-three seats in the 2010 midterms, creating the largest Republican House majority in more than sixty years, two top strategists for the National Republican Congressional Committee explained the secret to their success in a *Politico* op-ed. Mike Shields and Brad Todd explained that it hadn't really been anything they did. President Obama had done all of the work for them with Obamacare:

> While independents objected to Democrats' spending and debt, we found it was the health care vote that caused them to give up

on the party as a congressional majority.... When asking voters an open-ended question about their greatest hesitation to supporting their local Democratic candidate, the phrase "health care" came up more often than any other—besides "Democrat." In our most difficult races, we closed the campaign on health care.[56]

One advantage the Republicans had, in addition to the public's antipathy toward the bill itself, was that Obamacare's first regulations went into effect in late September 2010. And around the same time, several insurers announced large premium rate hikes

In Washington State, several major insurers raised premiums by double-digit amounts. Regence BlueShield raised them by 16.5 percent; Asuris Northwest Health by 23.7 percent; Group Health Options by 22 percent. In California, Blue Shield announced a 59 percent rate hike, citing the health care law as one of its reasons.[57] Increased expenses from Obamacare, the company said, meant it would lose money even with the hike, which the state forced it to delay for two months.[58] Connecticut's largest insurer, Anthem Blue Cross and Blue Shield, had to raise rates by 23 percent just to pay for one of Obamacare's provisions—the elimination of lifetime coverage limits.[59]

When the insurers cited Obamacare as one major reason for the price hikes, Obama's Health and Human Services (HHS) Secretary, Kathleen Sebelius, responded with a bullying letter to the top lobbyist for the health insurers' trade group.[60] It was typical gangster government, essentially telling the insurers to shut up: "There will be zero tolerance for this type of misinformation and unjustified rate increases," Sebelius wrote. "We will not stand idly by as insurers blame their premium hikes and increased profits on the requirement that they provide consumers with basic protections." Sebelius also threatened to exclude from Obamacare's still-to-be-formed insurance exchanges any insurers who were so unwise as to inform customers of Obamacare-inspired rate increases.[61] So not only has the First Amendment stopped working, but transparency in pricing is no longer a virtue. Not when it embarrasses President Obama.

But what had Sebelius and Obama expected? The insurers were raising prices because their costs were rising with the first raft of Obamacare regulations. Obamacare required lower co-pays, the extension of coverage to 26-year-old "children," and would force insurers over time to spread the risk of their older and less healthy patients to their younger and healthier ones. They were losing their ability to limit liability with annual and lifetime coverage limits. What's more, the insurers faced a looming excise tax bill that begins at $8 billion and rises to $14 billion annually. All of these changes add costs for the insurance business, and cost increases lead to price increases.

There are other, less obvious reasons why Obamacare is causing rate hikes. One example is the rule forcing insurers to spend 80 or 85 percent of the premiums they collect on health care. Although all of the largest insurers approach or meet this 85 percent threshold on a nationwide basis, Obamacare's regulations actually require them to meet the ratio *in each individual state*. This is a much higher bar. For example, UnitedHealth spent 84 percent of its premiums on health care nationwide in 2009. But during the same year, its Golden Rule subsidiary in Florida spent less than 65 percent.[62] So even if this provision causes some Floridians to get a better deal, one way for the company to make up lost profits in Florida is to raise premiums in other states.

The Obamacare-induced hikes in insurance premiums were bad news for consumers in general, but there was even worse news for retirees at some of America's largest companies.[63] When the GOP Congress had passed its Medicare Prescription Drug program in 2003, it had made a deal with these companies. In order to prevent them from dumping hundreds of thousands of retirees into the Medicare program—which would have cost the government dearly—Congress agreed to subsidize the companies' retirement health plans, tax-free. The thinking was sound, the *Wall Street Journal* editorialized, because it would cost the government five times as much to cover these retirees under Medicare as it would to give their companies a small tax break: "$233 in corporate tax breaks [per employee] to avoid spending $1,209 seems like a deal."[64]

Unfortunately, one of Obamacare's hidden provisions, buried in the thousands of unread pages, undid this deal. The bill did not actually curtail the subsidies, but instead taxed them, beginning in 2013. This burned a new $14 billion hole in several large companies' balance sheets, including Verizon, AT&T, Boeing, Valero, and John Deere. There was a strong possibility that the companies would respond by terminating their retiree coverage and sending their pensioners into the Medicare program.

The executives of these companies had warned the Obama administration in advance, but White House officials arrogantly ignored their concerns and rebuffed them. The *American Spectator*'s "Prowler" quoted an anonymous senior lobbyist who had seen the intransigence of gangster government:[65]

> Most of these people [in the Administration] have never had a real job in their lives. They don't understand a thing about business, and that includes the President....My CEO sat with the President over lunch with two other CEOs, and each of them tried to explain to the President what this bill would do to our companies and the economy in general. First the President didn't understand what they were talking about. Then he basically told my boss he was lying. Frankly my boss was embarrassed for him; he clearly had not been briefed and didn't know what was in the bill.

After Obamacare passed, these same CEOs were required by other laws to restate their earnings projections; this revealed that this simple change in Obamacare would cost them a combined $14 billion. The White House responded by launching a bullying counterattack against the companies, with White House chief of staff Rahm Emanuel and Obama senior advisor Valerie Jarrett calling the CEOs and chewing them out for embarrassing the president.[66]

But as it turns out, the companies were right. At first, Congressional Democrats, led by Democrat House Energy and Commerce Chairman Henry Waxman of California, had announced that the CEOs would have to justify their earnings re-statements in congressional testimony. The Democrats demanded mounds of documents, many of which the companies considered proprietary, dating back to 2009.

And then Waxman, whose zeal for investigating corporations normally knows no bounds, suddenly backed off. The reason was that if the re-statements were embarrassing to the Obama administration, then the hearings would be even more so. He canceled the show-trial.

The details of the bill suddenly mattered, because it became painfully obvious that Democrat members of Congress had voted for the bill without reading or understanding its contents.

During the health care debate, House Speaker Nancy Pelosi famously said: "We have to pass the bill so that you can find out what is in it," which could stand as the maxim of gangster government. Thanks to this formula of blindly legislating, a litany of unexpected Obama surprises suddenly presented themselves:

- The period an employer could hire a seasonal employee before having to pay him health insurance had been quietly shortened through the reconciliation process from 150 to 120 days. This put the tourist industries of several states at risk.
- Because of a drafting error, Obamacare did not immediately require coverage for children with pre-existing conditions—something President Obama had repeatedly promised. In order to remedy the error, the White House had to cut another unlegislated deal, this time with the insurance industry it had been demonizing.
- After the bill passed, state governments noticed changes to Medicaid law, so that states had to guarantee not only payment but *treatment*. Given the number of doctors who refuse to see Medicaid patients, cash-strapped state programs could soon find themselves in court, being forced to ramp up Medicaid payments substantially.[67]
- Rather than decreasing medical costs, Obamacare was now predicted to raise medical costs by about $311 billion over ten years. The Congressional Budget Office, meanwhile, raised the estimated cost of the bill by another $115 billion, pushing it beyond the trillion-dollar mark.

- Another hidden cost to small business, already reeling in a bad economy: Obamacare required small businesses to file IRS 1099 forms for every vendor with whom they do more than $600 in business. This provision would not raise much money, but it would dramatically increase compliance costs for 30 million U.S. businesses. Its repeal seems likely, but the fact that it was ever included shows just how tough Obama and his party were willing to be on businesses in order to make their bill appear deficit-neutral.

RULE BY BUREAUCRAT

As this book goes to press, four federal district courts have ruled on Obamacare. Two of them saw no conflict between the constitutionally limited powers of the federal government and the law's requirement that all Americans purchase health insurance. Two of them found that provision unconstitutional, and one of these—in the Northern District of Florida—struck down the entire bill. A final decision by the Supreme Court is almost inevitable, and the outcome cannot be guessed in advance. Even if the high court strikes down the individual mandate, a substantial portion of the law could remain intact.

Meanwhile, the ship of Obamacare sails on. Bureaucrats are issuing regulations and rulings, and making key decisions that will affect every American's health coverage and care for decades to come, unless the measure is ultimately repealed.

Among these bureaucrats is Donald Berwick, whom President Obama appointed as Administrator of the Centers for Medicare and Medicaid Services in July 2010. Berwick is known for praising Britain's troubled National Health Service at the expense of America's health care system.

"I am romantic about the NHS; I love it," he said in Britain in 2008. "All I need to do to rediscover the romance is to look at health care in my own country."[68]

Berwick's speeches suggest that he favors socialized medicine and sees health insurance as a means of economic redistribution:

> Any health care funding plan that is just, equitable, civilized, and humane must, must redistribute wealth from the richer among us to the poorer and the less fortunate. Excellent health care is by definition redistribution.[69]

Berwick is a recess appointment, which means he will hold his post only until January 2012. But it also means that he got to skip Senate confirmation.

Obama's decision to make a recess appointment was unusual. There was no filibuster against Donald Berwick. His statements, while perhaps outside of mainstream American thinking, could surely have been explained in a hearing.

But Berwick, then CEO of a non-profit called the Institute for Healthcare Improvement, was never even scheduled for a hearing. As for the reason why, my *Examiner* colleague, Byron York, has probably come closer than anyone else to giving a decent explanation:

> As it turns out, Berwick himself does not have to deal with the anxieties created by limited access to care and the extent of coverage. In a special benefit conferred on him by the board of directors of the Institute for Health Care Improvement, a nonprofit health care charitable organization he created and which he served as chief executive officer, Berwick and his wife will have health coverage "from retirement until death."[70]

Berwick's lifetime health benefit, York reported, came "on top of the $2.3 million in compensation the nonprofit gave Berwick in 2008, the $637,006 in compensation he received in 2007, and the $585,008 he received in 2006." So Obamacare will be developed and run in large part by man who is not only an ideological zealot, but possibly a non-profit profiteer as well.

So where did this charity's $12 million in 2008 grants come from? Who was essentially paying Berwick $2.3 million, just before he would take a position from which he will have great power over the health care of millions of Americans?

Uncomfortable questions like these could have arisen in a hearing. In fact, it was weeks after a Republican senator sent written questions about the nonprofit's finances that the recess appointment was suddenly announced. Tim Carney called it "an Obama innovation in presidential power: While George W. Bush used recess appointments to install officials who couldn't clear a Democratic filibuster, Obama ... uses recess appointments to avoid embarrassing floor debates and spare his party's senators from embarrassing votes."[71]

Four months after he received his job without congressional approval, Berwick made his first trip to Capitol Hill to testify. He pleaded that he could not produce information on the organization he had founded. It would be a conflict of interest for him to request it, he said, now that he heads CMS.[72] So transparency is a conflict of interest, but it is not a conflict of interest for Berwick to receive a lifetime of free health care from this group.

It is fitting that such a man was appointed, in such an underhanded way, to such an important post, with no transparency or consultation, to implement a vitally important law that was crafted and passed in much the same way. Gangster government shuns the light and operates in the shadows, cuts deals with favored businesses, writes provisions known only by a select few, offers legislative and regulatory exemptions to friends, and threatens opponents with death by regulation.

CHAPTER FOUR

THE MOST EXPENSIVE STORY EVER TOLD

"Our policy problem today is that the bill that was actually passed into law was both so expensive and so badly flawed that it gives the whole concept of macroeconomic stimulus a bad name."

—Former White House economic advisor Lawrence Lindsey, writing in **The Weekly Standard**[1]

"Look, all governors like 'free money' coming to the state," said Republican Senator Jon Kyl of Arizona.[2] "My governor is no different. But the reality is that it has added to our deficit. We're now going to have a $1.8 trillion deficit this year."

Kyl was discussing the American Recovery and Reinvestment Act—the stimulus package—on *This Week with George Stephanopoulos*. Today, that law is maligned, dubbed "porkulus" and known mostly for its less defensible grants and projects, such as research on cocaine-addicted monkeys and expensive, handicapped-accessible sidewalks that literally lead into ditches. The result is that the Obama administration has come to hate the word "stimulus" almost as much as it hates the word "Obamacare."

But at the time Kyl was speaking—July 12, 2009—Americans were definitely still giving stimulus a chance. So Kyl was going out on a limb when he said that the package:

...promised to create or save 4 million jobs. We've now lost another two million jobs. Unemployment is two points higher than it was when the president took office. And even with the stimulus, it's higher than they said that it would be without the stimulus.

The reality is it hasn't helped yet. Only about 6.8 percent of the money has actually been spent. What I proposed is, after you complete the contracts that are already committed, the things that are in the pipeline, stop it.... [W]e're digging this deficit hole even deeper than we have today.

He went on to mention something that would later be found within the volumes of spreadsheet data collected by the government: some of the grants were actually being spent on grant writers. "It was interesting—a bit amusing—to find that some of the jobs created by the stimulus bill were to hire people to apply for more federal grants. That's not the kind of jobs that we want to create."

No sooner had Kyl uttered his criticism than the wheels of gangster government were set in motion. The following day, Arizona's Republican governor, Jan Brewer, received letters from four of President Obama's cabinet secretaries—Agriculture, Transportation, Interior, and Housing and Urban Development. Each letter asked whether she would like the $521 million in Arizona stimulus projects to be withdrawn from the state.

It was a tacky but darkly humorous political stunt—a bit of hardball with Rahm Emanuel's name all over it. It was also a veiled threat against legislators who criticize the stimulus package in the future, and consistent with President Obama's answer to Republicans when they had objected to some of the stimulus provisions in January 2009: "I won."[3]

The implication of the letters is that gangster government is going to waste your money, and if you criticize, then it will waste the money only on other people. But the story only begins there. It ends with one of Obama's cabinet secretaries trying to save face for the White House, and apparently lying to Congress.

One of the letters to Governor Brewer was from Obama's Transportation Secretary, Ray LaHood. LaHood had been a moderate Republican member of Congress from Illinois for seven terms before joining the cabinet. He came from Peoria, not Chicago, but was of the same Illinois political stock and felt right at home in the Obama administration.

As a member of the House Appropriations Committee, he had been a key ally for Chicago's Democratic Mayor, Richard M. Daley, whose endless drive for more federal money to expand O'Hare International Airport was a point of personal pride. The City of Chicago's website still boasts of his commitment to complete this project "at no cost to local or state taxpayers."[4] And sure enough, a November 2010 Department of Transportation press release from LaHood announced ("gloated" might be a better word) that the project had received $800 million so far, making it the most heavily federally subsidized airport project in the history of the United States.[5]

LaHood, a notorious pork-barreler during his time in the House, had steered $9 million of his $60 million in earmark requests in 2008 to campaign donors, according to the *Washington Post*.[6] He was the ideal administrator for the transportation dollars that would play such a prominent role in the stimulus package.

The Peoria *Journal-Star* had once quoted LaHood explaining his reasons for seeking a seat on the powerful House Appropriations Committee, which has the first say in all government spending: "The reason I went on the Appropriations Committee, the reason other people go on the Appropriations Committee, is they know that it puts them in a position to know where the money is at, to know the people who are doling the money out and to be in the room when the money is being doled out."[7]

In 2005, as Congress was considering a relief package after Hurricane Katrina, some members had discussed paying for it by removing their own earmarks from that year's transportation bill. LaHood was not one of them. He told the *Chicago Tribune*, "It's a little unrealistic for us to be sitting around at this moment having a lot of heartburn about the deficit."[8] LaHood had his own agenda for Hurricane Katrina. He wanted to use the disaster as an excuse to steer relief funds to his own rural Illinois district, on the grounds that the storm had disrupted grain shipments.

For this, and for the $44 million in pork projects he slipped into the 2005 transportation bill, he had been named "Porker of the Month" by the watchdog group Citizens Against Government Waste.[9] The group was also put off by LaHood's bitter fight to prevent the closure of 700 of the federal Farm Service Agencies' 2,351 offices that year. LaHood won that fight, and as of this writing, the agency (which most Americans have never heard of) has 2,346 offices nationwide.[10]

LaHood also fit well into ObamaLand because he had no qualms about embracing a less-than-conservative vision for transportation. Instead of facilitating travel, the LaHood Department of Transportation has tried to discourage people from driving. As LaHood told George Will on one occasion, "I think we can change people's behavior," prompting a horrified Will to call him "the Secretary of Behavior Modification."[11] LaHood did not shy away from this criticism, either, telling a reporter about his department's "livable communities" initiative: "It's a way to coerce people out of their cars, yeah...and the only person that I've heard of that objects to this is George Will."[12]

LaHood would later propose a federal ban on holding hands-free cell phone conversations while driving. In a November 2010 appearance on MSNBC's *Morning Joe*, he said that the federal government was exploring the use of scramblers to disable drivers' cell phones. "There's a lot of technology out there now that can disable phones and we're looking at that," he said.[13]

So LaHood wasn't too far out of his comfort zone defending the stimulus from criticism by writing a retaliatory letter against someone who had publicly voiced fears about waste, and deficits, and contributing to the growth of government. LaHood wrote to Governor Brewer that Senator Kyl had "publicly questioned whether the stimulus is working and stated that he wants to cancel projects that aren't presently under way....If you prefer to forfeit the money we are making available to your state, as Senator Kyl suggests, please let me know."[14]

When four different cabinet secretaries send a letter just like this at the same time, it's not too difficult to figure out that it came straight from the top. And the Obama White House was not shy about its role in this bullying effort, either. In fact, the White House proudly took credit for it and made sure it appeared in the press. *Politico* reported: "[A]fter seeing Kyl and House Minority Whip Eric Cantor (R-Va.) again paint the legislation as a failure on Sunday talk shows, White House chief of staff Rahm Emanuel directed that the letters from the Cabinet secretaries be sent to Brewer, according to two administration officials."[15]

Jonathan Alter's *The Promise* also credits this brilliant tactic to Rahm Emanuel: "When Jon Kyl of Arizona, the Senate Republican whip, criticized the stimulus, Rahm called him on it by arranging for a letter to be sent from the federal government to Arizona Governor Jan Brewer asking which billion in stimulus spending the state chose not to receive."[16]

This example of gangster government got really interesting when a member of Congress decided to ask LaHood about it during a congressional hearing. Because apparently, LaHood had not gotten the memo about Emanuel taking public credit for the whole thing.

On July 24, 2009, eleven days after the four secretaries wrote Brewer, LaHood appeared before the House Budget committee. Republican Congressman Scott Garrett of New Jersey asked him about the letter.

> **Garrett:** Is it appropriate for a cabinet secretary to contact the governor of that state to request whether the money should come back? Could you see that as a veiled threat from the administration? Could you see that if you were still a member of Congress?
>
> **LaHood:** Not at all.
>
> **Garrett:** You wouldn't think that?
>
> **LaHood:** Not at all.
>
> **Garrett:** Should I have any concerns that I even raise this? That I would get a letter sent to Governor Corzine of New Jersey saying, "Well, the Congressman voted against the stimulus, and so therefore we're wondering whether you want to receive the money?"

LaHood played dumb, not even trying to present a plausible explanation. He cast his letter to Brewer as a sincere expression of concern about whether Arizona really wanted its money. And then it got testy:

Garrett: Did anyone else in the administration or outside the administration encourage you to write the letter?

LaHood: I don't need any encouragement to write letters to governors, Congressman.

Garrett: Did anyone inside or outside the administration contact you or encourage you to write that letter?

LaHood: I don't need any encouragement from anybody to write letters, Congressman. My job is to work with governors.

Garrett: Just answer that question. Did anyone else inside or outside the administration encourage you to write that letter, whether you needed…?

LaHood: Congressman, my responsibility is to work with governors…

Garrett: Would you answer the question?

LaHood: Let me answer it.

Garrett: It's a yes or no. Did anyone in or outside the administration encourage you to write that letter?

LaHood: I don't need any encouragement—

Garrett: Can you answer the question? Whether you needed the encouragement or not, did anyone…

LaHood: I don't need any encouragement. That's my answer.

Garrett: Mr. Chairman, would the witness please answer the question? Did anyone inside or outside the administration encourage you to write that letter? Whether you needed the encouragement or not, did anyone encourage you to write that letter?

LaHood: No.

Garrett: Did anyone talk to you about writing that letter?

LaHood: No.

Garrett: It was all, entirely your decision?

LaHood: Congressman—

Garrett: That's…

LaHood: Do you want me to answer, or do you want to go on?

At least Garrett only had to ask the question seven times to get an answer from LaHood. And never mind that if any of the reporting surrounding the incident is true, this "straight answer" was straight fib.

Why should Obama administration officials care about telling the truth to Congress? After all, "they won," didn't they?

WE JUST WASTED A TRILLION DOLLARS?

The month President Obama was inaugurated, January 2009, an incredible 779,000 jobs disappeared, making it the worst month of the Great Recession.[17] Obama made it clear to Congress, even before he was sworn in, that he wanted a large stimulus package. Days after taking office, he addressed the need for stimulus in Elkhart, Indiana:

> You didn't send us to Washington because you were hoping for more of the same. You sent us there with a mandate for change.... That is why I put forth a Recovery and Reinvestment Plan that is now before Congress. At its core is a very simple idea: to put Americans back to work doing the work America needs done.... The plan will save or create three to four million jobs over the next two years.[18]

So what was the American Recovery and Reinvestment Act of 2009? In the sense that it was a proposal for tons of deficit spending, it was "more of the same." Since 2002, both Republican and Democratic congresses had accumulated an impressive $3.3 trillion in deficits, not even counting the TARP spending binge at the end of President Bush's term and the second dose of TARP at the beginning of Obama's.[19] Obama just wanted to open the spigot further.

In the sense that it contained billions in infrastructure spending, it was also more of the same. In 2005, Congress had passed a $286 billion transportation authorization bill that ran through 2009. The 2009 stimulus package promised more than $105 billion for infrastructure, dedicating about $48 billion to roads and $18 billion to sewer and water projects.

Nearly every Republican voted against the stimulus, but there was little serious resistance to the package, given Obama's stratospheric post-inaugural popularity—not to mention the administration's propensity to send letters to critics' home-state governors. Besides, a stimulus package is not a terribly hard sell in tough times.

Days after his speech in Elkhart, Obama signed the stimulus package, an $814 billion spending bill that contained some of Congress's annual routine business (a patch on the Alternative Minimum Tax, for example), but was mostly a grab bag of different programs designed to stimulate demand in the economy. There were modest tax credits, new subsidies, and billions of dollars for government projects that were supposedly ready to begin right away— "shovel-ready projects," as Obama liked to say.

> [M]y economic team, which I'm going to be meeting with today, is helping to shape what is going to be a bold agenda to create 2.5 million new jobs, to start helping states and local governments with shovel-ready projects—rebuilding our roads, our bridges... putting people back to work, getting businesses to start seeing some increase in demand, so that we can get, instead of a downward spiral, start getting on an upward spiral.

Twenty months later, Obama was a much wiser man. As he told *The New York Times Magazine*: "There's no such thing as shovel-ready projects."[20]

The real question is, did we get anything more than that realization for our $814 billion?

Many liberals and mainstream media pundits take it on faith that the American Recovery and Reinvestment Act was necessary to save the world, even if they acknowledge that it has fallen out of favor with the public. Jonathan Alter writes that the package "was poorly framed politically and too slow in creating jobs. But without it, the country would have likely stayed mired in a deep recession or even slipped into a depression."[21]

This is not a popular view—in October 2010, 68 percent of Americans rejected it out of hand, telling the *Washington Post*-ABC News poll that the stimulus money had been "mostly wasted."[22] But some people, especially members of Obama's administration, will tell you it has created hundreds of thousands or millions of jobs. In fact, sometimes they each make up a different number.

"Two million," said strategist David Axelrod.[23]

"One point five million," said spokesman Robert Gibbs.[24]

"Thousands and thousands," said adviser Valerie Jarrett, whose imagination was apparently more limited.[25]

Those figures were all conjured from thin air on the same day—January 24, 2010. The three Obama administration officials actually appeared on three different Sunday talk shows and made up three different numbers.

The burden of proof for the stimulus package's success lies squarely with those who spent $814 billion and failed to create any significant number of new jobs. They haven't produced much proof yet. Obviously, stimulus grants went out, and the money was used to hire some number of people—that much is not in dispute. But that's not necessarily the same thing as "creating" net jobs. And even assuming that the stimulus has funded some worthwhile road projects, and alleviated some people's suffering in hard economic times, that's not the same as claiming that a stimulus package can end a recession or create millions of jobs.

When Congress voted to borrow and spend $814 billion, they did not know—and we cannot know for sure—what would have happened if all or part of it had been invested in private ventures instead of the Treasury bonds that paid for the grab bag of fiscal measures that was the stimulus package. That is to say nothing of the man-hours and private investment that were lured away from productive, useful things that meet actual consumer demand, and invested instead in chasing after stimulus subsidies. We also do not know whether or to what degree businesses had to raise wages to compete with stimulus hires, resulting in less hiring.

The most recent study on the stimulus—the only one so far to try to measure its success based on post-stimulus events, rather than pre-stimulus assumptions—found that the package caused about 2 million "short-lived" jobs to appear and then rapidly disappear within a matter of months.

And finally, we can be quite certain that the jobs "created or saved" by the package cost a lot of money. If the package had lived up to its minimum billing and created or saved 3 million more jobs than it destroyed, it would have done so at an average cost of $271,000 per job. If it was less effective, as most Americans suspect, then each job obviously cost more than that.

Voters are now skeptical of stimulus packages, in part because of recent experience. In the Recovery Act's first twenty-one months, a net 3 million jobs were lost. We can never know for sure what would have happened without the Recovery Act, but we can look at what some parts of it did to see whether there are any good arguments that it was a success, or even what sort of "success" it was actually driving at. Was the goal to create new jobs period, or was it to create the sorts of jobs that Barack Obama thought should be created?

Beyond questions of success or failure, and beyond the obvious accusation—that this was an attempt to appease voters with taxpayers' money—the stimulus is a tool of gangster government. It has provided President Obama with financial leverage to re-shape the economy to meet his own very specific and narrow vision of America's economic future. He sees a future America in which unionized workers build renewable energy products that thrive from taxpayer subsidies—an America in which drivers abandon their cars and ride on expensive high-speed rail lines. It is an unsustainable future, and it is the opposite direction from where our economy (where it is free and undirected by gangster government) and the rest of the world are headed.

Obama's vision has come at a great cost, steering billions of dollars to areas where there is not enough consumer demand to justify private investment. To the extent that it has done this, the money probably undermined rather than boosted recovery. But it did provide billions in subsidies to the Obama administration's allies.

The final act of the stimulus saga—the most expensive story ever told—is a strange and unexpected twist. "Stimulus"—a perfectly acceptable word in public life as recently as 2008—has become an obscenity that members of the administration won't even use when describing the Recovery Act.

Who ever thought the idea of free money could become so unpopular?

BORROW AND SPEND

Stimulus packages are nothing new. They have been tried before by congresses and presidents of both parties. President George W. Bush signed one as recently as 2008—you may remember receiving a check in the mail for some amount between $300 and $1,200.

President Obama's stimulus package was much larger. Its original $787 billion price tag was later revised to $814 billion by the non-partisan Congressional Budget Office. Although there are many ways of dividing its parts and describing it, it is probably easiest to look at these three main categories:

- First, there were direct attempts to stimulate demand among consumers. These included a $116 billion refundable tax credit—meaning that it also went to some families that don't pay income taxes. This category also includes entitlement spending—extended unemployment benefits, food stamps, insurance subsidies, and one-time $250 payments to Social Security recipients.
- Second, there was money for states and municipalities, to spur government purchases and prevent huge budget cuts and layoffs. This came to $144 billion in the original stimulus package; in August 2010, Congress added a $26 billion state bailout.
- Third, there were grants, loans, and contracts for specific projects—the category that got the most (and the most negative) publicity.

"IT'S LIKE A BUDGET NUMBER"

The problem with deficit-spending stimulus packages is that they amount to robbing Peter to pay Paul—they merely divert money from the private sector to government-supported projects. They redistribute demand in the economy instead of creating it. But that hasn't stopped the Obama administration from trying to manufacture evidence that the stimulus was successful.

The first attempt involved stimulus reporting. From the moment the package passed, the White House was eager to show results. So the Recovery Administration contracted a Maryland firm called Smartronix to build and maintain the Recovery.gov website for the astoundingly high price of

$18 million.[26] The price tag was eye-popping, but the website was not, especially at first. In its first incarnation, the search function was nearly useless, and the results pages impossible to navigate. To find the important information, users had to make several counterintuitive clicks and navigate around several hundred words of confusing, page-filling bureaucratese.

The site's real virtue was that it allowed users to download Excel spreadsheets of stimulus reports—something that anyone reasonably familiar with a PC could have set up in 1996 for a day's pay.

But far worse than the website's technical shortcomings, which were later mitigated, were the outlandish early claims for jobs created by stimulus programs. The White House naturally embraced positive numbers as signs of progress. But federal departments had given contractors and loan recipients confusing or conflicting instructions on how to report data. So we started seeing stories like this one:

> About two-thirds of the 14,506 jobs claimed to be saved under one federal office, the Administration for Children and Families at Health and Human Services, actually weren't saved at all, according to a review of the latest data by The Associated Press. Instead, that figure includes more than 9,300 existing employees in hundreds of local agencies who received pay raises and benefits and whose jobs weren't saved.[27]

The number of jobs actually created in that pool? About nine.

And then:

> In June, the federal government spent $1,047 in stimulus money to buy a rider mower from the Toro Company to cut the grass at the Fayetteville National Cemetery in Arkansas. Now, a report on the government's stimulus Web site improbably claims that that single lawn mower sale helped save or create 50 jobs.[28]

And there were plenty of other examples:

New numbers released by the federal government Friday estimate that the federal stimulus package has helped create or save 34,500 total jobs in Washington, making it the state with the third-largest reported number of stimulus jobs behind California and New York. But there's a caveat on those job creation numbers: 24,000 of them probably weren't in danger in the first place.... Without that funding, the money to pay the teachers would have come out of the state general fund, said Jill Satran, Gov. Chris Gregoire's main adviser on stimulus projects.[29]

And:

Up to one-fourth of the 110,000 jobs reported as saved by federal stimulus money in California probably never were in danger, a [*Sacramento Bee*] review has found. California State University officials reported late last week that they saved more jobs with stimulus money than the number of jobs saved in Texas—and in 44 other states. In a required state report to the federal government, the university system said the $268.5 million it received in stimulus funding through October allowed it to retain 26,156 employees. That total represents more than half of CSU's statewide work force. However, university officials confirmed Thursday that half their workers were not going to be laid off without the stimulus dollars.... "This is not really a real number of people," CSU spokeswoman Clara Potes-Fellow said. "It's like a budget number."

As much as that last quote says about budgeting at California's universities, it says a lot more about the government's methods of stimulus reporting. So does the fact that such stories were so common.

My colleague Mark Hemingway and I compiled a running tally of jobs "not really created or saved" as reported in the media, and we also combed through the Recovery.gov spreadsheets to see what else we could find. Our analysis, which was by no means complete, identified at least 95,000 of the reported jobs to be bogus.[30] In addition to the inaccuracies already reported by the press, we found many entries that specifically stated they had counted small raises as new jobs; jobs that hadn't actually been created yet (and were not supposed to be reported yet under Recovery.gov rules); and jobs that paid impossibly small amounts (less than $2,000) but were counted as full-time equivalents anyway. Several thousand of the jobs created were just part-time work-study jobs on college campuses, which are more accurately described as a form of financial aid.

In some states, though, the job count did provide some useful data. The *Boston Herald* reported in February 2010 that 71 percent of the jobs "created or saved" in Massachusetts at that point were government jobs.[31] In New Hampshire, the initial numbers suggested that 90 percent were government jobs. As in California, it was not at all clear from New Hampshire's report that the 2,700 government jobs had ever been at risk.[32] But gangster government has a soft spot for supposedly "saved" government hiring.

CAN OPENER

The line in the White House was that "while the data may be imprecise," the stimulus' effects were "irrefutable."[33] And they became truly irrefutable after that, because the Obama administration turned to another bogus way of proving that the stimulus was creating jobs: they began *assuming* it.

On December 1, 2009, the respected, non-partisan Congressional Budget Office (CBO) produced a report estimating stimulus job creation at between 600,000 and 1.6 million jobs to date. Vice President Joe Biden, dubbed the "stimulus sheriff" by President Obama, was quick to pounce when he saw something that looked like vindication:

> This new report from the Congressional Budget Office is further evidence of what private forecasters and government economists have been saying: the Recovery Act is already responsible for more than 1 million jobs nationwide. From independent economists to Congress's own nonpartisan research body, the experts have

spoken and the debate is no longer whether the Recovery Act is creating and saving jobs, but how we provide even more opportunities to drive growth and support American workers. This early progress less than halfway through the program is encouraging, but we're just getting started.[34]

Unfortunately, these job-creation claims were a lie. It's not that the CBO is unreliable—to the contrary, there is no reason to believe the report was not 100 percent accurate. The problem was that it did not say what the White House wanted it to say.

In the stimulus package, Congress required the CBO to produce quarterly comments on its progress, *but not on how the economy or the unemployment rate reacted to the stimulus*. The non-partisan watchdog's reports looked primarily at how much money the stimulus had spent and then factored in how many jobs *might* have been created for each category of spending.

Before the stimulus passed, the CBO developed a formula that assumed, for example, that each dollar of spending on government purchases was worth between $1 and $2.50 in the economy, and that each dollar given through the Making Work Pay tax credit was worth between 60 cents and $1.50.[35] These figures are based on historical studies of previous government programs. But they also don't take into account such factors as current economic output, unemployment, or GDP growth.

Each quarter, the CBO asked two questions—how many stimulus dollars went out the door, and what were they spent on? They adjusted for a few factors (interest rates, for example) and then multiplied according to their formula for the net effect of such government spending and, *voila*, an estimate of the number of jobs.

If, by some fluke, the unemployment rate had suddenly fallen to just 4 percent in June 2010, the CBO would have produced exactly the same report it did, positing the creation of 1.4 million to 3.3 million jobs. And if unemployment had increased to 50 percent in June 2010, CBO would still have said exactly the same thing.

CBO's director, Doug Elmendorf, made this clear after a March 2010 speech, when he explained to a questioner how the CBO simply uses "multipliers" based on studies of previous spending bills and their believed economic effects. He said the CBO was "repeating the same exercises we [already] did rather than an independent check on it."[36]

He was then asked: "If the stimulus bill did not do what it was originally forecast to do, then that would not have been detected by the subsequent analysis, is that correct?"

"That's right."[37]

So while the CBO was honest, the Obama administration was not—it kept trotting out these job figures as if they were proof of success. Writing about another stimulus report that used the same method of assuming its conclusion, former Bush economic advisor Lawrence Lindsey provided an apt analogy in *The Weekly Standard*: "This is the economic equivalent of assuming there are 1,000 angels on the head of a pin, observing that we have 10 pins, and therefore calculating that we must have 10,000 angels. The math is fine. But it sheds no light on the key policy issue."[38]

Obama and Biden must have heard the old joke about the economist who is stranded on a desert island with nothing but a can of food. He *assumes* a can opener. Obama and Biden put a gangster government spin on this, assuming they could fool all the people all the time.

NET ZERO

The stimulus package, as the *Wall Street Journal* noted, was "aimed in large part at preventing public-sector layoffs."[39] How was that money spent? According to John Cogan, a former White House deputy budget director, and John Taylor, a Stanford economics professor, state and local governments actually spent less money after the stimulus package than before. Taylor and Cogan found that instead of spending all the extra stimulus cash, states and cities used federal stimulus funds to avoid borrowing more money. "The bottom-line is the federal government borrowed funds from the public, transferred these funds to state and local governments, who then used the funds mainly to reduce borrowing from the public. The net impact on aggregate economic activity is zero...."[40]

In other words, when it comes to the stimulus for state and local governments, the stimulus package was really just a debt balance transfer to Uncle Sam—a simple bailout that accounted for $170 billion, or one-fifth of the entire stimulus package, transferred from bureaucrats to bureaucrats.

Other attempts to measure the stimulus' effectiveness have produced similarly disappointing results. In January 2009, prior to President Obama's inauguration, incoming White House economic advisors Christina Romer and Jared Bernstein authored a paper stating that with a stimulus package, the unemployment rate would top off below 8 percent in the middle of 2009 and then fall precipitously to below 7 percent by the time this book is published.[41] This did not happen—instead, unemployment broke 10 percent briefly, then hovered above 9 percent throughout 2010.

But out of fairness to Romer and Bernstein, they had an excuse for being wrong. At the time they published their report, they could not have been aware that the unemployment rate was already 8.2 percent, much worse than they believed. And so Bruce Lindsey, writing in *The Weekly Standard*, recalculated their estimates accordingly. What he found is that after the stimulus package passed, the unemployment rate easily exceeded their prediction, adjusted accordingly, for what would have happened *without* a stimulus package.[42] This calls into question the entire model the administration used in developing the package.

The most serious scholarly attempt to measure the stimulus' effectiveness was an October 2010 study by Daniel Wilson, an assistant director at the Federal Reserve Bank in San Francisco.[43] Wilson was the first to measure the stimulus against a reality-based hypothetical scenario in which no stimulus had passed. In order to do this, he carefully examined the variations in stimulus spending between different states, to see how great the effects were over time of more or less stimulus funding.

Wilson's 40-page paper, filled with economists' jargon and equations with Greek letters as variables, comes with 40 additional pages of charts and tables. It is not a fun read. But its conclusion is extremely enlightening. He writes that the Recovery Act "...created or saved about 2.0 million jobs, or 1.5% of pre-ARRA employment, in the total nonfarm sector by early 2010.

However, the results indicate that many of these ARRA-generated jobs were short-lived, as the estimated employment impact fell to just 0.8 million (0.6% of pre-ARRA employment) by June 2010 and to essentially zero by August 2010."

Wilson also observed that "ARRA spending appears to have increased both jobs gains (from opening/expanding businesses) and job losses (from closing/contracting businesses)." In terms of net job creation, this would suggest that the package has been a costly failure.

LEARNING FROM SPAIN

As President Obama put it, his goal was to create "not just any jobs [but] jobs that meet the needs we've neglected for far too long and lay the groundwork for long-term economic growth."[44] This is called central planning. The stimulus gave Obama $814 billion in borrowed cash to spend, and he took it as an opportunity to throw billions of dollars at bad liberal ideas in order to change the way America works. Obama now had significant leverage to steer markets and industries in directions he wanted—to re-shape the economy to support expensive boondoggles that had no demand in the free market.

President Obama invoked the European experience several times, and Spain in particular, as he tried to sell Americans on the idea of a future green economy full of new, well-paying jobs. Weeks before his inauguration, he spoke in Bedford Heights, a suburb of Cleveland: "And think of what's happening in countries like Spain, Germany and Japan, where they're making real investments in renewable energy. They're surging ahead of us, poised to take the lead in these new industries."[45]

Indeed—look at Spain. That nation had taken its commitment to renewable energy very seriously, offering massive and very-long-term subsidies for wind and solar producers. One result was that heavily subsidized wind farms cropped up on picturesque hillsides. But the subsidies were heaviest in solar, and so was the growth in production capacity.

Beginning in 2007, the Spanish government reimbursed and subsidized utilities for the much higher costs of producing energy from "renewable" sources, and by government decree, every spark of electricity produced from renewable operations had to be purchased by a utility company at above market rates for twenty-five years. This locked in a guaranteed market for the investors' higher-priced power, and a guaranteed return on investment: an investor in solar power could reap a 17 percent return on his investment with (at least in theory) the same level of security as a Spanish government bond.[46] That's a big enough return to increase any investment 50-fold over the 25-year guarantee period.

All these incentives of guaranteed, no-risk profit attracted a lot of investment to the green power sector. Spain not only led the world in solar investment in 2008, but demand for solar panels there actually exceeded demand for the entire rest of the world.[47] In some cases, Spaniards took huge mortgages on their homes to buy and install new panels.[48] Growth in solar electric generation increased 35-fold in Spain between 2006 and 2008.[49] By President Obama's stimulus logic, you'd expect Spain's economy to be humming along. After all, people had to build all of those panels and install them—just think of all the jobs they were creating!

Unfortunately, things don't work that way in the real world. Spain's unemployment rate currently stands at 21 percent; its government is on the edge of default; and the huge subsidies for renewable energy only created a massive asset bubble, steering investors' billions away from where there really was consumer demand, where investment made real sense, and sustainable jobs could be created.

Spain's free-money program was riddled with corruption from top to bottom, and led to the arrests of dozens of public officials and industry insiders—gangster government at its finest.[50] But things got much worse than that. By the end of 2008, Spain had become a world leader in solar power, second only to Germany. Yet its socialist government recognized that the pace of its investments was completely unsustainable, and so it scaled back the subsidies for new solar installations, and then capped the amount of new solar generation it would subsidize for the year. The global market for solar components suddenly collapsed—prices plummeted and jobs disappeared.[51]

And then it got even worse. In 2010, just as Greece's fiscal situation was coming apart at the seams, the Spanish government saw its credit rating slashed. Its budget was weighed down in part by its high levels of spending on electricity subsidies—a staggering $37 billion in eight years. Looking for areas to cut costs and stave off a total panic, the government began reopening the 25-year subsidy agreements that had been made prior to 2009, with a view of cutting back subsidies for existing firms.[52] The subsidized companies countered that if the government reneged on its promises, the solar projects wouldn't be sustainable and there would be a new wave of defaulted loans.[53] They threatened legal action.

In March 2009, economist Gabriel Calzada of King Juan Carlos University in Madrid released a damning study on the government's renewable energy program, concluding that it had killed 2.2 jobs for every "green" job created, just through misallocation of the government's funds and workers' productive capacity.[54] He didn't even hazard a guess at how many additional jobs had been lost because investors' private money was being lured out of economically productive pursuits.

Calzada also found that each "green" job was costing the government a staggering $775,000 on average. And Spain's initiatives in wind power, which had been far more efficient than solar in terms of subsidies per megawatt hour, were nonetheless extremely inefficient in terms of creating jobs. Each job "created" in wind power cost the government $1.4 million.

The solar industry and the Spanish government actually tried to force the university to disavow Calzada's study.[55] But a leaked memo from the Spanish cabinet later showed the government essentially admitted that Calzada had been correct.[56]

In the United States, the supposedly science-friendly Obama administration was not about to accept Spain's failure as evidence of anything. White House spokesman Robert Gibbs was asked if he thought the study was wrong. "I haven't read the study," he said, "but I think, yes."[57]

(His boss had once given a similar answer when asked about the conduct of the Cambridge police in the arrest of Henry Louis Gates: "Now, I don't know, not having been there and not seeing all the facts, what role race played in that, but I think it's fair to say…that the Cambridge Police acted stupidly.…"[58] Gangster government has its friends and its enemies, and they need to be looked after or put in their place. The facts really don't matter.)

The Obama administration immediately reached out to the American Wind Energy Association (AWEA), a trade group, and to left-wing groups in an attempt to defend its policies. The bureaucrats' emails, later revealed through a Freedom of Information request by the Competitive Enterprise Institute, showed a bureaucracy completely co-opted by left-wing activists and what *Washington Examiner* reporter Tim Carney calls "subsidy sucklers."

Investor's Business Daily provided a sample of the emails among bureaucrats and industry insiders.[59]

> "The AWEA policy people are quite concerned about a recent report published in Spain…"

> "It is critical that we respond, this thing won't die and its (*sic*) doing a good job of undermining our green job message."

> "The AWEA folks are wondering what we'll do, so if this is our plan, I'll let them know."

And later, as the administration's response was being prepared:

> "Is it okay if we send out our response to colleagues at AWEA and CAP [the liberal Center for American Progress]? We promised it to them many weeks ago. It will soon be irrelevant.…"

The end result was a white paper from the National Renewable Energy Laboratory that attempted to refute Calzada's work by criticizing him for actually taking into account that government spending comes with opportunity costs, something subsidy-sucklers don't want to understand: money spent subsidizing their special interests is money that is denied to other enterprises.[60] When gangster government picks winners, it also creates losers.

Columnist George Will summed up the government's initial reaction to the Spanish study thus: "A sobering report about Spain's experience must be false because otherwise the behavior of some American importers, seeking to cash in on the U.S. government's promotion of wind power, might be participating in an economically unproductive project."[61]

In fact, there would be further evidence of this, and it would come from within the White House itself.

THE ANSWER IS BLOWING IN THE WIND

In October 2010, White House economic advisor Larry Summers and two other White House aides penned a memo that circulated in the White House and on Capitol Hill. It outlined some of the problems with stimulus funding for green energy projects, including that they allowed private firms outsized profits without any risk and generated little if any overall economic benefit for the country.

What's more, solar and wind power companies, which had a long experience with government subsidies, were gaming the system, putting as little as ten percent of their own equity into projects subsidized by the government, double-dipping on multiple subsidy programs, and taking government subsidies for projects that didn't need them because they were already financed and underway.

To illustrate the point, Summers pointed to one project in Oregon, the Shepherds Flat wind farm, which is being developed by Caithness Energy, LLC, and General Electric Energy Financial Services. They had applied for a $1.3 billion loan guarantee, worth $300 million in savings on interest.[62] The wind farm will have an 845 megawatt capacity, but its developers' energies have been primarily directed toward securing various government subsidies.

The project was already benefiting from a federal cash grant, federal and state bonus depreciation tax breaks, a state tax credit, and a state requirement (the power is to be sold into California) that the wind-generated electricity be purchased at above-market rates for the next twenty years. (Note the similarity to the policy in Spain.) When all of the subsidies were taken together, Summers wrote, they came to a rather shocking $1.2 billion. That's for a single wind farm which, according to a Department of Energy press release, will hire only thirty-five workers permanently, and 400 construction workers for installation.[63] Just for reference's sake, $1.2 billion divided by 435 is $2.8 million in subsidies per job. Thanks to the government, the developers of Shepherds Flat put down only about 10 percent of the project's equity and could count an estimated return of 30 percent on their investment—not bad for a project that would not have survived in the free market. The developers of Shepherds Flat were the government-chosen winners, and the consumers who had to buy higher-cost electricity were the government-chosen losers.

But were the environmental benefits worth the cost? Not even the Obama administration could truthfully argue that. According to the memo: "Carbon reductions would have to be valued at nearly $130 per ton CO_2 for the climate benefits to equal the subsidies"—or "more than 6 times" the value that the government actually puts on carbon reductions for regulatory purposes.

While Spain, Germany, Italy, France, and the Czech Republic are all cutting their subsidies for "green" power, the Obama administration was promoting its own vision at the economy's expense, in addition to looking out for its friends and keeping the money flowing.[64]

The quarterly stimulus reports from the White House's Council of Economic Advisers (CEA) provide a broader picture of how badly the stimulus is causing good money to be misallocated. CEA estimated that as of July 2010, the stimulus package had diverted $134 billion in private investment into "clean energy," a field whose economic benefit, and whose ability to sustain long-term jobs, is not at all evident.[65] The makers of windmills, insulation, high-speed rail components, and double-pane windows can rejoice at government-inflated demand for their products, and at the additional $52 billion in government spending that was supporting them, but their celebration comes at the expense of sustainable job creation in sectors that actually meet market demand.

NO JOBS HERE[66]

In the rush to throw money at renewable energy projects, the stimulus package didn't just line the pockets of big subsidy winners. It also threw good money after bad companies that were hemorrhaging cash and in no position to create jobs.

Solyndra, a solar panel manufacturer, was the first recipient of a stimulus loan guarantee from the Department of Energy, to the tune of $535 million. Loan guarantees give borrowers better rates because the government (i.e., taxpayers) agrees make to make up the difference if they fail to repay the loan.

In late May 2010, Obama came to the Silicon Valley to praise his own stimulus package and the new factory it was helping to build for Solyndra. "[T]hrough the Recovery Act, this company received a loan to expand its operations. This new factory is the result of those loans. Since the project broke ground last fall, more than 3,000 construction workers have been employed building this plant. Across the country, workers in 22 states are manufacturing the supplies....Solyndra expects to hire 1,000 workers to manufacture solar panels....[C]ompanies like Solyndra are leading the way toward a brighter, more prosperous future."

And how bright the future seemed—a major expansion and 1,000 new, long-lasting jobs!

Fast-forward just six months to November 2010, however, and Solyndra was a deeply troubled company, making huge cuts in cost and production in order to mollify itchy investors. Instead of expanding into the new factory Obama had visited as planned, the company was now going to close its old factory. It was delaying any planned expansion, cutting production goals in half, laying off workers, and terminating 150 of its subcontractors.[67]

Oh, and it wouldn't be hiring those 1,000 workers Obama talked about, either.

The government's choice of Solyndra as a winner was not an inspired one—but it was driven less by economic sense than by the political desirability of subsidizing solar power, and quickly. It is axiomatic that government "invests" taxpayers' money less prudently than private investors invest, or risk, their own.

If the government had thoroughly examined Solyndra's books, it might have found what PriceWaterhouseCoopers did five months after its loan guarantee, when it performed an audit ahead of the firm's planned (but later scrapped) initial public offering of stock. Solyndra had accumulated losses of $558 million over its five-year lifetime.[68] It's a pretty bad sign when you lose that much money selling a product that the government already subsidizes. The auditing firm warned that Solyndra's financial situation was so bad that there was "substantial doubt about its ability to continue as a going concern." [69]

How did Solyndra get half a billion dollars and Obama's blessing? It is no corporate titan. According to the Federal Election Commission, its employees had not contributed huge sums to political candidates. But Solyndra did hire people that are listened to in Washington. It spent $340,000 on lobbyists in just the first three quarters of 2010. Solyndra's most prominent representative in Washington is Steven McBee, a former Democratic Hill aide whose firm did $8 million in lobbying business in the first three quarters of 2010. He has contributed about $250,000 to politicians and political action committees (mostly Democrats) since 1999.[70]

As it sought approval for its first Department of Energy loan, Solyndra hired lobbyist Deana Perlmutter, then-wife of Democrat Congressman Ed Perlmutter of Colorado. As election time approached, the company hired an additional firm, the Washington Tax Group. The issues on which the company lobbied are not difficult to guess: the stimulus, an energy subsidy bill, and the cap-and-trade bill, all of which stood to benefit them.

This is the process by which government selects economic winners, and it's not pretty. It is a different world from the free market, where investors study a company's finances and products carefully before putting their money at risk, and resist being taken in by pipe-dreams.

When Solyndra received its loan guarantee, Vice President Biden said the project was "exactly what the Recovery Act is all about." He was right. Solyndra is Obama's vision of America's economic future—a future that is always one subsidy check away from becoming bankrupt.

HIGH-SPEED RAIL

To serve Obama's green agenda, the stimulus allocated a lot of money in many ways that don't make sense economically. For example, $1 million went to build bike lockers in Portland, Oregon.[71] The stimulus weatherization program set out with $5 billion with a goal of weatherizing 600,000 homes—

at an average cost of *$8,000 per home*, even though weatherization is only expected to save the average household $350 per year.[72]

Another large part of President Obama's green energy vision that doesn't make economic sense is high-speed rail. It threatens to saddle states with billions in short-term cost overruns and long-term operating losses that will require hundreds of millions in annual subsidies.

Obama rolled out his rail program with a major speech highlighting its significance:

> Our highways are clogged with traffic, are costing us $80 billion a year in lost productivity and wasted fuel. Our airports are choked with increased loads.... What we need, then, is a smart transportation system equal to the needs of the 21st Century, a system that reduces travel times and increases mobility. A system that reduces congestion and boosts productivity. A system that reduces destructive emissions and creates jobs.[73]

This sounds wonderful—no more waiting in traffic, and as Obama promised in his 2011 State of the Union address, you won't even be patted down before boarding the train.

But Obama's $13 billion stimulus rail proposal is one of the biggest boondoggles in the stimulus package. After Republican governors took over in Florida, Ohio, and Wisconsin, they cancelled the stimulus rail projects in their states and happily forfeited the funds. The planned rail lines would have duplicated existing highways while doing little or nothing to decrease traffic on the roads. The reason is that these projects are usually premised on unwarranted optimism about ridership, construction costs, and future ticket prices. Such irrationally optimistic promises—really lies—had been needed to convince voters in California to narrowly approve a rail project that the stimulus is now funding.

Take, for example, the high-speed project in California that is now receiving $2.4 billion in stimulus help. The project was originally sold to voters in 2008 with a total price tag of $33.6 billion. Within two years, the state raised the cost estimate to $43 billion.[74] To make up for the higher costs, California's rail authority also changed its projection for one-way ticket prices—the trip from Los Angeles to San Francisco went from $55 to $105, which makes a round trip far more expensive than most round-trip flights.

Because of the ticket price increase, California officials have also scaled back their ridership projections to a still-unrealistic 40 million annual passengers by 2030. For an idea of how optimistic this is, consider that California's entire population is today 37 million, and will still be only 46.4 million in 2030, according to U.S. Census projections.[75] A study by America 2050, a group that strongly supports high-speed rail, reported that there are only 8.4 million annual airline trips taken between all of the cities along the planned California corridors.[76]

In Florida, Obama committed $1.25 million for a high-speed rail line that was to include Tampa, Orlando, and Miami. The Reason Foundation's Wendell Cox released a study in January 2011 warning that the 84-mile, $2.7 billion Tampa-to-Orlando line, all by itself, could suffer cost overruns of between $1 billion and $3 billion, if it falls in line with previous international experience.[77] The current official ridership estimate, at 2.4 million, is four times the annual air traffic between the two cities.

The White House promised on its website that this rail segment would reduce the trip-time between Tampa and Orlando, from ninety minutes to less than an hour, but that's only the time between train stations.[78] Cox also estimated door-to-door travel times under various scenarios between destinations along all points of the rail line. Assuming it would take only ten minutes to change from car or cab to train at one station, and ten minutes from train to car at the other, he found that almost any high-speed rail trip would take longer than simply driving door-to-door. In his sample Orlando-to-Tampa trip, which ends in a residential neighborhood near the University of South Florida's Tampa campus, he found that the rail trip would take thirteen minutes longer. If the traveler takes mass transit from the new train station, the trip takes almost twice as long as driving.

Even America 2050 gave the Florida projects low marks, citing the "lack of a single dominant city" in the state, and the fact that even Miami "is not large enough on its own to drive ridership."[79]

President Obama wants to go much further with rail projects than his $13 billion commitment through the stimulus package. He now wants to throw an additional $53 billion into it over the next six years.[80] The irony, as with green energy, is that the very Europeans often cited as the model for high-speed rail have been moving in the opposite direction for decades. Transportation expert Randall O'Toole wrote in 2008 that despite massive government subsidies for rail, Europeans are migrating toward air and car travel. Rail's share of passenger travel in Europe declined between 1980 and 2005 by nearly 30 percent, with automobiles and intra-European air travel picking up the slack.[81]

Obama's stimulus is paying top dollar to take American transportation backwards, not forwards. When gangster government chooses winners and losers this way, taxpayers are always losers.

FROM CRISIS TO WASTE

During the fifty minutes Vice President Biden kept his audience waiting on August, 23, 2010, about 2,500 newly jobless workers applied for unemployment benefits. By that date, most of the money from Obama's $814 billion stimulus package had already been spent, putting hardly a dent in the nation's unemployment rate, which was 9.5 percent and rising. But Biden's late-morning speech proved that the nation's economic decline had not caused a corresponding decline in wishful thinking:

> Nobody anymore argues whether or not there would be 3 million fewer people working today than there are now working but for the Recovery Act. No serious economist is making that argument any longer. The economy has been growing for a full year.[82]

This was simply false, and yet it might have been the closest thing to a true claim in his entire speech, which consisted of one fairy tale after another. Gangster government knows how to make big promises when an election is approaching. Biden claimed that thanks to the stimulus package, America's renewable-energy consumption—which had grown by only 18 percent in the previous twenty-five years—would *double* in the next two years.[83] By 2015,

Biden promised, the stimulus would cut the cost of solar power in half, and the cost of electric car batteries by 70 percent. Electric vehicles, he said, would soon be cost-competitive with your average gasoline-powered Honda Civic. Not only that, but the Energy Department's stimulus spending would make it possible to map out your entire genetic code for less than $1,000 by 2015, down from the current cost of $48,000.

But the most far-flung claim that Biden made was about the possibility of waste, fraud and abuse in the stimulus package. "Thus far," he said, "that dog hasn't barked. Under one percent of all the money that's been spent has even been questioned as to whether or not...it is being spent appropriately."

By the time Biden spoke, his former Senate colleague Republican Tom Coburn of Oklahoma had authored three separate reports questioning the appropriateness of $14.4 billion in stimulus spending on 300 different projects. The plain fact was that waste from the stimulus package was obvious and widespread.

Back in March 2009, before he had begun minimizing stimulus waste in his public appearances, Biden had been warning against it: "We will take a spotlight and a bullhorn to anything we don't believe is fulfilling the purpose of this legislation," he said.[84] He explicitly warned, "No swimming pools in this money." And the law itself contained some controls, forbidding funding for any "casino or other gambling establishment, aquarium, zoo, golf course, or swimming pool."[85]

Even that was not enough to stop stimulus money from funding the operation of swimming pools in Youngstown, Ohio, and Evanston, Illinois, training at an Indian casino in Minnesota, an instructional golf program in Oregon, an aquarium at Northwestern University, and the National Zoo in Washington, D.C.[86] And where the guidance was less explicit, the waste was more egregious. The most absurd examples of stimulus waste—of projects with no apparent economic value—came in the form of stimulus spending to advertise the stimulus itself. Stimulus road signs popped up everywhere, some of the larger ones costing grateful taxpayers $10,000.[87] At first, some agencies within Ray LaHood's Transportation Department actually required that state governments post the signs on work projects—a requirement they later relaxed after public reports on the signs' cost.[88] The signs were essentially advertisements for Obama's re-election, which prompted some to ask why Obama didn't use his campaign money for them.[89] It was an old Chicago game—why spend campaign dollars when you can leverage millions in tax dollars to promote yourself?

In addition to signs, stimulus funding was paid to publicity firms. In Pennsylvania, Democrat Governor Ed Rendell put a "part-time" consultant on retainer for $100,000, to help him *promote stimulus spending*.[90]

Some PR firms were hired with stimulus money to promote other government policies. The New York firm Ketchum, Inc., won a $25.8 million contract to promote a controversial government health information program.[91] The same firm had been skewered by the Government Accountability Office for producing fake news reports that promoted President Bush's Medicare prescription drug program, and for paying radio host Armstrong Williams $240,000 to promote the No Child Left Behind Act.

When the government spends money, the politically connected tend to do well. Burson-Marsteller, a PR firm operated by noted Washington pollster Mark Penn, received a $6 million stimulus contract to publicize the transition to digital television. (At the time, Hillary Clinton's 2008 presidential campaign still owed Penn's separate polling company—a subcontractor on this project—nearly a million dollars.)[92]

Vice President Biden, who at times lets his mouth run too freely, once expressed the idea of the stimulus package in this way:[93]

"Well, people when I say that look at me and say, 'What are you talking about? You're telling me we have to go spend money to keep from going bankrupt?' The answer is yes, I'm telling you."

Here are just a few examples of how we're "avoiding going bankrupt":

- The General Services Administration is spending $121 million to wrap the federal building in Cleveland in glass and aluminum. This fix is projected to save $700,000 a year in heating and cooling costs. The project will pay for itself…sometime in the twenty-second century.[94] (If the building lasts that long.)

- Have you heard the one about the wasteful stimulus project? Northwestern University scientists received $713,000 to create "machine-generated humor"—a comedy computer.[95]
- How did the turtle cross the road? The stimulus put $3.4 million into building a tunnel for turtles to cross underneath Highway 27 near Tallahassee, Florida.[96]
- A researcher at Wayne State University in Michigan received $2.6 million to help train prostitutes in China to drink more responsibly.[97]
- In Washington, D.C., the American Legacy Foundation received $977,000 for a unique smoking cessation program. In order to help smokers quit, they give them free Blackberries.[98] (Yes, you really paid for this.)
- The Department of Transportation spent $350 million in stimulus funds to upgrade tiny airports that are seldom used by the public, and which are dedicated primarily to corporate and private aviation. For example, in Alaska, the tiny, remote towns of Ouzinkie, Akiachak, and Fort Yukon—combined population: under 1,500—received a total of $45 million to upgrade their three airports.[99] In upstate New York, an airport owned and mostly used by members of a private pilots' club got $400,000.
- Another $128 million has been dedicated to build a massive, five-mile bridge between Palm City and Stuart, Florida. They already have one bridge between them, and it's less than two miles away from the newly planned one, which will require the seizure of dozens of homes through eminent domain. Palm City and Stuart have a combined population of less than 40,000.[100]
- In Hillsborough, New Hampshire, $150,000 in stimulus funds was used to resurface an old stone bridge that only extends halfway across the Contoocook River. The old bridge, which is within yards of a functioning modern bridge that *does* cross

the river, has no possible use except for scenery—and it boasts lovely views of a strip mall, a gas station, and an automotive dealership.[101] This project somehow took priority, despite the fact that one-third of the *real* bridges in New Hampshire are considered "structurally deficient or obsolete" according to a 2010 report by the non-profit Road Information Program.[102]

- Montana's state-owned liquor warehouse received $2.2 million to install skylights.[103]

- In the small town of Boynton, Oklahoma, the stimulus package paid $90,000 for new handicapped-accessible sidewalks along state highway 72. The new sidewalk literally leads into an impassable ditch.[104] According to local news reports, there is hardly any pedestrian traffic in the area, and the old sidewalks had just been installed five years earlier. A resident remarked to a local television station that it was "one hundred percent a waste of money," and added, "When you don't find anybody that's for this, here in this town, it's pretty bad."

- In remote North Dakota, $6.1 million in stimulus dollars built a new "green" visitors' center for the Audubon National Wildlife Refuge, complete with wind turbines and parking spots reserved for energy efficient vehicles only. About eighty people visit the 15,000-acre refuge each day, but the center keeps bankers' hours (8:00 a.m. to 4:30 p.m.), and it's closed on weekends and federal holidays when most people might want to visit it.[105]

- The stimulus paid $500,000 for Dayton, Ohio, to purchase 10,000 recycling bins with RFID chips to track residents' recycling habits.[106] It's estimated that the program will, in the long run, cut costs for the city and should break even and produce an economic benefit…in about nineteen years or so.

- The "Dance Draw" project at the University of North Carolina-Charlotte got more than Dayton's trash-tracker: $775,000, for dancers to "wear wireless computer mice on their chests and wrists to 'draw' abstract geometric shapes on a computer screen."[107]

- Among the dozens of absurd-sounding studies the stimulus has funded is one at Syracuse University, on "the prevalence of hookups in the first year of college" among 500 freshman females.[108] Researchers were awarded $219,000 to satisfy their curiosity in this area.

- Researchers at Wake Forest received $72,000 for the now-famous study that got monkeys high on cocaine.[109]

- And to cap it off, the best stimulus study of all: researchers at three Texas universities received a $194,000 grant to study "the impact of stimulus funds on the perceptions of citizens and the choices of local community decision makers."[110]

FREE MONEY ISN'T FREE

In 2009, the Department of Homeland Security announced that it was spending $77 million on stimulus upgrades at five little-used checkpoints on Montana's Canadian border. Montana's Democrat senators, Jon Tester and Max Baucus, proudly took credit for bringing this stimulus pork avalanche back to their state. Tester issued a press release in April 2009, which read in part:

> Tester, a member of both the Senate Homeland Security Committee and the Homeland Security Appropriations Subcommittee, also pushed Napolitano for funding. He also urged the federal government to invest in new facilities while touring the Port of Scobey with then-Deputy Homeland Security Secretary Paul Schneider last summer.
>
> "This is another reason I supported and voted for the Jobs Bill," Tester said. "Investing in these ports strengthens our homeland security and increases our commercial opportunities.... This will pay off for generations to come by creating new jobs and opportunity that will benefit all of Montana."

For reference, the Scobey checkpoint mentioned in the press release sees about twenty travelers per day in the summer and almost none in the winter.[111] It was getting a $15 million upgrade. The nearby Whitetail checkpoint, which the press release said would also get $15 million, serves somewhere between two and five border-crossers per day, on average, depending on whose estimate you trust. In all of 2008, it saw $63,000 in freight cross into the United States.[112] At night, when this checkpoint closes down, its agents put three orange traffic cones in the middle of the road. The Associated Press described the Whitetail checkpoint as getting a new facility "the size and cost of a Hollywood mansion."[113]

The news coverage of this boondoggle generated public outrage. Senator Tester doggedly defended the projects, telling the press, "The northern border tends to be forgotten, and it shouldn't be," and, "I think, absolutely, it's going to create jobs and build the infrastructure."[114]

By April 2010, the Department of Homeland Security had scaled back "stimulus" for Montana border checkpoints to $23 million, but little Whitetail was still slated to get $8.5 million. "For the security of our entire country, all of Montana's ports need to be updated in order to keep out the threats of the 21st Century," Tester said in another press release.[115]

Over the summer of 2010, construction began in Whitetail. After about $1.3 million had been spent, the federal government announced that the project was being suspended because the checkpoint was probably going to be closed. The Canadian government had suddenly decided to shut down its checkpoint on the other side, citing the lack of traffic. So the Americans had to choose between closing Whitetail or having it as a one-way port of entry.[116]

Tester, who faces re-election in 2012, now talks about the need to close the checkpoint to which he once bragged about funneling pork. "We can't keep open an unsafe port that doesn't meet today's security needs, and with Canada's recent decision, we can't afford upgrading it."[117]

In one form or another, something like this has been happening all over America. Obama expected voters to support stimulus projects when they saw signs and ads promoting government spending. Instead, the voters have gotten a little wiser. They've noticed that their money is being wasted before their very eyes, with little improvement to their own situations.

President Obama's ambitious agenda has cost a lot, and added substantially to the nation's debt. It prompted him in early 2010 to present a budget that the CBO says will increase the national debt by $9.7 trillion over the next ten years.[118] Over the last forty years, the size of our nation's publicly held debt has been, on average, 36 percent of our economy. At the end of 2008, when President George W. Bush left office, that debt equaled 40 percent of GDP. After two years of Obama, and thanks in large part to the stimulus package, the federal debt is 62 percent of GDP—"the highest percentage since shortly after World War II," the CBO says—and it is on its way to 87 percent by 2020, unless taxes are raised again to Clinton-era levels.[119]

If the federal government wasted much or all of the money in the stimulus package, it is not a victimless crime: it has cost taxpayers money when they could least afford it, it has diverted capital from productive uses where it could have created lasting jobs, and it has placed an outrageous burden of debt on our children and grandchildren. We have met the victims of gangster government, and they are us.

CHAPTER FIVE

WE'RE GONNA HELP OUR FRIENDS: BIG LABOR

*"Imagine having a president whose life work
was your work."*

— Senator Barack Obama, Democrat, Illinois,
in a 2007 speech to the SEIU Political Action Conference

The Obama presidency is already a failure.

That is not to say that President Obama hasn't successfully moved several major pieces of his agenda through Congress. It is not to say he cannot win re-election or somehow manage to restore his popularity.

But Obama's presidency has failed in the sense that he is not achieving the goals he promised the public he would tackle.

For example, President Obama signed a stimulus package promising that it would create jobs and keep unemployment low. Neither of these things happened, and only the most sharply partisan and flawed analyses suggest otherwise.

Consider also that Obama signed a health care reform bill, promising that it would bring down costs and make Medicare more sustainable in the long run. Yet just weeks after its passage, we learned from the actuary of Medicare, Richard Foster, that the bill's new entitlements will gobble up all of the government's expected savings and then some. Six months after that, in August 2010, we learned from the same source that most of the savings themselves are just an accounting fiction anyway.[1] So far, for most Americans, Obamacare has only resulted in higher insurance premiums, higher taxes on medicines and medical devices, and higher tax-compliance burdens for small businesses.

The reason President Obama can't deliver on hope and change is that, in true gangster government fashion, he's delivering it to his friends instead. The special interests that elected Obama are now receiving their reward. They are devouring the savings that were supposed to be achieved by the health care bill. They are absorbing whatever benefits the stimulus package might have had to offer.

One reason Obamacare now threatens to bust the federal budget—despite its supporters' mathematically dubious claims to the contrary—is that the very unions who lobbied the hardest for it were spared the shared obligation of paying for it. For parliamentary reasons, it proved impossible to grant them a total exemption from the so-called "Cadillac Tax" on the high-priced insurance policies unions negotiate, which few other Americans have. So President Obama agreed to delay implementation of the tax until 2018, adding $120 billion to the bill's net cost. Unions now have eight more years than other Americans to prepare for Obamacare's harmful effects.

As we will see in the next chapter, Obama also deliberately left open a $56 billion hole in the health care industry, so that trial lawyers can continue to exploit the defects of our medical malpractice laws. It was a blatant case of President Obama rewarding one of his party's most loyal and most generous constituencies, to the detriment of the public and the promises he had made.

As for the stimulus package, it came from the least business-experienced administration since 1900,[2] and was inevitably at cross-purposes with the administration's actions to reduce demand—higher taxes on cigarettes, medicines, medical devices, and even tanning.[3]

But that's just the beginning. Federal agencies are also deliberately wasting billions of stimulus dollars to pad construction contracts, by requiring that they go to the Obama administration's friends, the labor unions.

President Obama's lofty rhetoric invokes the common good—reducing health care costs, creating jobs—but his overriding goal is helping those who have helped him most: labor unions, trial lawyers, government employees, and other special interest groups of the Democratic Party. This is gangster government at work.

In his campaign stump speeches, Obama said, "When special interests put their thumb on the scale, and distort the free market, the people who compete by the rules come in last."[4] During the health care debate, he expressed similar sentiments on multiple occasions: "I will not stand by while the special interests use the same old tactics to keep things exactly the way they are."[5] And in the 2010 election cycle, Obama went so far as to bring up special interests and remark, "They talk about me like a dog."[6]

And it's true. Obama's favored special interests say "fetch," and he does.

THE SEIU AGENDA IS MY AGENDA

On February 6, 2009, President Obama signed Executive Order 13502, authorizing federal agencies to require all contractors on construction projects larger than $25 million to sign "project labor agreements"[7] that force contractors to use union labor.[8] Anything to help a friend.

In April 2001, within months of taking office, President George W. Bush had banned federal agencies from requiring project labor agreements (PLAs). The reason was simple: they are union featherbeds that discriminate against the 86.9 percent of private sector construction workers who don't belong to unions. They drive up costs (borne by taxpayers) by 12 to 18 percent, in part by reducing the number of bidders, and in part because union wages are 51 percent higher. Moreover, using union workers increases the chances of labor disputes.[9] As one recent study by the libertarian CATO Institute put it, "A decision by public owners to enter into a PLA is a signal that they are willing to subordinate the interests of the general public to those of the unions."[10]

For example, the federal General Services Administration awarded a contractor with a PLA the job of renovating the Lafayette Building in Washington, D.C., home to the Veterans Administration and the Export-Import Bank of the United States; the PLA will add an estimated additional $3.3 million taxpayer cost to the project.[11]

Government-wide, PLA contracts amount to a multi-billion-dollar favor to unions. And why shouldn't Obama grant it? He has always identified public service and the service of big labor unions as one and the same. In his

speech to the Service Employees International Union political action conference in 2007, Obama made it clear where his loyalties lie:

> But the question I do want SEIU to ask yourselves is not who's
> talking about your agenda, but who can change our politics in
> Washington so we can make your agenda a reality... I'm not just
> asking you to bet on me—I'm asking you to bet on us.... That's
> what you did with me in 2004. Because I probably wouldn't be
> standing here if it hadn't been for the SEIU endorsement back
> then. And the fact that all these folks sitting here—right here—
> they walked doors for me, they made phone calls for me, they
> turned out the vote for me.

Here, the crowd burst into chants of "Yes, we did!" And it was true—they had.
Obama's rise in Illinois was aided by the fact that Obama's mentor, Illinois
State Senate President Emil Jones, made him chairman of the state Senate's
Health Committee. From that perch, Obama demonstrated his unquestion-
ing fealty to the state's powerful SEIU chapter and its 100,000 members—or
as David Mendell of the *Chicago Tribune* put it, he "carried SEIU's water."[12]
The union, in turn, played a huge role in putting Obama over the top in his
2004 Senate primary election against two other serious candidates.

Obama was their guy.

Obama went on to explain to the SEIU crowd why its Illinois chapter had
supported him then, and why they should support him again for president.
The reason (apparently) was that he had never made a decision without
consulting the SEIU:

> The reason they did it was because we have fought together. We
> have stood side by side.... We have worked together. And you have
> seen that I was willing to stand by your side even when it wasn't
> politically convenient. Your agenda has been my agenda in the
> United States Senate. Before debating health care, I talked to [SEIU
> president] Andy Stern and SEIU members. Before immigration
> debates took place in Washington, I talked to [SEIU International

Secretary-Treasurer] Eliseo Medina and SEIU members. Before
the EFCA [Employee Free Choice Act, the "card check" bill for
organized labor], I talked to SEIU. So we've worked together over
these last few years. I'm proud of what we've done. I'm just not
satisfied. Because I know how much more we could accomplish
as partners in an Obama administration. Just imagine what we
could do together.... Imagine having a president whose life work
was your work.

We don't have to imagine anymore. In February 2008, the SEIU endorsed
Obama over Hillary Clinton. They proceeded to provide $60 million and
100,000 volunteers—3,000 of them full-time—to help Obama against John
McCain. They won, and now they're owed.[13]

When the SEIU gave Obama its official endorsement, its president, Andy
Stern, made it quite clear that Obama had not been exaggerating in his 2007
speech: "There has never been a fight in Illinois or a fight in the nation where
our members have asked Barack Obama for assistance and he has not done
everything he could to help us."[14]

This continues to be true. And it matters, because all the favors are coming at your expense.

PAYING HIS DEBTS WITH YOUR MONEY

Stern, who until 2010 served as the SEIU's president, visited the White
House nearly sixty times during President Obama's first two years in office.
He had eighteen visits with President Obama himself and three with Vice
President Joe Biden. Richard Trumka, head of the AFL-CIO since September
2009, visited the White House forty-eight times, meeting with Obama seven-
teen times and with Biden three times.

Organized labor owns the Obama White House in a way no other special
interest can claim to own it. Obama does not make comments like this one,
from the August 2007 presidential debate hosted by the AFL-CIO, for just
anyone: "I want to be absolutely clear that the reason I'm in public life, the
reason I came to Chicago, the reason I started working with unions, the reason

I march on picket lines, the reason that I am running for president is because of you, not because of folks who are writing big checks."[15]

Of course, the people he was addressing were the ones writing the biggest checks of all. When President Obama awarded the Presidential Medal of Freedom to former AFL-CIO president John Sweeney, he was giving this high honor to a labor leader who had spent $53.4 million to elect Obama in 2008.[16] The AFL-CIO's political expenditures for that fiscal year far exceeded the money they spent representing their workers, according to reports filed with the Department of Labor. And the AFL-CIO went so far into debt electing Obama that its $103 million in liabilities actually exceeded its assets by $21 million when it filed its 2009 financial disclosures.[17] Election spending in 2007 and 2008 had helped obliterate the $21 million surplus that the union enjoyed as recently as mid-2006.

Obama isn't even slightly ashamed of the transactional relationship he enjoys with unions. Here is how he describes it in *The Audacity of Hope*, after noting all the help the unions had given him in the course of his political career up to that point: "So I owe those unions. When their leaders call, I do my best to call them back right away. I don't consider this corrupting in any way…"[18]

Obama was in debt, and he began paying off right away by giving a plethora of top jobs and responsibilities to labor leaders.

- Stern, the SEIU president, was given a seat at President Obama's 2009 "Fiscal Responsibility Summit." In 2010, Obama appointed Stern to the National Commission on Fiscal Responsibility and Reform—though perhaps Stern was there to represent the voice of fiscal irresponsibility, given that half a dozen local chapters in Stern's union had been suing the State of California to prevent needed budget cuts[19] before the state ran out of cash and actually had to issue IOUs to vendors.[20]

- SEIU secretary-treasurer Anna Burger and SEIU healthcare chair Dennis Rivera were given prominent roles in Obama's health care summit. Burger served on the President's

Economic Recovery Advisory Board, the website of which describes her as "an outspoken voice on the role unions can play to restore economic fairness."[21]

- Obama appointed Patrick Gaspard, a former political director for the SEIU in New York, as his White House political director. A registered lobbyist, Gaspard was paid $37,000 by the SEIU for "carried over leave and vacation" during 2009, even as he was serving in the White House.[22] Obama later made Gaspard the executive director of the Democratic National Committee for his re-election effort.

- President Obama named SEIU associate general counsel John Sullivan to a seat on the Federal Election Commission (FEC). The appointment was something of a surprise, because Sullivan was a harsh critic of the McCain-Feingold law's restrictions on unions' political coordination with candidates. Sullivan had also represented the SEIU when one of its political affiliates, America Coming Together, had been fined $775,000—the third largest fine in FEC history—for laundering less-regulated state campaign funds into its federal election activities.[23] (Unfortunately for Sullivan, he was never confirmed because of a turf dispute over other unfilled openings at the FEC.)

- Obama appointed labor attorney Mark Pearce to the National Labor Relations Board. Frank Ervolino, a crooked union president in Buffalo, had hired Pearce during the 1990s to help prevent members of his hotel union from seeing its books because he was embezzling hundreds of thousands of dollars.[24] Before the embezzlement was exposed, Pearce decried the transparency effort in public as "a fishing expedition."

- Craig Becker, a former academic and an attorney for the SEIU and AFL-CIO, used to write controversial articles on labor issues that suggested employers be completely silenced during union elections.[25] He even mused about the possibility of legally forcing all workers to join unions.[26] Such writings made his Senate confirmation impossible, and forced Obama to give him a recess appointment to the National Labor Relations Board. His appointment expires at the end of 2011. Becker signed Obama's standard agreement not "to work on regulations or contracts directly related to your former employer for two years."[27] But he maintains that his recusal obligation does not apply to cases involving the SEIU's local chapters, even though the SEIU's constitution says the national union has "jurisdiction over its affiliated bodies and all Local Unions." Becker has participated in at least seventeen rulings and decisions involving the SEIU since taking his seat. I could find only one case in which he ruled against them.[28]

- Obama did not neglect to fill minor positions with unionists, either. In December 2010, Obama's was forced to recess-appoint William Boarman, vice president of the Communications Workers of America, to run the Government Printing Office (GPO). Boarman's nomination had hit a snag when it was revealed that he had received $3,700 in improper payments from the GPO. Despite having been on unpaid leave from the agency for more than twenty years—he had left to work for the union—Boarman cashed three checks he received from the GPO between 2004 and 2007.[29]

When Obama chose a secretary of Labor, he chose the unions' secretary of Labor. Democrat Congresswoman Hilda Solis of California is the daughter of two union workers, and has always attributed her family's relative prosperity to organized labor.[30] She kept a low profile during her eight years in Congress, sponsoring few major bills, but she amassed a rigidly liberal record (her American Conservative Union lifetime rating is 2 percent).

Obama was going to pick a pro-union Labor secretary in any event. But in Solis, the unions got a fanatical true believer, known for giving strident speeches describing how all budget cuts and all Republican policies and appointments disproportionately hurt women and children.[31]

Stern was ecstatic at her appointment: "On every issue that's important to us, she has stood up for an America where everyone's hard work is valued and rewarded.... As opposed to some candidate [for whom] this would have been just a job, for Hilda Solis it's the fulfillment of a life-long dream.... She probably will be the labor secretary that has been on more picket lines and rallied more in support of workers' rights than potentially anyone in American history."[32]

For such a favorable candidate as Solis, Big Labor wasn't going to let a small matter like her husband's tax problems—he paid $6,400 in years-old IRS liens when she was nominated—get in the way. Nor would they let it sink her nomination that she was serving as the treasurer of a union front group that was lobbying Congress, even as she was serving in Congress. Stern denounced such concerns as "an insult to every working person in America."[33]

During the 2008 presidential election, Obama had often recycled the joke that he wanted the Department of Labor to stop being "the Department of Management." What he created instead was a Department of Reviving Dying Unions. In January 2011, Solis released the Department of Labor's strategic plan and demonstrated her great value to the SEIU. The document reads like a love letter to an institution that is irrelevant to 93.1 percent of Americans working in the private sector:

> Union jobs are, by and large, good jobs. Employment in a unionized workplace has been associated with higher wages, better health and retirement benefits, and quality training. Unionized workplaces typically have formal channels by which workers can report violations of safety or other labor standards and seek redress, reducing the need for government enforcement of the relevant laws and regulations. Unions also help educate workers about their rights under federal and state employment laws. Unions also promote good jobs through apprenticeship programs (jointly sponsored with employers) which allow apprentices to earn while they acquire an in-demand skill. Thus, many of the Department's outcome goals are furthered by high rates of union membership.[34]

Obama's Labor Department views the union shop as the ideal employer, and is undeterred by the fact that the nation has been moving away from that model for decades. As a result, Obama is now using the White House in every conceivable way help the cause—to pay back a special interest whose fortunes have waned and whose membership now stands at a historic low. Big Labor spent $400 million on the 2008 election—nearly all of it on Democrats[35]—and Obama isn't about to let them go down without all the help that he can force taxpayers to muster.

THE HEART OF THE MATTER

Just what are the unions getting for their investment in Obama? They have gotten something out of nearly every action Obama has taken in office. His legislative agenda, his executive orders, his administration's regulations and rulings, and his big spending bills have almost all included union giveaways. He began his presidency by bailing out the UAW. And beyond that, he had a number of tools to help unions further.

Thanks to Obama, unions have been shielded from Obamacare's most immediately harmful provisions and from basic standards of transparency that are required under labor law. He has altered in their favor the interpretation of laws that have governed their operations for decades. Unions have been granted special privileges in seeking not only stimulus contracts but all federal government contracts, despite the fact that they make up a small and dwindling share of the American workforce.

But the dirty secret behind all of these favors is that it goes beyond simple favoritism. It is really a question of mutual self-preservation. Democrats need unions, and unions, on the verge of collapse in America, will disappear as a political force unless they get lots of help from Democrats, and fast.

Labor unions are less attractive to American workers today than they have been in a century. The numbers tell the story: in 1954, unions accounted for 39 percent of the American workforce.[36] By 2010, the number was just 11.9 percent overall, with just 8 percent of workers under age thirty-five joining unions.[37] Most troubling for the labor movement is the fact that in the private sector, union members now account for just 6.9 percent of the workforce. The only place unions remain strong is in government jobs, where they represent 36 percent of all workers. And even here, their ranks have slightly thinned since 2000.[38]

Workers are no longer attracted to labor unions for workplace improvements because labor laws have already caught up with the times, and then some. Many union pension plans, which were once a selling point for workers, are now underfunded and extremely risky. And although union members still make more money than their non-union counterparts—a lot more in some industries, like construction—the overall advantage is less than you might expect. The Labor Department estimates that union members make 20 percent more per week, but that is less impressive than it looks for two reasons.[39] First, the union population is disproportionately old—more than half of all union workers are over forty-five years of age and in their peak earning years.[40] Second, union members are disproportionately concentrated in high-income states: one-third live in California, New York, or New Jersey, which account for only one-fifth of the U.S. population.

Employers have also soured on unions. Take Boeing, for example, which has used union labor for decades. In 2009, the company was preparing to create at least 1,000 new jobs to build the first 800 of its 787 Dreamliner airplanes. But Boeing had been suffering delays in production because of strikes at its union facilities in Washington State—including one that lasted fifty-two days. The company's management could not extract a promise of a labor peace from the machinists' union, so they simply decided to create the new jobs in Charleston, South Carolina, where workers at one of their plants had just voted to get rid of the union.[41] Boeing is not alone among manufacturers in moving to southern "right-to-work" states, where it is illegal to make union membership a condition of employment.

The lack of interest in unionization is having two profound effects on big labor unions. First, it threatens to diminish their political influence—a fact that has Democrats taking notice, since unions loyally and lopsidedly support them. Second, it is devastating union pension plans. With few young members coming in, and more older members retiring, these funds are, in many cases, teetering with dangerously low levels of funding. This creates a vicious cycle because risky pension plans in turn make unionization less attractive. Even worse, this situation is beginning to threaten many unionized companies that are paying into those pension plans.

Many labor unions that have members working for several companies rely on something called the "multi-employer pension plan." The federal Pension Benefit Guaranty Corporation (PBGC)—the government agency that partially insures pensions—says there are 10.1 million union workers and retirees covered by about 1,500 multi-employer plans today.[42] The idea behind such plans is that a union negotiates with several major companies in an industry and gets them all to contribute to a single plan for union members. The members, in turn, can accrue pension credits even if they change companies.

But these plans have serious downsides. One is that the age pyramid in many of them are beginning to resemble the critical late stage of a Ponzi scheme. Another is that if such a plan goes completely bust, the federal Pension Benefit Guaranty Corporation will only pay benefits up to $13,000 per year—and it's only that generous for retirees who worked thirty years.[43]

Whenever a multi-employer pension plan's funds fall below 80 percent of what it needs to pay its promised benefits, it is required to inform beneficiaries and the Department of Labor that it is officially "Endangered." When a plan falls below 65 percent of its needed funding, it must publish a notice that it is "Critical." In 2010, 177 out of the nation's 1,500 pension plans were endangered, and an additional 255 were critical.[44] Add it up, and nearly one-third of all multi-employer pension plans are in serious enough trouble that the government has stepped in to demand changes. In some cases, plans have been forced to reduce benefits on their own by 50 or even 75 percent just to avoid being handed over to the Pension Benefit Guaranty Corporation.[45]

In May 2010, Charles Jeszeck of the federal Government Accountability Office offered a few alarming notes in congressional testimony on the subject.[46] As of 2006, the last year for which data was available, all multi-employer plans were, on aggregate, only 66 percent funded. That was *before* the recession and the downturn in the stock market. One number that Jeszeck did not mention was the one contained in the Pension Benefit Guaranty Corporation's 2006 annual report—that the aggregate unfunded liabilities of multi-employer plans stood at $150 billion.[47] The PBGC has since stopped publishing this statistic in its annual reports, but today, it is probably higher.

Jeszeck also reported that beginning in 2001, current workers have been outnumbered by retirees or vested employees in these funds who are no longer contributing to them. The percentage of active workers in the plans has fallen in every subsequent year, and the percentage of retirees collecting benefits has risen.

For an example of a troubled pension plan, look no further than President Obama's appointee to head the Government Printing Office, William Boarman. His responsibilities with the Communications Workers of America included the chairmanship of the CWA/ITU[48] pension fund, which the Department of Labor declared to be in "critical" condition in 2010.[49] The plan, to which 349 different employers contribute on behalf of union workers, was forced to raise its minimum retirement age by two years, end its five-year guarantee of benefits for surviving beneficiaries, and change the rules to make it harder for older workers to become vested before they retire.[50] According to its IRS filings, the CWA pension plan is severely demographically challenged. It receives contributions for only 5,500 active workers, but pays 17,000 retirees and 3,500 surviving family members. The plan will also have to provide benefits later to 8,600 additional workers who are no longer contributing.[51] The plan paid out $90 million to retirees in 2009 and took in only $14 million in contributions.[52]

Multi-employer pension plans are also albatrosses for employers because of what is known as the "last-man-standing" rule. If fifty employers contribute to one of these union funds, and ten go bankrupt, the other forty become responsible for the bankrupt company's retirees. If forty of the fifty go bankrupt, then the last ones standing inherit all of the liability.

To give some idea of how bad the situation is, consider that UPS agreed in late 2007 to pay $6.1 billion just to extract itself from the Teamsters' Central States multi-employer pension plan. Four months after UPS bailed out, the plan was declared "critical," despite all the new money, and it is in desperate shape today.

The situation is about to get even worse for businesses that are stuck in union multi-employer pension plans. The Financial Accounting Standards

Board, a private, self-regulating board that determines accounting practices, is expected this year to adopt a new standard that requires companies paying into multi-employer pension plans to be more transparent with the potential liabilities they pose.[53]

In the short term, the change will burn a hole in the books of several unionized companies, hurting their shareholder value, threatening their ability to borrow money, and possibly putting some out of business altogether. In the long term, the change gives companies an additional and very strong incentive to avoid joining union pension funds, at all costs. The transparency will also likely destroy many union jobs. And this, in turn, makes it more difficult for the unions to do what they need to do: keep as many working bodies in these plans, and find as many new ones as possible in order to prop them up.

This is where President Obama—the man the unions spent over a hundred million dollars to elect—is supposed to step in. His Plan A, which he has long championed and which he vigorously promoted in his first two years in office despite public opinion, was the inaptly named Employee Free Choice Act. EFCA is best known for its "card-check" provision, which deprives workers of the right to vote on unionization in a secret-ballot election. Card-check allows union organizers to take over a shop by gathering signatures individually among employees, a process which, unlike a secret ballot, often involves significant pressure and coercion.

But another important part of EFCA is that it can force companies unionized through this process into binding arbitration with the union whenever a contract cannot be reached within 120 days. Arbitrators set the terms of the contract, and both the company and the workers are stuck with it for two years.

So here's the rub: under President Obama's plan, you could return from your vacation and suddenly find yourself a member of a union, thanks to a card check campaign. And then, thanks to binding arbitration, you could also find yourself—without even an opportunity to vote on your contract—locked into terms of employment that include a multi-employer pension plan which arbitrators force your employer to join. Not only would you no longer be able to contribute to your 401(k) or receive an employer match, but you might also discover that in fact you are just being used as cannon fodder—that the union that was just certified without your input, using a contract you did not approve, is taking your retirement contributions to pay its current retirees, and you are likely to get little or nothing out of the deal.

Sound like gangster government? You bet it does.

That was Plan A for solving the unions' pension problem—one of many problems they currently face. But it failed to pass Congress in Obama's first two years for lack of sixty votes in the Senate. Its chances of passage in the 112th Congress are zero.

Plan B is a straight-up bailout, and Democrats in Congress are already on the case. Democrat Senator Bob Casey of Pennsylvania proposed a bailout bill in Congress last year, which would put taxpayers on the hook for all of the unions' deadbeat pension plans, at a likely cost to taxpayers of $165 billion or possibly more. As my colleague Mark Hemingway put it: "Casey's bill is an entitlement for the 7 percent of Americans still in labor unions."[54]

Yes—but with gangster government, the important thing is that it's the *right* 7 percent getting the entitlement.

FAVORS AMONG FRIENDS

One rule of gangster government is that when you can't win, you change the rules.

When he bailed out the automakers by abusing the bankruptcy process, President Obama did not consult Congress. And even in situations where the legality of executive action is less dubious, Obama's appointees do not necessarily have to consult Congress to change rules in order to benefit unions.

Here are a few small but noteworthy examples of how Obama has helped tilt the playing field in the area of labor relations.

1. The National Rail Act: Obama appointees on the National Mediation Board, the federal panel that oversees labor disputes in the airline and railway industries, changed the long-standing rules of union elections in May 2010. In doing so, they overturned 76 years of legal precedent in order to make it easier for unions that were having a hard time convincing employees to join.[55]

Under the Railway Labor Act, unions have always been required to win majority support among a company's workers (or among the class they wish to represent) in order to be certified as their monopoly bargaining agent. But with its decision of May 3, 2010, Obama's National Mediation Board declared that unions now only have to win a majority of the ballots cast, instead of a majority of all the workers. This reinterpretation was a special favor for the pilots', machinists', and flight attendants' unions. Naturally, Obama had not neglected to appoint unionists to the panel who would make it happen— Linda Puchala, former president of the Association of Flight Attendants, AFL-CIO, and Harry Hoglander of the Airline Pilots Association. On two previous occasions, the flight attendants' union had lost elections among Delta employees under the old rules. Delta had treated its employees well enough that they simply did not want union representation.

As it happened, Obama's special favor wasn't enough to put these particular unions over the top. The flight attendants rejected the union for a third time in November 2010.[56] Weeks later, Delta's ground workers also voted against joining the machinists' union.[57] But you can be sure that the unions will be back soon, and one of these days, they'll win with a majority vote because of low election turnout.

2. Dana Corporation: There is one case from which Craig Becker, Obama's recess appointee to the National Labor Relations Board, did indeed recuse himself, on the grounds that he had previously been litigating it on behalf of unions. In *Dana Corporation*, which was decided in December 2010, a three-member panel of the NLRB ruled 2-to-1 (two Obama appointees formed the majority) that employers can secretly collude with unions that don't even represent their workers in order to force the workers into a union— and into a contract—that the employer likes. Dana Corporation wanted to let the UAW organize its employees. It made a secret deal with the union, setting forth some terms for a future contract—including terms regarding "attendance, classifications, compensation, healthcare, mandatory overtime, team-based work schemes, and work incentives."[58]

With its agreement in hand, the company helped the union win monopoly representation rights over its workers using card check. When the workers found out about the collusion, three of them filed a complaint and asked for an election to decertify the union. In December 2010, Obama's NLRB ruled that they would have to wait until their contract expires.

Such collusion is—or at least was—considered a violation of the law. But the *Dana* case overturned an important 1964 precedent called *Majestic Weaving*, in which the NLRB had protected workers from such employer-union schemes at their expense.

3. TSA: Despite the possible lack of flexibility that might result, and the implications for national security, President Obama's Federal Labor Relations Authority gave the 50,000 workers of the Transportation Security Administration the green light to unionize. The deal will be worth as much as $30 million per year in union dues to the American Federation of Government Employees, whose boss, John Gage, announced that it would negotiate new deals on "seniority, shift biddings, transfers and awards."[59] CNN reported that the union would not be allowed to bargain "on any topics that might affect security," which, for the Transportation *Security* Administration is…every topic related to employment.

TSA unionization was a promise Obama made during the 2008 election. "I will work to ensure that TSOs [Transportation Security Officers] have collective bargaining rights," he said, calling it a "priority for my administration."[60] Fittingly, his TSA has achieved this goal while making air travel more burdensome for passengers under Obama. And as an additional favor to the union, Obama's TSA announced in late January that it would block any further airports from transitioning to private screening companies—something many airports want to do, and which the law allows.[61]

4. Transparency: In 2008, former Labor Secretary Elaine Chao had issued rules, five years in the making, to improve the transparency of union finances. Among the new items subject to transparency requirements were pension plans, training funds, and other union trusts. The hope was to stop the many cases in which top union officials embezzle or mismanage workers' money, and to give union members a better idea of how safe their pensions and benefits funds are.

It's hard even to imagine who could oppose such a thing, aside from union bosses who are genuinely crooked. But two people who oppose it are Barack Obama and his Labor secretary, Hilda Solis. Shortly after taking office, Solis temporarily halted several union transparency rules from going into effect. In her report on her first 100 days in office, she referred to these rules as "burdensome" and "ineffectual." And finally, in November 2010, the rule on reporting of union trusts using the Department of Labor's standard T-1 form was simply eliminated altogether.[62] The effect is more chances for corruption, nepotism, and waste of rank-and-file union workers' money.[63]

These changes are not winners among union rank and file. One survey of union members showed 89 percent in support of putting all union finances on the Internet.[64] Republican Congressman John Kline of Minnesota, who is now chairman of the House Labor Committee, released this statement at the time:

> Once again the Obama administration has decided to limit work- ers' ability to know how their union dues are used by labor offi- cials. This is the latest in an ongoing effort by the administration to tilt the balance of power in favor of Big Labor and against rank-and-file workers. Regrettably, this decision will roll back commonsense financial reporting and disclosure requirements that would have given workers a better understanding of how union dues are spent.

Although Kline is expected to push back against this change in the new Con- gress, the story demonstrates again what a sympathetic administration (or gangster government) can do to help its friends—with or without the legisla- tive branch.

5. NLRB: Craig Becker and his colleagues at the National Labor Relations Board are already attempting to impose one new requirement on employers that does not exist in law. In addition to all the other workplace notices about minimum wage and unemployment benefits, employers would not only have to post signs telling employees that they have a right to unionize, but possibly also distribute the notice by email and all other means used to distribute work- place messages. If the employer fails to adequately promote unionization, or to deliver the message in all of the workers' native tongues, it would be consid- ered an "unfair labor practice" and grounds for bringing a case before the NLRB.

In addition to this, the board has threatened to sue four states that recently added provisions to their state constitutions requiring that all workers, when deciding whether to unionize, be given the opportunity to vote in secret-ballot elections.

6. Obamacare: Unions were already effectively exempted from paying for the Obamacare law, for which they lobbied heavily. But more than that, they have been disproportionately exempted from one critical Obamacare requirement that will cause the health insurance premiums of non-unionized workers to rise.

In order to keep their insurance premiums low, SEIU nursing home workers in New Jersey negotiated a plan with a very low annual benefits limit—just $50,000. Such arrangements were common. But Obamacare now forbids them unless you have a federal waiver. And the administration seems especially willing to give waivers to its union friends. Obamacare otherwise demands that companies dramatically *raise* the maximum annual benefits they offer. A spokeswoman for the union local told CNS News that less than 1 percent of the union's members had ever exceeded the cap, and that the union had made other arrangements to help them.[65] This system offered the best value to the beneficiaries. It allowed workers to get health coverage and pay much less for it. It stands to reason, given that very few people actually need $1 million worth of health care in a single year. Most people would rather not pay for benefits they will likely never use.

But if you're not part of a government-favored union or a lucky company, Obamacare denies you this flexibility and requires your insurance policy to have very high annual limits, which means you will pay more. For 2011, the minimum limit is $750,000. For 2012, it must be at least $1.25 million, and then $2 million in 2013.

Until 2014, the Secretary of Health and Human Services can grant special exemptions.

The Obama administration's dispensations from the rules do not fall evenly. Among the 729 exemptions that had been granted as of January 2011, 166 of them went to union benefit funds. And these accounted for 40 percent of the 2 million employees affected by all of the exemptions. This means that so far, 870,000 out of 13.6 million unionized, non-federal workers in the United States have been exempted. They are being exempted at six times the rate of non-union workers.[66] And why not? President Obama and his family and the staffers who wrote Obamacare are also exempted from the bill—so why shouldn't their friends be exempt as well?

UNION TOADY TASK FORCE

President Obama is on your side. He's thinking of you. He cares about your family and your economic priorities.

Perhaps you got this feeling when you heard the news that Obama had set up a "White House Task Force on the Middle Class" on January 30, 2009.[67] The new president, at least, was hoping you would get that feeling. Obama established it "to ensure that the economic challenges facing the American middle class, challenges that predate the recession that was deepening as the Task Force was formed, always remain front and center in the work of the Administration."[68]

From this description, you wouldn't guess intuitively that the task force is just a group of union lackeys with few serious or meaningful proposals to help the 93 percent of private-sector workers who don't belong to unions. But that is, indeed, the panel Obama created in your name. It speaks volumes that the tickets to the panel's official February 2009 kick-off in Philadelphia were given away to environmental and labor groups, that the panel consisted of union bosses and Democrat politicians, and that every member of the panel—and all of the union bosses that addressed it—had annual salaries greater than $150,000.[69] This includes Andy Stern, SEIU president, who was making $260,000 in salary (plus a $46,000 expense account), and Anna Burger, SEIU secretary-treasurer, who was making $229,000.[70]

In February 2010, the Task Force on the Middle Class released its first annual report. It bears no resemblance whatsoever to the needs of the real-life "middle class." Instead, it is a laundry list of union priorities, with a few "regular people" items thrown in as camouflage.[71] Even here, as he pretends to reach out to regular people, Obama is really just serving his favorite special interest.

For example, when is the last time your family sat down at the kitchen table and discussed how important "Project Labor Agreements" are to your future? These union featherbeds are a top priority for this task force.

Or maybe you count the hours at work, wishing someone would come along and demand that you sign a card to authorize a union. The organizers are friendly—they might even visit you at your home, repeatedly, until you finally give in. Or maybe they won't be so friendly. Maybe they'll tell you that you'll be fired (or even deported) unless you sign. It's happened.[72] If this is what you think will help your family, then you share the same priorities as the White House Middle Class Task Force.

Are you one of the roughly 10 million Americans who work as independent contractors? In 2005, the last time the Bureau of Labor Statistics produced a report on the matter, contractors made up 7.4 percent of the workforce—a larger share than private-sector union members make up today.[73] According to the BLS survey, less than ten percent of contractors are interested in being someone's employee.

If you're a contractor, then President Obama's Middle Class Task Force cares about your situation, but not in the way you might hope. They're worried that you've been "misclassified," and they want to make you an employee again so that you can be coerced into joining a labor union. This is a perennial left-wing cause, and well out of place, considering that independent contracting is increasingly popular for small businesses, thanks to the expensive taxes and time-consuming legal requirements of hiring of regular employees, imposed over the years by liberal politicians. If you make the economically rational choice, it is a high priority of Obama's Middle Class Task Force to have the Department of Labor scrutinize your contracting decisions.

The Middle Class Task Force also cares a lot about "responsibility in federal contracting." That could be a good thing—after all, taxpayers should be worried about getting a good deal. But as you might have guessed, that's not what it's about. "[T]he Task Force is looking at ways to improve the procurement process by making it less likely that irresponsible businesses will get Federal contracts and by allowing procurement officers to consider job quality when awarding contracts while not raising the quality-adjusted costs of contracts." What you see here are two code words: "quality-adjustment" and "irresponsible." These represent something called "high-road contracting." Although it has been dropped for now—the public and private sector unions can't agree on this one—the idea is to make it easier to funnel government contracts to firms that use union labor, even if their bids represent a worse deal for the taxpayer. Surely, this is on the minds of most middle class Americans, don't you think?

So what will Obama do for middle class Americans? Just look at his task force for the answer. He will ignore their needs and accommodate unions in their name. Once again, the drive to save the economy looks suspiciously like a drive to save Obama's friends.

THE PRESIDENT'S BUDGET INCREASE PANEL

In many states, public employee unions have worked the political system so their members have much higher pay and better benefits than private sector employees. That's put taxpayers potentially on the hook for the unfunded pension liabilities of states and municipalities—now estimated to be $3.5 trillion.[74]

President Obama's stimulus package was specifically designed to protect state government workers who might otherwise have been laid off—even if their jobs were jobs that states needed to cut, and desperately. In April 2009, Governor Arnold Schwarzenegger tried to buy time for cash-strapped California by instituting a $2-an-hour cut to the state's subsidy for unionized home healthcare workers. But their union, the powerful Service Employees International Union, was having none of it. They lobbied the Obama administration, which rushed to the union's aid.

At the SEIU's urging, Obama officials convened a conference call with California officials and threatened to cut off $6.8 billion of the state's stimulus funding—certain doom for flat-broke California under the circumstances— unless Schwarzenegger reconsidered.[75] The Obama administration had actually invited SEIU's general counsel in Washington and two SEIU officials in California to participate in the conference call. California Secretary of Health and Human Services Kim Belshe remarked, "This was really atypical and outside any norm I am familiar with."[76]

When it became clear who was pulling the strings, the White House was forced to back down.[77] It was one of those cases where gangster government was just too unsubtle to be effective.

But where the Obama administration can really deliver the bacon is with the Federal employee unions. Federal employees are generally paid better than state employees, and thanks to the pension reforms of the Reagan era, they enjoy a more stable retirement system. They're also far better off than private sector employees. Federal workers' salaries exceed those of private sector workers in similar professions by 20 percent on average.[78] If you combine salaries and benefits, the average federal worker receives $123,000 a year, more than twice as much as the average private-sector worker's $61,051.[79] Even with President Obama's late November 2010 promise to freeze federal employees' cost-of-living pay increases, two-thirds of federal employees remained eligible for step-increases worth a combined $2.5 billion.[80] And those federal workers enjoy much more job security than employees in the private sector. Out of 2 million civilian federal employees, only 11,275 were fired for cause in 2009—about 0.5 percent—and layoffs were practically non-existent at just 400.[81] Private employees are historically three to four times as likely to lose their jobs.[82]

President Obama has responded to this growing problem…by helping federal employee unions strengthen their hands. On December 9, 2009, he issued Executive Order 13522, which, among other things, formally gives the unions that represent federal workers a seat at the table when it comes to negotiating policy, which includes budgets.[83]

The order does two things of significance. First, it creates a federal labor-management panel that includes seven seats for union bosses. Second, it deems the advice they give to be "pre-decisional"—a term of art which shields the panel's procedures from public scrutiny. The "pre-decisional" nature of the consultations allows the Obama administration to invoke executive privilege if citizens ever try to get details about what this panel is doing.

The executive order states that its provisions do not "impair or otherwise affect" the White House budget director's authority, but that really hangs on the meaning of the word "affect." On January 19, 2011, White House Personnel Director John Berry released a memo on referring back to Obama's executive order, again highlighting the "pre-decisional" nature of the unions' consultations and encouraging the unions to interfere in budget negotiations:

> During the budget development phase, before the President sub-mits the Budget to Congress, management develops proposed funding levels and draft programmatic narratives to be included in the budget document. At this stage, management has the option to solicit input from employee representatives. If management chooses to solicit such input, it should be limited to high-level discussions of goals and strategies. Moreover, to the extent that anyone receives confidential pre-decisional, deliberative informa-tion during this budget-development period, such information remains subject to the long-standing OMB policies on preserving the confidentiality of the deliberations that lead to the President's budget decisions.[84]

In other words, President Obama has given federal employee unions a for-mal role in clamoring for larger agency budgets. He has also shielded their involvement from citizens' eyes by exempting them from the Freedom of Information Act. This works against his oft-stated goal of cutting the defi-cit—a goal that you could argue has been unserious all along, considering the massive debt Obama has accumulated. But as we have seen, public promises mean little to gangster government when there is a favored special-interest group involved.

CHAPTER SIX

WE'RE GONNA HELP OUR FRIENDS: THE TRIAL LAWYERS

"At an intimate, $2 million fundraiser put on by a group
of trial lawyers in a private home in Washington, D.C.
last week, [Joe Biden] boasted that he had 'done more than
any other senator' for trial lawyers. There are 'two groups that
stand between us and the barbarians at the gate,' he professed.
'It's you and organized labor.'"

—**The Boston Globe**, *October 1, 2008*

In September 2010, the journal *Health Affairs* published a study on America's medical liability system and the burden it places on Americans each year. The answer: $56 billion, or 2.4 percent of all health care spending in America.

The study found that defensive medicine—"the prescription of extra tests and treatments by physicians primarily to reduce the likelihood of malpractice lawsuits"—dominates the equation, accounting for 82 percent of the added cost.

Unfortunately, the fact that America is a uniquely litigious society weighs heavily upon American doctors and hospital administrators. Magnifying the size of the malpractice insurance premiums doctors must pay is this dooms-day scenario: a mistake, or even a judgment call that goes the wrong way in an unclear medical situation, could become grounds for a multi-million dollar pain-and-suffering jury reward.

Some cases are even decided against doctors despite a lack of medical evidence that they did anything wrong. Junk science and medical theories concocted by creative trial lawyers can often carry the day in courtrooms, where non-expert jurors are the final arbiters of key questions of fact. Former Democrat Senator John Edwards of North Carolina, for example, made his fortune from multi-million dollar cases based on now-discredited ideas about cerebral palsy in infants. His ability to sway jurors was enough to set two new records in North Carolina—he secured a $23 million award in one 1997 case.[1] And even in cases where patients genuinely deserve awards, juries often grant them far in excess of what would be reasonable.

The results are high malpractice insurance premiums for doctors, and lots of defensive medicine, which drive up health care costs for everyone. The chief beneficiaries are trial lawyers, and their rewards come at the expense of consumers and taxpayers in the form of higher health care costs. In states where limits have been placed on medical malpractice lawsuits, costs have plummeted, and doctors (who were fleeing) have returned.[2]

The American Association for Justice, the chief trade group of trial lawyers in the United States, countered the *Health Affairs* study on the enormous costs posed by the trial lawyers not by discrediting it, but by asserting that a $56 billion annual leak in the health care system is simply not a big deal. The group blithely asserted that the study "shows that limiting the rights of injured patients will do practically nothing to lower health care costs."[3]

Actually, what the study showed is that placing reasonable limits on jackpot jury awards could save Americans more on health care costs than the annual gross domestic product of Bolivia; nearly twice as much as the Bear Stearns bailout cost; and more than the National Football League's entire revenue for 2009.

Fifty-six billion dollars a year is more than a half trillion dollars over ten years. The trial lawyers' argument that this isn't real money hinges mostly on the fact that it's a small annual percentage of health care costs, which the government had estimated at $2.4 trillion in 2008.[4] If $56 billion "only" accounts for 2.4 percent of all medical spending, then it's barely worth touching, right?

Unfortunately, this argument undercuts the entire rationale for passing Obamacare. In December 2009, the President's Council of Economic Advisers generated estimates—probably overly optimistic ones—of how much the Senate version of Obamacare would save Americans on health care costs.[5] If you work out the math based on current estimates of medical inflation, they promise that under Obamacare, annual health care costs will increase by only 23.2 percent between 2013 and 2018. The entire savings implied in that figure is almost exactly identical to the amount that the 2.4 percent added cost of our medical malpractice system will add to health care costs during the same period—23.3 percent by 2018.

Malpractice reforms would not have required Obamacare's $770 billion in tax increases, nor the creation of 159 new bureaucracies, nor the perverse incentives against hiring that Obamacare's mandates and fines are already creating for employers. A malpractice reform bill would not have run thousands of pages. It would not have created an unprecedented requirement that all Americans purchase a commercial product as a condition of being alive. It would not have required shady back-room deals with special interest groups, drug-makers, or senators intent on leveraging taxpayers' money to win re-election.

But trial lawyers, like a few other key special interest groups, hold unusual clout in the Obama White House. That's why malpractice reform was never seriously considered. The best Obama ever did was to pay it a bit of lip-service, and to promise "demonstration projects" that will never affect any law or policy. It is worth mentioning the fact that his Secretary of Health and Human Services, Kathleen Sebelius, who will be responsible for the demonstration projects, is a former executive director of the Kansas Trial Lawyers' Association.

In his 2011 State of the Union Address, President Obama went so far as to say he was "willing to look at other ideas to bring down costs, including… medical malpractice reform to rein in frivolous lawsuits." But even here, Obama had not deviated from the trial lawyers' standard line. The real problem in the world of medical liability is not "frivolous" cases—these are rarely brought, due to the money and strong legal teams that malpractice insurers have at their disposal. The real problem in medical liability is that even legitimate cases end with the kind of excessive and disproportionate jury awards that John Edwards was known for winning. This leads malpractice insurers to settle more cases for larger amounts. You will not see President Obama advocate caps on damage awards, no matter how much he talks about "frivolous lawsuits."

During the 2004 presidential campaign, Democrats Edwards and John Kerry embraced the same line Obama used. They advocated punishments for lawyers who file "frivolous" suits and supported independent examination of all cases by a qualified medical specialist.[6] This did not cause them to suffer any loss of support from trial lawyers, who do not fear toothless measures. None of John Edwards' suits would have been considered "frivolous," so why should they worry?

THE SPECIAL-EST INTEREST

Moreover, that train had already left the station a year earlier, with Obamacare's passage. And the complete omission of tort reform provides a strong example of the underlying contradiction in Obama's governance. Here, again, we have an example of Obama helping his friends, even at the expense of his own stated goals.

Obama is acting on many fronts to expand businesses' vulnerability to lawsuits—another anti-stimulative act whose sole purpose is to benefit a special interest that is especially generous to the Democratic Party.

In 2008, the Boston Globe reported on an excessively candid statement that then-Senator Joe Biden of Delaware made at a Washington fundraiser, which illustrates the importance of trial lawyers for the Democratic Party and for Obama's success in 2008:

> At an intimate, $2 million fund-raiser put on by a group of trial lawyers in a private home in Washington, D.C. last week, [Joe Biden] boasted that he had 'done more than any other senator' for trial lawyers. There are "two groups that stand between us and the barbarians at the gate," he professed. "It's you and organized labor."[7]

One would be hard pressed to find an interest more special than the trial lawyers, whose well-being outweighed a national reduction of health care costs. This was an unmistakable special-interest favor, recognized as such by none other than former Democratic National Committee Chairman Howard Dean, a medical doctor: "The reason tort reform is not in the [health care] bill is because the people who wrote it did not want to take on the trial lawyers in addition to everybody else they were taking on. And that's the plain and simple truth."[8] But it wasn't just a question of not making new enemies. Why would he ever hurt them? Trial lawyers were Obama's friends.

At the *Washington Examiner*, we conducted a detailed analysis of contributions by the top 112 plaintiffs' firms during the 2010 election cycle. We found that the employees and partners of these firms gave $7.3 million to candidates for Congress. Fully 97 percent of the money in our sample went to Democrats, to help Obama keep control of Congress and guarantee that the good times of jackpot jury verdicts would keep rolling. And if you think the remaining 3 percent went to Republicans, you'd be wrong. About half of it went to Charlie Crist, the former Republican who ran as an independent candidate for Senate in Florida. (Crist, an attorney, joined a personal injury law firm based in Orlando after he lost the election.)[9] The remaining 1.5 percent went to GOP candidates. The American Association for Justice, the trial lawyers' trade group, donated an additional $2.7 million to federal candidates, 99 percent of which went to Democrats.

The omission of malpractice reform from Obamacare is perhaps the most glaring example of pandering to this small but very powerful special interest. But that isn't the only thing they've managed to wrest from the Obama White House.

The very first bill that Obama signed as president was the Lilly Ledbetter Fair Pay Act, overturning a 2007 Supreme Court ruling. The Court had ruled the Lilly Ledbetter, who had sued her former employer over a decades old act of alleged discrimination by a supervisor, had no grounds for suing because the 180-day deadline for her lawsuit had passed many years earlier.

In response, the American Association for Justice (AAJ) lobbied for the Ledbetter law, which completely abolishes the statute of limitations for pay-discrimination lawsuits for current employees. Companies must now live in fear of sleeper plaintiffs waiting to sue until retirement or separation. As the *Wall Street Journal* editorial board explained, "For the tort bar, this is pure gold. It would create a new legal business in digging up ancient workplace grievances."[10] Decades after an act of discrimination occurs, perhaps by supervisors now long dead or retired, any employee can go to the courts in search of an extra severance package. Large, mysterious potential liabilities now exist on the books of every company in America, based on any of thousands of routine decisions so old that none of the companies' current owners or officers might have had any part in them.

Consider also the WalMart case that is currently bouncing around the federal court system. Class-action suits are the most efficient kind for trial lawyers—they can produce huge contingency fees, even if individual plaintiffs get little or nothing. And sure enough, the Lilly Ledbetter law gave birth to its first class-action case very quickly. By December 2010, the issue had reached the Supreme Court, which agreed to decide whether such a mass lawsuit can be filed on behalf of 500,000 female WalMart employees at stores across America. It could produce a multi-billion-dollar award, and massive attorneys' fees.[11]

Ninth Circuit Chief Judge Alex Kozinski, who dissented from the opinion that allowed the class-action case to go forward, implied suspicions of trial lawyer gold-mining, given that the employees in question worked under widely varying conditions:

> Maybe there'd be no difference between 500 employees and 500,000 employees if they all had similar jobs, worked at the same half-billion square foot store and were supervised by the same managers. But the half-million members of the majority's approved class held a multitude of jobs, at different levels of Wal-Mart's hierarchy, for variable lengths of time, in 3,400 stores, sprinkled across 50 states, with a kaleidoscope of supervisors (male and female), subject to a variety of regional policies that all differed depending on each class member's job, location and period of employment.

The WalMart case is the most extreme example of how this law is already being abused, but it actually poses a much greater threat to small employers—WalMart's "mom-and-pop" competitors who cannot afford to lawyer up. It adds one more reason, in addition to the many taxes, expenses, and workplace rules created over the years, for small businesses to avoid taking on employees as long as possible, and to avoid hiring more of them if at all possible. It certainly works against President Obama's stated goal of job creation.

TAX CUTS FOR A FEW RICH

How many times have we heard President Obama say that he opposes tax cuts for millionaires?[12] Obama once famously said of the rich: "At a certain point you've made enough money."[13] In his September 25, 2010, weekly radio address, he went so far as to accuse Republicans of promoting the "same worn out philosophy: cut taxes for millionaires and billionaires; cut the rules for Wall Street and the special interests; and cut the middle class loose to fend for itself…."[14]

But it really depends on which millionaires you're talking about. If they happen to be trial lawyers, they stand a decent chance of getting their taxes cut, and an act of Congress might not even be necessary. In July 2010, trial lawyers began a premature celebration over just such a tax cut, which might have been the only reason Obama couldn't give it to them.

The American Association for Justice (AAJ) was holding its annual convention in Vancouver, British Columbia. It was a star-studded event in the world of the plaintiffs' bar—the sort of thing that anyone who's anyone attends. Twelve Democrat senators showed up to raise money from a crowd that was more than happy to open their wallets for good friends.[15]

But these politicians did not produce the big news of the convention. That came in a closed-door session with AAJ's top lobbyist, John Bowman. Bowman announced to the crowd that Obama's Treasury Department was about to give trial lawyers a tax break worth $1.6 billion, and that this would be done administratively, without Congress. Apparently, the group had failed to keep moles out of its conference, because word spread quickly. *Legal Newsline* reported:

John Bowman, the Director of Federal Relations for the AAJ, said in response to a question from a state delegate regarding recruiting new members that an administrative order from the Treasury Department could come as soon as tomorrow....Sources also said Bowman cautioned AAJ members not to go public with the news the order would soon be issued, for fear of raising public ire to the proposal.[16]

Although it is impossible to know for sure, the breaking of this story might have prevented the trial lawyer tax cut from going through in 2010. It may still go through at any time, but this incident put a chill on it.

The reports from Vancouver immediately prompted two dozen Republican members of Congress, led by Senator Charles Grassley of Iowa, to write Treasury Secretary Tim Geithner and object. "We urge you not to make such changes in the government's enforcement of the tax laws, absent a clear direction from Congress or to comply with court decisions," they wrote, noting that Congress had already considered and failed to pass a similar measure.[17] They demanded documents related to administration officials' communications on this matter, which were never provided.

The tax change, which Treasury officials had been considering since at least May 2010, would have allowed trial lawyers who work for contingency fees (collecting a share of a successful plaintiffs' settlement or judgment) to write off the expenses of ongoing cases in the same year they are incurred. Under current law, the up-front expenses of such cases are considered loans to clients, and can only be deducted when a case is won or lost, which can be years later.

An administrative ruling from the IRS could have simply allowed this write-off, which no other lender enjoys. But more importantly, it would have changed the assumptions under which plaintiffs' lawyers operate. When they decide whether to take a case, they have to make complicated calculations based on chances of success, expenses, and the likely size of the award. The tax break, which would reduce effective expenses of litigation by 30 to 40 percent, would allow trial lawyers to take cases that are slightly less serious or slightly less lucrative.

In short, it was a tax subsidy that would help expand the lawsuit industry. This is why the American Medical Association strongly opposes the change.[18]

The fact that Obama even considered doing this is a testament to just how much power the trial lawyers hold within the Obama White House and the Democratic Party. But this change was an important one for AAJ. Although the plaintiffs' bar does not suffer the same challenges as the labor movement, AAJ's membership has fallen off in recent years. It had suffered a 33 percent drop in membership dues collection between 2005 and 2008. The tax break, which would have applied to a much larger number of lawyers than many of AAJ's other agenda items, was meant to be a recruitment tool.

PREEMPTION

Beyond merely fighting for special favors for its members, and against any new limits to lawsuits, the AAJ also lobbies for laws that create new legal vulnerabilities for deep-pocketed potential defendants.

In the automotive safety bill of 2010, for example, the AAJ lobbied for language that would have held automakers and rental car companies vicariously liable when irresponsible drivers caused accidents with their rented or leased vehicles. Democrat Congressman Bruce Braley of Iowa, a former president of the Iowa Trial Lawyers' Association, attempted to add this language in the Energy and Commerce subcommittee. He also tried to add language that would have allowed lawsuits against automakers for the designs of their vehicles—even if those designs meet federal safety standards. The effect would have been to let state juries, instead of federal regulators, decide what features make a car safe.

The automakers are currently protected by "federal preemption," which prevents state legislatures and courts from adding to federal regulations. It is a principle that President Obama has attempted to weaken in a number of areas. Because the issue is an obscure one, few voters probably noticed the executive memorandum on federal preemption that Obama signed in May 2009. This document attempts to expand legal liability and create new business for trial lawyers.

This memorandum was in response to lobbying from the AAJ, which had made the repeal of preemptive laws and regulations a top priority. They were especially interested in using laws and executive orders to overturn a major 2008 Supreme Court case, *Riegel v. Medtronic*.[19] A heart patient from New York had sued the manufacturer of a balloon catheter which, despite meeting rigorous federal standards of design, had failed him on the operating table when it was used inappropriately. The high court's 8-to-1 majority, citing the clear preemption language in the federal law that covered this device, disallowed the lawsuit insofar as it faulted the device's manufacture, labeling, and design, all of which met federal standards.

Preemption rules did not just arise out of a vacuum—they exist for a reason. As the Supreme Court's majority opinion noted in the *Riegel* case, a large number of products would never be created or would have to be taken off the market if not for preemption, due to potential liability. Justice Scalia, writing for the eight-justice majority, made what he characterized as an educated guess about Congress's intent in creating a preemptive law for medical devices: "[T]he solicitude for those injured by FDA-approved devices ...was overcome in Congress's estimation by solicitude for those who would suffer without new medical devices if juries were allowed to apply the tort law of 50 States to all innovations."

AAJ made the repeal of preemptive laws and regulations a top priority in its $4 million lobbying campaign of 2010. In January 2009, just days before Obama became president, AAJ's Director of Regulatory Affairs, Gerie Voss, sent a draft of an executive order on preemption to Obama's transition team. AAJ's draft order would have blocked executive agencies from including preemption language in new rules and regulations. It would have also required agencies to review the rules and regulations enacted during the George W. Bush years, and to begin purging any preemption language that could be found in them.

When Obama released his preemption memo on May 20, 2009, it was almost identical in substance to the AAJ's suggestions, even if it was just a "memorandum" and not the "executive order" they had requested. As a memorandum, it remains in effect only as long as Obama is president, but it also generated a lot less attention than an executive order would have. And

Obama upped the ante—asking that preemptive language be purged going back a full ten years—back, in other words, to the tail end of the Clinton administration.

The memorandum, which went almost unnoticed by the press, came out twelve days after the second visit recorded in the White House visitor logs that year by then-AAJ lobbyist Linda Lipsen. She made eleven visits in all during 2009.

You know you have real clout when you get to write the president's memoranda. It's a privilege Obama extends only to his closest friends, like the trial lawyers.

FAVORS AMONG FRIENDS

Michael Cembalest, the chief investment officer for JP Morgan Private Bank, examined the backgrounds of 432 cabinet secretaries past and present to size up the Obama administration. His idea was to look at every person who, since 1900, had held nine of the top executive branch jobs that most affect American businesses, to see how many of them had experience as business decision-makers—people who understood what makes for prosperity in the free market.

Cembalest published his findings in *Forbes* in November 2009, stacking up nineteen presidential administrations based on the business experience of their secretaries of State, Commerce, Treasury, Agriculture, Interior, Labor, Transportation, Energy, and Housing and Urban Development during that period. He found Obama's cabinet to be the least experienced in business matters, with fewer than 25 percent having run companies.[20] But Cembalest might have overstated the case. He acknowledges that in studying the issue, he awarded partial credit for private sector legal experience—a significant fact, because two of Obama's cabinet picks are trial lawyers. What their legal experience tells us is that Obama's top appointees have about the same amount of experience *suing* businesses as they have running them.

Like other "friendly" special interest groups, trial lawyers have received key appointments in the Obama administration. Secretary Sebelius may have the highest profile and the most power, but there are obscure appointees as well who make the bureaucracy friendlier to trial lawyers. In one case, Obama chose a trial lawyer to regulate an industry he used to sue.

The Grain Inspection, Packers and Stockyard Administration (GIPSA) seems an unlikely tool for trial lawyers, but gangster government has not neglected even this remote corner of the executive branch. Obama's appointee, J. Dudley Butler, has brought the agency far more notoriety, because he has issued new regulations that will make it easier for cattle and poultry producers to sue meat packers.

Eight circuit courts—every circuit court that has addressed the issue in recent years—have ruled that when meat and poultry producers allege "unfair" practices by meat packers, they must show that the actions in question hurt or were likely to hurt competition.[21] Practices are not "unfair" simply because they cause prices to go down. In response to the court cases, Butler proposed new rules at GIPSA that eliminate this requirement. The effect would be to make more of these lawsuits succeed and create more paydays for trial lawyers. The new proposed rules adopt the notion that: "A finding of harm or likely harm to competition is always sufficient, but not always necessary, to establish a violation of sections 202(a) and/or (b) of the P&S Act."[22]

To understand what's at stake, consider this: in one case, which the 11th Circuit Court later reversed, a jury awarded *$1.3 billion* to a class of cattle ranchers. The award was made on the sole grounds that these ranchers were getting lower prices on the spot market because other producers were selling through long-term contracts. That's a gold mine if you're a trial lawyer.

Democrat Congressman David Scott of Georgia, one of the rare Democrats in Congress who routinely bucks trial lawyers, was irate over the rules when Butler appeared before his House Agriculture Subcommittee on July 20, 2010. He accused Butler of deliberately thwarting congressional intent:

> A number of these provisions had previously been rejected, their amendments on the floor, in the Senate process, and certainly in the farm bill. They were rejected strongly during the last farm bill deliberations. So the question is, why are they here? Is this an end-run around Congress?

...This proposed rule goes well beyond—well beyond—what Congress intended. It eliminates the required showing of competitive injury....These are the most sweeping changes to the Packers and Stockyards Act in nearly 100 years.... [23]

On June 22, 2010, the very same day the proposed rules were released, 115 members of Congress wrote to Obama's Secretary of Agriculture, Tom Vilsack, complaining that GIPSA was going far beyond its legal mandate and making "proposed regulations that greatly exceed the mandate of the Farm Bill."[24]

Although the period for public comment on the rules was eventually extended, these members of Congress should not necessarily expect a sympathetic reception. Vilsack is himself a former president of the Iowa Trial Lawyers' Association.

MR. LEAD PAINT GETS A NOMINATION

Naturally, the most important appointments for the trial bar are judicial nominations, and here President Obama has outdone himself. He has nominated a multi-millionaire trial lawyer who boldly tried to take liability where it had never gone before, and nearly succeeded.

To fill a vacancy in Rhode Island's federal district court, the state's Democrat senators urged President Obama to pick Jack McConnell—which he did. McConnell, a trial lawyer, was given a mediocre rating by the American Bar Association ("substantial majority: qualified, minority: unqualified"), but he had the most important qualification of all: McConnell and his wife had contributed nearly $700,000 to Democratic candidates at the federal level since 1993, and another $74,000 to state level candidates.[25] The beneficiaries included President Obama and four of the Democrats who were serving on the Senate Judiciary Committee at the time of his nomination.[26]

At the *Washington Examiner*, we studied the precedents for political giving by judicial nominees and found this to be highly unusual. Only four of President George W. Bush's 261 district court nominees had given more than $20,000 to candidates (many had given nothing). The most generous donor had been a former Republican Party county chairman from Ohio, who had given $83,000.

McConnell was not only notable for his political generosity, but also for the fact that he was a litigious trailblazer. He made a fortune in the tobacco settlement of 1998, and he went on to champion a new and dubious theory of lead paint liability. He and other partners at the Motley Rice law firm decided that lead paint is not just a dangerous product, but an actual "public nuisance." The distinction is very significant. Public nuisance law covers cases where someone deprives others of a public common-law right. It can be invoked when factories spew black smoke into the sky, or when someone dams up a river on his property and causes a flood. It is not often used against corporations that make dangerous products.

One must credit this public nuisance theory for its genius. If it could survive in court, it would be like a trial lawyer's license to print money. Public nuisance cases are less difficult to prove than product liability cases, and they have no statute of limitations. To apply public nuisance law to lead paint would open up entire new horizons of liability for trial lawyers that no court had ever imagined. More important, it would create an opportunity for nine- or even ten-figure contingency fees. Why file relatively unprofitable lawsuits against landlords who fail to remediate lead paint in their buildings, when you can instead launch a single multi-billion dollar lawsuit against dozens of deep-pocketed paint manufacturers? And the companies being sued don't even have to make lead paint. They could also be the successors of long-defunct corporations that stopped making lead paint decades ago.

In 1999, McConnell was given the opportunity to launch just such a case in Rhode Island—a lawsuit to make paint companies pay to remove every chip of lead paint in every building in the state. The liability would be in the billions of dollars. The Ocean State's then-attorney general—Sheldon White-house, who is now a Democrat senator, a recipient of McConnell's campaign donations, and a supporter of his nomination—hired Motley Rice to take the case, with an agreement that the firm could take one-sixth of whatever the state won.

After a decade of costly litigation, one mistrial, and a successful 2006 jury verdict for McConnell, Rhode Island's Supreme Court unanimously slapped down this public nuisance theory as "antithetical to the common law." The court noted that what McConnell was attempting "would lead to a widespread expansion of public nuisance law that never was intended."[27] The court even quoted Edmund Burke's adage that "bad laws are the worst sort of tyranny," and forced the state of Rhode Island to pay for part of the defendants' expenses. As of this writing, the paint companies are still in court trying to recoup more of their legal expenses.

McConnell's firm did not just fight this battle in Rhode Island. It made itself into a veritable public nuisance over the course of a decade, filing similar lead-paint lawsuits on behalf of several states and cities with similar fee agreements. Others, including the city of Saint Louis, brought similar cases. The City of Chicago tried to use public nuisance law to sue gun-makers.

And in state after state—New Jersey, Illinois, Missouri—their theory was defeated as a matter of law. Ohio's attorney general fired McConnell and dropped a similar case after the Rhode Island decision was issued.[28] As of this writing, Motley Rice is involved in the only remaining lead-paint public nuisance case, in California.

McConnell succeeded only in that these frivolous cases hurt businesses and stunted job growth, causing paint companies' shareholders to lose billions of dollars in equity—for nothing.

McConnell was rewarded by President Obama with a lifetime appointment to the federal bench. If he is ever confirmed, he might be helping Obama's friends long after Obama's presidency is over.

THE OBAMA ANTI-STIMULUS

President Obama ran up a great deal of debt with stimulus incentives and giveaways. But as we have seen in both this chapter and the last, he was doing favors for friends in organized labor and on the plaintiffs' bar that were simultaneously un-stimulating the economy and stunting growth. He allowed unions to increase costs for stimulus projects, reducing hiring. Even as he dramatically altered the nation's health care system in the name of controlling health care costs, Obama protected one of the largest single sources of added costs—big paydays for trial lawyers in the area of medical malpractice.

These special-interest favors are helping his friends build and maintain the large inefficiencies in the economy and loopholes in the legal system that they have historically exploited at the expense of broader prosperity.

You might think that the Obama administration's stimulus and anti-stimulus measures simply cancel each other out. That may be true mathematically, but in the final analysis it is inaccurate. In this context, the simultaneous acts of giving with one hand and taking away with the other both accomplish something. Even if their actions net out to zero in economic terms, both hands are helping to increase the Obama administration's power over business, health care, the economy, and generally over people's lives.

And that's the whole point of gangster government.

CHAPTER SEVEN

"WE'RE GONNA PUNISH OUR ENEMIES"

*"The only way to get somebody to stop crowding the plate
is to throw a fastball at them."*

—White House spokesman Robert Gibbs

The author of the latest anti-Barack hit book is appearing on WGN Radio in the Chicagoland market tonight, and your help is urgently needed to make sure his baseless lies don't gain credibility.

David Freddoso has made a career off dishonest, extreme hate mongering, even calling legislation to protect people from hate crimes the "Thought Police." And WGN apparently thinks this card-carrying member of the right-wing smear machine needs a bigger platform for his lies and smears about Barack Obama—on the public airwaves.

Freddoso will be on WGN tonight from 9:00 to 11:00 to promote his new attack book against Barack.

Tell WGN that by providing Freddoso with airtime, they are legitimizing baseless attacks from a smear merchant and lowering the standards of political discourse.... Confront Freddoso tonight before this goes any further.

This was my first real taste of the future Obama presidency. His campaign—not some Democrat or left-wing group, but the actual campaign of the current president of the United States—sent this email to his supporters, encouraging them to call into a local Chicago radio show and shout me down. It's not uncommon for activists to organize call-ins, but until Obama 2008, I had never even heard of a presidential campaign doing anything quite like this.

Late in the campaign season of 2008, I had traveled to the Chicago area to visit friends and appear on Milt Rosenberg's show to promote *The Case Against Barack Obama*. The show's format was a debate between me and a young attorney who supported Obama. I thought it came off pretty well. We shook hands at the end, and I headed for the airport.

Unfortunately for those receiving the above marching orders from Obama for America, I was already back in Washington by the time the show aired, completely oblivious to their campaign of talk radio disruption. We had pre-taped the entire debate. In the final hour of his show, Rosenberg went live and invited callers to voice their comments. The goon squad quickly showed up, and several people who clearly had not read *The Case Against Barack Obama* called in and read from the same script.

This salvo was not really aimed at me, my career of "dishonest, extreme hate mongering" notwithstanding. The email message directed users to a page on Obama's website labeled "WGN Standards." The warning shot had really been aimed at Rosenberg, the Tribune company, and anyone else in the Chicago media who might consider giving airtime to any critic of then-Senator Obama.

I doubt that it had any serious effect, but it was a significant data point for understanding how Team Obama works. Someone in the Obama campaign had actually taken the trouble to write up an entire "ACTION ALERT" so that people could call in and berate me (or so they hoped) on air, lest I convince the Chicago area that their extremely popular, rock-star senator was a poor choice for the presidency.

I was not the first target of this sort of defamatory email "ACTION ALERT" from Barack Obama's campaign. My then-colleague at *National Review*, Stanley Kurtz, had been given his own creative set of epithets by Team Obama weeks earlier:

Right-wing hatchet man and conspiracy theorist, Stanley Kurtz is pushing a new crackpot smear against Barack falsely claiming he was a member of something called the New Party.... This isn't the first time Kurtz has ventured down this slippery slope—he has a history of telling these kinds of unsubstantiated tall tales.

Aside from the fact that Kurtz's writings about the New Party happened to be true—Obama had sought and obtained the New Party's endorsement in 1996 and was described in its newsletter as "a member"—the pejorative adjectival description of Kurtz is just absurd. He is a soft-spoken writer, an academic by training, fond of ideas, and prone to dogged, detailed document research. "Hatchet man" is probably the last thing that comes to mind. The document research underlying his new book on Obama's pre-political days, *Radical-in-Chief*, will generate historical interest for students of left-wing politics long after Obama is gone—probably even among liberals who dislike his conclusions.

Kurtz had actually been live on the air when the goons began calling in—people who clearly had no idea what he had written, recently or ever. But in a blog post afterward, he was admirably restrained about the attention he had received from Obama's smear site. His reply carries a relevant message even now, years later:

Ordinarily, a site that spewed this sort of odious and insulting nonsense would merit no reply. Given that it's being run in the name of the possible next president of the United States, however, it may make sense to respond...

Obama has been mightily helped during this campaign by his calm and apparently reasonable demeanor in debate. It's tough to believe a man this cool could be a supporter or practitioner of Saul Alinsky's militant intimidation tactics. Yet Alinskyite "direct action" is alive and well at Obama's "Fight the Smears" website. This site still seems committed to the proposition that I should be barred from radio, television, and media generally—or at the very least barred without direct supervision from an Obama campaign representative. The thugocracy lives at "Fight the Smears." This is the real Obama, even if most voters know nothing about it.[1]

Over a year later, in October 2009, *Politico* published a piece titled, "Obama strategy: Marginalize most powerful critics." In the context of Stanley's experience, it is a rather illuminating piece, suggesting that what we had witnessed in the 2008 campaign had been just trial runs for broader smear campaigns to be run from the Obama White House.

> President Obama is working systematically to marginalize the most powerful forces behind the Republican Party, setting loose top White House officials to undermine conservatives in the media, business and lobbying worlds....
>
> Obama aides are using their powerful White House platform, combined with techniques honed in the 2008 campaign, to cast some of the most powerful adversaries as out of the mainstream and their criticism as unworthy of serious discussion.[2]

This is what Stanley Kurtz had described and predicted; these were the methods of Saul Alinsky's *Rules for Radicals*: "Pick the target, freeze it, personalize it, and polarize it."[3]

Following that playbook, the White House chose numerous powerful targets. The most unusual had to be FOX News, on which it declared open war.

It began when President Obama unexpectedly captured the Nobel Peace Prize. White House Communications Director Anita Dunn celebrated by telling *Time* magazine that FOX News, which the administration treated dismissively, was "opinion journalism masquerading as news."[4] She followed up with an interview with Howard Kurtz: "The reality of it is that FOX News often operates either as the research arm or the communications arm of the Republican Party.... What I think is fair to say about FOX, and certainly the way we view it, is that it is more a wing of the Republican Party."

Kurtz asked whether Obama had snubbed FOX News because of the way it covered his Nobel Peace Prize, and Dunn said, "Yes." And in case she hadn't been clear enough, she added that FOX was "not really a news network at this point."

Why was Dunn upset? Because *FOX News Sunday* host Chris Wallace had *fact-checked* a member of the administration, Assistant Veterans' Affairs Secretary Tammy Duckworth, after she made an appearance on his show. Dunn was livid:

> We had told Chris Wallace that, having fact-checked an administration guest on his show—something I've never seen a Sunday show do. And Howie, you can show me examples of where Sunday shows have fact-checked previous weeks' guests, and I'd be happy to see those. We asked Chris for an example where he had done that to anybody besides somebody from the administration in the year 2009, and we're still waiting to hear from him. When they want to treat us like they treat everyone else—but let's be realistic here, Howie. You know, they're widely viewed as part of the Republican Party. Take their talking points, put them on the air, take their opposition research, put them on the air. And that's fine, but let's not pretend they are a news network the way CNN is.[5]

Other senior Obama administration officials carried the fight against FOX even further. David Axelrod appeared on *This Week with George Stephanopoulos* to urge all other news networks to stop treating FOX as a legitimate news source: "It's really not news, it's pushing a point of view and the bigger thing is that other news organizations like yours, ought not to treat them that way. And we're not going to treat them that way. . . ."[6]

Rahm Emanuel appeared on CNN and sounded a similar note, stating that President Obama does not want "the CNNs and the others in the world [to] basically be led in following Fox."

Dunn had said, "They are boosting their audience. But that doesn't mean we are going to sit back."[7] White House spokesman Robert Gibbs picked up on this theme, as if FOX was motivated by ratings in a way that other news outlets weren't, saying of FOX News, "I would say sometimes programming can be tilted toward accentuating those profits."[8]

It is entirely possible that Wallace was harder on Duckworth than he had been on other guests. But ask yourself this: Is it a good or a bad thing when journalists tell you, as a viewer, that you've been told something false by a White House official? Perhaps Wallace should have been doing this more often with other guests, but that doesn't create a legitimate reason for the White House to whine.

Perhaps this is why Howard Kurtz's last question to Dunn betrayed some incredulity: "To some extent—poll numbers being down, problems piling up—things are not going as well as you would probably like for the administration. I'm wondering whether the people at the White House are just a little shell-shocked, because Barack Obama got such good coverage during the campaign, and now he's getting pretty typical presidential coverage, which is to say, pretty rough coverage."

For his part, FOX's Wallace summed it up pretty well with this description of the Obama administration: "They are the biggest bunch of crybabies I have dealt with in my thirty years in Washington."[9] In fact, the crybaby strategy was a calculated one. With the correct whines against the correct targets, the White House was seeking to boost its political fortunes and shore up its base.

BOGEYMAN OF THE WEEK

In 2007, biographer David Mendell was the first to comment on a less-known side of Obama's personality: "What the public has yet to see clearly is his hidden side: his imperious, mercurial, self-righteous, and sometimes prickly nature, each quality exacerbated by the enormous career pressures that he has inflicted on himself."[10] Two years into the Obama presidency, this description certainly resonates.

In 2000, when George W. Bush had won his election, he promised to be "a uniter, not a divider."[11] He still divided America—as all presidents do—with controversial policy decisions. He invaded Iraq. He cut taxes. He pushed for a guest-worker program. He passed a new Medicare benefit. In each case, people loved it or hated it.

President Obama has likewise divided Americans with his policies, but he has also divided them with demeaning rhetoric, often directed at entire classes of people. His predecessor simply never showed any behavior analogous to this.

He came to office after his famous put-down of working class (presumably non-unionized) Americans: "It's not surprising then that they get bitter, they cling to guns or religion or antipathy to people who aren't like them or anti-immigrant sentiment or anti-trade sentiment as a way to explain their frustrations."[12]

Of neighbors too dumb to support him in 2008, he said: "I want you to argue with them and get in their face."[13]

Of Republicans, he said: "They can come for the ride, but they gotta sit in back."[14]

Again, of Republicans: "I don't want folks who created the mess to do a lot of talking. I want them to just get out of the way so we can clean up the mess. I don't mind cleaning up after them, but don't do a lot of talking."[15]

Of the Cambridge, Massachusetts, police officer who arrested a black college professor outside his home: "I don't know, not having been there and not seeing all the facts, what role race played in that. But I think it's fair to say…that the Cambridge police acted stupidly."[16]

Of pro-lifers, he once wrote: "Most antiabortion activists, for example, have openly discouraged legislative allies from even pursuing those compromise measures that would have significantly reduced the incidence of the procedure popularly known as partial-birth abortion, because the image the procedure evokes in the mind of the public has helped them win converts to their position."[17]

In its first two years, the Obama administration has shown an amazing, even Nixonian propensity to pick fights and lash out against perceived enemies. Obama, who as a candidate had complained about "phony and foolish diversions" in politics, stands atop an administration that spends as much or more time creating them than any in recent memory.[18] Who could forget about his White House's call to report "fishy emails" from detractors of his health care reform bill? In lashing out against its enemies, the Obama administration often shows the same characteristics that Mendell identified. Attacks on political enemies are the weapon of choice for shoring up the president's support among his left-wing base. At times—especially leading up to the 2010 election—such attacks were nearly all Obama had to offer.

If Obama is willing to demean secured creditors, ordinary Republican voters, and police officers trying to do their jobs, it goes without saying that the usual political targets are going to get their fair share of White House barbs. Depending on what week it was, the White House might have been targeting FOX News, oil companies, Karl Rove, John Boehner, Dick Cheney, or even billionaire conservative philanthropists David and Charles Koch (whose tax information was divulged in a White House press briefing[19]) as the cause of the nation's problems.

There was a method to the madness of whining as an argument, but it didn't seem to have proven terribly effective in the 2010 election.

Shortly after Obama's inauguration, when the Obama administration chose Rush Limbaugh as a target, it was because polls suggested that this would help strengthen Obama's footing. As Jonathan Martin reported in *Politico*, the White House chose this line of attack when polling showed Limbaugh's low approval numbers among voters under age forty: "Democrats realized they could roll out a new GOP bogeyman for the post-Bush era by turning to an old one in Limbaugh, a polarizing figure since he rose to prominence in the 1990s."[20]

Far more interesting, and unusual, was Obama's direct attack on the Supreme Court in his 2010 State of the Union address, delivered with six justices seated immediately in front of him. Obama attacked the Court for its recent *Citizens United* decision on campaign finance law: "Last week the Supreme Court reversed a century of law that I believe will open the floodgates for special interests—including foreign corporations—to spend without limit in our elections. Well I don't think American elections should be bankrolled by America's most powerful interests, and worse, by foreign entities."[21]

While behaving in typical gangster government style, bullying a coequal and non-political branch of government, Obama also displayed a complete misunderstanding of the decision he was deriding. Former Federal Election Commission Chairman Bradley Smith explained at *National Review*'s "The Corner":

> The Court held that [the law] which prohibits all corporate political spending, is unconstitutional. Foreign nationals, specifically defined to include foreign corporations, are prohibited from making "a contribution or donation of money or other thing of value, or to make an express or implied promise to make a contribution or donation, in connection with a Federal, State or local election" under 2 U.S.C. Section 441(e), which was not at issue in the case. Foreign corporations are also prohibited, under 2 U.S.C. 441e, from making any contribution or donation to any committee of any political party, and they are prohibited from making any "expenditure, independent expenditure, or disbursement for an electioneering communication."

Smith wrote that Obama's comments were "either blithering ignorance of the law or demagoguery of the worst kind."[22] The latter appears more likely because it better explains the White House smear campaign that followed. As the 2010 election grew nearer, Republican-aligned groups and donors would become subject to a strong xenophobic smear campaign run out of the White House.

The bogeymen were conservative political groups that raised money in unlimited amounts. Democrats formed similar groups—and they always had a built in advantage thanks to labor unions' election spending—but they were having less success than the GOP in 2010. Newly formed groups like American Crossroads were, for once, allowing Republicans to match organized labor's massive expenditures. So Obama trotted out a false smear that the Chamber and other groups were spending "foreign money" in elections.

For example, while campaigning for Alexi Giannoulias, the losing Democratic Senate candidate from Illinois, he delivered this speech:

> Right here in Illinois, in this Senate race, two groups funded and advised by Karl Rove (American Crossroads and Crossroads GPS)

have outspent the Democratic Party two to one in an attempt to beat Alexi—two to one. Funded and advised by Karl Rove. Just this week, we learned that one of the largest groups paying for these ads regularly takes in money from foreign sources.... That's not just a threat to Democrats. That's a threat to our democracy.[23]

Obama repeated the same formula in a campaign stop in Philadelphia: "It could be the oil industry, it could be the insurance industry, it could even be foreign-owned corporations. You don't know because they don't have to disclose. Now that's not just a threat to Democrats, that's a threat to our democracy."[24]

It was Obama's xenophobia election strategy. And it had absolutely no basis in reality.

Obama and his administration's officials leveled this smear against several groups, but the biggest fish of all was the U.S. Chamber of Commerce. The Chamber is a pro-business organization, but not always a conservative one. It had supported Obama's stimulus package, which was larded with goodies for well-placed contractors. But it had also come out very strongly against Obamacare. Even worse, the Chamber was in the process of spending $75 million in the 2010 election, the overwhelming majority of it in support of Republicans.

The Chamber is a 501(c)(4) organization—a tax-exempt membership group, consisting mostly of businesses who value the group's clout in Washington. As with political campaigns and committees, donations to such groups are not tax-deductible, nor are they taxed upon receipt. Unlike political groups, they are forbidden to exhort voters directly to support or oppose candidates. But what they can do and have done, especially before the McCain-Feingold campaign finance law of 2002, is buy ads that provide "educational" statements about candidates, usually to portray them in a negative light.

The Chamber of Commerce happens to be an international group, collecting some $300,000 in annual dues from foreign companies—a tiny part of its $200 million annual budget. Like all other 501(c)(4) groups, it is not required to reveal the names of donors publicly.

So the Obama White House added one and one together to come up with four. They promoted an insidious smear campaign: *Foreigners are buying our election through the U.S. Chamber of Commerce!*

If it matters at all, it wasn't true. As the *New York Times* reported, "a closer examination shows that there is little evidence that what the chamber does in collecting overseas dues is improper or even unusual, according to both liberal and conservative election-law lawyers and campaign finance documents."[25] But this did not prevent Obama himself, Vice President Joe Biden, and several senior White House officials from making spurious accusations about foreigners buying the election.

"I challenge the Chamber of Commerce to tell us how much of the money they're investing is from foreign sources," Biden said.[26]

White House advisor David Axelrod told ABC's Jake Tapper:

> Well we certainly do know about the Chamber, that they have foreign affiliates and they do raise money for the organization that way. What we don't know is where the millions of dollars $75 million, is coming from that they are using to fund these campaigns. And the question back to them keeps coming back from us and others is why not simply say? What is it that is so nefarious about the sources of their money that they won't reveal it? And that's true with all these organization.... It is a insidious, dangerous thing when people can contribute huge sums of money to run negative ads in campaigns and never confess or allow to their participation. It opens the door to all kinds of chicanery.[27]

Of course, Democrats had also funded campaigns using 501(c)(4) groups. Democratic National Committee spokesman Brad Woodhouse, who in 2010 hypocritically denounced this kind of spending in the *New York Times*, had actually run a group that did the exact same thing during the 2008 cycle, funding campaign ads and a bus tour to highlight "the destructive results of the conservative policies and ideologies implemented under the Bush administration."[28]

But Axelrod was a particularly unfitting spokesman for the White House's "hidden money" allegations. In a 2008 piece in *Newsweek*, Michael Isikoff had detailed how Axelrod's firm ran a scare campaign using undisclosed corporate money, in order to drum up public support for an electricity rate increase in Illinois.[29] Commonwealth Edison, the utility, wanted an increase in electricity rates, so it hired Axelrod's Chicago firm, ASK Public Strategies. ASK helped them set up a dummy Astroturf organization called Consumers Organized for Reliable Electricity (CORE) to obscure the campaign's source of funding. As Isikoff wrote in 2008:

> CORE ran TV ads warning of a "California-style energy crisis" if the rate increase wasn't approved—but without disclosing the commercials were funded by Commonwealth Edison. The ad campaign provoked a brief uproar when its ties to the utility, which is owned by Exelon Corp., became known. "It's corporate money trying to hoodwink the public," the state's Democratic Lt. Gov. Pat Quinn said. What got scant notice then—but may soon get more scrutiny—is that CORE was the brainchild of ASK Public Strategies, a consulting firm whose senior partner is David Axelrod, now chief strategist for Barack Obama.

The fact that Illinois law did not require donor disclosure in the CORE campaign had been good enough for Axelrod when his firm was using a phony front group to scare Illinoisans into embracing higher electricity rates. Not so for the Chamber to spend its own money on elections, openly. Gangster government jealously guards its privilege of playing by a different set of rules.

CONTEMPT

When the U.S. government is found in contempt of court for acting in bad faith, it is something of an embarrassment to the nation. It's even worse when officials fall under this sanction because they are using dishonest means to impose scientifically unsound and ideologically-based policies, all in the name of demonizing an industry. This was the end result of the Obama administration's blanket moratorium on deep-water oil drilling in the Gulf of Mexico.

During the 2008 presidential campaign, Republican candidate John McCain called for a cut in the corporate tax rate. In the time since, President Obama has also called for a cut in the corporate tax rate. But during the campaign, Obama framed McCain's plan by saying, he wanted to give "$4 billion to the oil companies." Of course, the tax cut would have applied to *all* companies. But oil companies are especially easy for a demagogue to demonize. They evoke images of monopolistic practices, corporate greed, and destruction of the environment, all at the same time.

And Obama was sure going to show the oil industry—one of the few large industries that consistently gives 70 to 80 percent of its political donations to Republican candidates. After the BP spill occurred on April 20, 2010, his Interior Department had a new crisis of which to take advantage. In late May, Interior Secretary Ken Salazar issued a blanket moratorium, halting all drilling in the Gulf of Mexico in depths greater than 500 feet.

This moratorium threatened the livelihood of thousands of oil workers, and presented the possibility that oil rigs used for domestic production would be sent abroad to places like West Africa and the Middle East.[30] It has already caused at least one Houston-based firm to fold.[31] It was likely to wreak further economic havoc on a region already reeling from the sudden destruction of its coastline and the crippling of its fishing industry. And it came at the expense of companies which had behaved much more responsibly than BP.

For the moratorium to survive, Salazar knew that he would have to justify his actions before a court. And so in order to give it a veneer of scientific credibility, he presented a report on May 27 that had been reviewed by a team of scientists. The report that Salazar presented included the moratorium, as well as new safety procedures for offshore oil rigs.[32]

The only problem? The scientists had not actually been told about this blanket moratorium. The draft that they saw made much more modest recommendations—a "temporary pause" in current drilling operations to test the rigs currently operating, and a six-month moratorium on permits for depths greater than 1,000 feet.

Eight of the scientists, upon noticing this discrepancy, released a statement pointing out that their names and reputations were being used to justify a policy they had not endorsed:

> A blanket moratorium is not the answer.... This tragedy had very
> specific causes. A blanket moratorium will have the indirect effect
> of harming thousands of workers and further impact state and
> local economies suffering from the spill.... A blanket moratorium
> does not address the specific causes of this tragedy.... We encour-
> age the Secretary of the Interior to overcome emotion with
> logic...[33]

Months later, the Interior Department's Inspector General would report that it
had been White House officials, including Obama's climate change czar Carol
Browner, who had edited the report in a way that gave the false "implication that
the moratorium recommendation had been peer reviewed by the experts."[34]

On June 22, Louisiana Federal District Judge Martin Feldman ruled that
Salazar had not justified the moratorium from a scientific perspective. He
issued a preliminary injunction, forbidding the government from imposing
the moratorium. After losing a quick appeal, Salazar rescinded the moratorium, but he also instructed his department to draft a new blanket moratorium. He made it clear to the oil industry that a new moratorium would be
coming any day. Despite the court's order, he did not want the oil rigs to start
up operations.

On July 12, 2010, Salazar issued the new moratorium, which the court
would later describe as "substantively identical" to the one that had just been
struck down. He would officially rescind this second moratorium on October
12—the same day the Interior Department was due to file a brief in court
defending it.

Judge Feldman considered the government's behavior in this case to be
outrageous enough that he found the United States in contempt of court. In
a ruling issued February 2, 2011, he wrote:

> [T]he government did not simply reimpose a blanket morato-
> rium; rather, each step the government took following the Court's
> imposition of a preliminary injunction showcases its defiance: the
> government failed to seek a remand; it continually reaffirmed its
> intention and resolve to restore the moratorium; it even notified

operators that though a preliminary injunction had issued, they could quickly expect a new moratorium. Such dismissive conduct, viewed in tandem with the reimposition of a second blanket and substantively identical moratorium and in light of the national importance of this case, provide this Court with clear and convincing evidence of the government's contempt of this Court's preliminary injunction Order.[35]

For gangster government, misrepresentation of science and defiance of federal courts come all in a day's work. It's too bad for Obama that he doesn't control the courts.

NOT A FRIEND? OUT OF LUCK.

David Hamilton was a young Protestant seminarian in Louisville, Kentucky. In his spare time, he volunteered as a sidewalk counselor at the only abortion facility in town. He would stand outside the abortion center for long stretches, praying. When women approached to enter the clinic, he would try to convince them that there were better options than abortion.

This sort of work is common in the pro-life movement. Sometimes it becomes lively, with preachers bellowing about the value of innocent human life in the womb. Sometimes, as with many other kinds of protests, it becomes a bit too lively, with emotional words exchanged. Most often it is a lonely vigil by a few quiet people praying. In any case, it is an activity protected by the First Amendment.

Many abortion clinics—including Louisville's EMW Women's Surgical Center—draft volunteer escorts to hurry potential customers inside before the sidewalk counselors can approach them.

Hamilton was dedicated to a cause he believed in. At worst, he might have been a bit of a nuisance. He had no history of violence. He never attempted to block any patient's way into the clinic.

But David did make a mistake one day. On January 30, 2010, as a clinic escort guided a patient into the EMW Center, she threw her arm up to block him from speaking to the patient. According to the report in the Louisville *Courier-Journal*, he brushed the escort's arm aside.[36] According to Hamilton, at no point did he attempt to harm the woman seeking an abortion or her escort.

The clinic is the site of such protests every Saturday, and so the police are usually on hand, just in case. The officer who cited Hamilton for disorderly conduct reportedly had not seen what happened, but he wrote up the misdemeanor citation anyway.

"I never touched the girl going into the clinic....I didn't come close to touching her. I said what I had to say and kept walking," Hamilton would later tell the Louisville *Courier-Journal*.[37]

Before the misdemeanor case went to trial, Hamilton and his attorney made a good-faith offer to prosecutors. He would do eight hours of volunteer work at his church if they would just drop the charges. The prosecutor agreed. It wasn't much of a case anyway. No one had been hurt or threatened, and no one's access to the clinic had been blocked. There had been no violence. The incident had been so minor that the director of the clinic, Anne Ahola, did not even remember it when the Louisville *Courier-Journal* asked her about it in December 2010.[38]

Even as misdemeanor disorderly conduct cases go, this was a relatively minor one, though the heated nature of abortion politics inflated its importance. Hamilton performed his community service, and that should have been the end of it.

But it wasn't. Hamilton graduated from seminary in the spring of 2010 and moved to Houston. On December 21, 2010, he received a terse official message, which began: "A lawsuit has been filed against you." At the bottom of the page was the name of the plaintiff: The United States of America.

There was no shortage of tasks for Obama administration officials in December 2010. There were actual wrongdoers to bring to justice—people who had actually hurt other people. There were billions of dollars in stimulus spending being wasted on projects forbidden by the stimulus law. There were thousands of unresolved oil spill claims in the Gulf region. There were two wars going on that Obama had promised to end.

Yet Hamilton's case somehow became a top priority for federal prosecutors—not for the U.S. Attorney in Kentucky, but for Obama's Department of Justice team in Washington. The trial attorney who signed the document, and who demanded a reply within twenty-one days of service, was Aaron Fleischer, who works at the Civil Rights Division of the Department of Justice, headquartered seven blocks from the White House. Obama's Justice Department, which was at that very moment defending the health care reform law in court, had apparently been keeping its hawkish eye on the misdemeanor docket of Louisville's local courts. Perhaps it had to do with the Obama administration's presumption, based on an April 2009 report on "Right-Wing Extremism," that individuals who are opposed to abortion are particularly prone to terrorism.[39]

The Justice Department's court complaint against Hamilton demands $20,000 in fines and compensatory damages, making this perhaps the most expensive arm-brushing that the Western District of Kentucky has adjudicated in some time. In the words of Hamilton's attorney, Vincent Heuser, the complaint "takes an ordinary, nice kid who is concerned about society, and makes him look like some kind of national monster." The lawsuit states that Hamilton used "force against a volunteer clinic escort," and says that he "attempted to, and did injure, intimidate and interfere with persons attempting to obtain and provide reproductive health services."[40] Moreover, "On information and belief, unless Defendant is restrained by this Court, Defendant will continue to engage in the illegal conduct averred herein."

To that end, the complaint demanded of the court "[a]n Order permanently prohibiting the Defendant, David Hamilton, from approaching within 8 feet of another person obtaining or providing reproductive health services (including, but not limited to, volunteer 'escorts'), unless such person consents, within a radius of 100 feet from any entrance to the EMW Women's Surgical Center." Of course, this was unlikely to happen anyway, since Hamilton had been living in Houston for some time—a development that the Justice Department had apparently missed in all of its painstaking research on the case.

But more to the point, they were literally making a federal case out of a harmless elbow bump.

Hamilton's attorney would not make him available for an interview. That's understandable, considering that Hamilton is now being sued by the world's most powerful entity, which enjoys limitless resources and can press any case, no matter how frivolous, to whatever limit the courts will allow. But when I asked the attorney whether Hamilton had $20,000, he laughed at me. "He just graduated from a protestant seminary," he said.

Hamilton's case calls to mind an incident that President Obama had recorded long ago in his 2006 book on political life, *The Audacity of Hope*. It was about a friendly confrontation he had with pro-life protesters during his Senate candidacy:

> I explained my belief that few women made the decision to ter-
> minate a pregnancy casually; that any pregnant woman felt the
> full force of the moral issues involved when making that decision;
> that I feared a ban on abortion would force women to seek unsafe
> abortions, as they had once done in this country. I suggested that
> perhaps we could agree on ways to reduce the number of women
> who felt the need to have abortions in the first place.
>
> "I will pray for you," the protester said. "I pray that you have a
> change of heart." Neither my mind nor my heart changed that day,
> nor did they in the days to come. But that night, before I went to bed,
> I said a prayer of my own—that I might extend the same presump-
> tion of good faith to others that had been extended to me.[41]

This kind of formulation has done much to advance Obama's career. He frames debates in a way that makes him sound very reasonable, even if his own view on an issue is extreme.

As I discussed in detail in *The Case Against Barack Obama*, our president is 100 percent pro-choice on abortion, and perhaps more committed to this cause than any other president since the *Roe v. Wade* decision of 1973. In 2002, Obama had been the only member of the Illinois state Senate willing to speak on the floor against a bill protecting premature infants born alive in the course of failed abortions. He had argued that to give such legal recognition to the humanity of a baby born so prematurely would threaten the right to legal abortion: "[W]hat we're really saying is, in fact, that they are persons that are entitled to the kinds of protections that would be provided a—a child, a nine-month old—child that was delivered to term. That determination, then, essentially, if it was accepted by a court, would forbid abortions to take place."[42]

But the point of his vignette in *The Audacity of Hope* was that we can disagree on an issue without hating those on the other side. At the very least, he is saying, we should engage political opponents on political questions with some degree of respect.

Unfortunately, this attitude is not reflected in the case against Hamilton, which seems designed primarily to harass citizens who exercise their First Amendment rights while being pro-life.

The federal Freedom of Access to Clinic Entrances Act of 1994 (FACE)—passed in the waning days of a decades-old Democratic congressional majority and signed by President Bill Clinton—gives the federal government special power to sue and disrupt the lives of people who peacefully protest on behalf of one particular cause and one cause only. A few tragic incidents of anti-abortion violence were cited as justification, but no analogous federal laws were enacted governing the conduct of union picketers, anti-globalism protestors, or eco-terrorists who have at various times killed people or taken hostages. FACE was signed into law as a favor to an abortion lobby that is very supportive of Democrats, and despite the fact that real anti-abortion violence is subject to the same state and federal laws that can be used vigorously against all political and protest violence.

In any case, FACE is on the books, and it has been upheld by the nation's courts. So technically, cases like this one can be brought. But even FACE requires some degree of prosecutorial common sense in its application. In this case, the act is being used to reopen a misdemeanor incident so minor that charges were dropped. "This is not an effort to punish any violation of the FACE act," Heuser told me. "This is a suppression of free speech. It's totally agenda-driven."

Unless you believe that bumping elbows with someone is justification for a $20,000 lawsuit, this case does look a lot like an attempt by a bureaucrat in Washington to harass, intimidate, and threaten a 23-year-old who hasn't hurt anyone. But whatever the merits of the Hamilton case, compare it to another, better-known case, also recently handled by the Obama Justice Department's Civil Rights division.

The now-famous Black Panther voter intimidation case began with an absurd and almost comical day of voter intimidation by two very hateful individuals. It ended with Obama appointees dropping a won case against three of four defendants—one of whom was a Democratic Party official. It ended with a weak and meaningless penalty imposed upon the fourth defendant, and then a cover-up of this special treatment of the defendants.

On election day, November 4, 2008, a college student caught two men—"King" Samir Shabazz and Jerry Jackson—on camera, standing directly in front of the doorway of the polling place at 1221 Fairmount Avenue in Philadelphia's fourth precinct,[43] wearing paramilitary attire and striking menacing poses. One of them—Shabazz—was carrying a billy club.

"I'm security," said Shabazz, as he stepped toward the student, brandishing his nightstick. He even shook it a few times for greater effect.

"I think it might be a little bit intimidating that you have a stick in your hand," the student said. "I mean, that's a weapon."

"But you have a camera phone," Shabazz replied.

"I do have a camera phone, which is not a weapon."

The camera did not capture their most outrageous behavior, but several witnesses did and submitted sworn affidavits describing it. Christopher Hill, a poll watcher, offered this account:

> I observed that the billy-club or nightstick was brandished about by the shorter man in uniform. He pointed it at me and my colleagues and smacked it into the palm of his hand from time to time in our presence. When I attempted to exercise my rights as a credentialed poll watcher, and enter the polling place, the two men formed ranks and attempted to impair my entrance into the polling place...I heard Defendant King Samir Shabazz make a variety of racially charged statements while at the polling place directed at me and my colleagues which included terms such as "cracker" and miscellaneous profanity.

Bartle Bull is an election lawyer who ran Robert F. Kennedy's 1968 presidential campaign in New York State. He had also participated in the dangerous task of helping black Americans to vote in the Deep South in the early 1960s. He happened to be at 1221 Fairmount Avenue that morning as a poll observer for John McCain. He testified to witnessing blatant voter intimidation:

> I heard the shorter man make a statement directed toward the white poll observers that "You are about to be ruled by the black man, Cracker."
>
> To me, the presence and behavior of the two uniformed men was an outrageous affront to American democracy and the rights of voters to participate in an election without fear. I would qualify it as the most blatant form of voter intimidation I have encountered in my life in political campaigns in many states, even going back to the work I did in Mississippi in the 1960's. I considered their presence to be a racially motivated effort to intimidate both poll watchers aiding voters, as well as voters with whom the men did not agree.

This was definitely a legitimate news story, although it should have been a brief one, with updates only once the government had finished off the defendants in court.

Was it a huge deal? Probably not. The New Black Panther Party members' actions had no significant effect on the election's outcome. No one reported being denied the right to vote, and certainly no one reported being beaten, although some did report that the men *attempted* to prevent them from entering the polling place.

On the other hand, their behavior was flagrant, clearly illegal, caught on tape, and corroborated by multiple eyewitnesses. It was a textbook case of voter intimidation. The violators' actions were so cartoonish that one could be forgiven for mistakenly thinking it was a prank. The Panthers' public comments and Internet videos betray a genuine hatred of white people. And the law forbids any attempt to intimidate a voter—something they clearly intended.

On January 7, 2009, the Bush Justice Department sued the New Black Panther Party, its chairman (who had allegedly aided in the intimidation scheme and who publicly endorsed it afterward), and the two men who had been on the site intimidating voters.[44] The defendants simply ignored the case against them, refusing to respond. The court issued a ruling of default in late April and asked the government to submit a proposed judgment against them.

In other words, the government had a won case on its hands. Career attorneys at the Justice Department's Civil Rights Division penned a memo on May 6, 2009, recommending that Justice seek an injunction against the three men and the New Black Panther Party that would bar them from bringing any weapon or wearing their paramilitary uniforms in any polling place, permanently.

On May 13, the trial team got the go-ahead from another career civil servant, the head of DOJ's Appellate division, Diana Flynn. She recommended they seek default judgment against all four defendants, adding that it would be "curious" to do otherwise under the circumstances.

Then, some of President Obama's high-ranking political appointees became involved, and on May 15, the case was abruptly withdrawn.

A year later, the head of the Civil Rights Division, Thomas Perez (an Obama appointee), was asked in a hearing before the United States Commission on Civil Rights whether this decision had involved any political appointees. His answer was a firm "no." But the correspondence surrounding the case suggested a different series of events.

A subsequent Freedom of Information request by the group Judicial Watch revealed that two Obama appointees—Deputy Associate Attorney General Sam Hirsch and Associate Attorney General Thomas Perelli—had been far more involved in the case than Perez had let on. Hirsch had been editing the proposed injunction against Shabazz right up to the night before the judge received it.[45] In the end, it was weakened so that Shabazz was only given a three-year ban on taking weapons into polling places within the City of Philadelphia.[46]

The Department of Justice, for its part, stonewalled and refused to cooperate substantially in the investigation that the Civil Rights Commission initiated. It withheld documents and emails containing many of the deliberations that would make clear what involvement Obama's political appointees had in letting three defendants off the hook in a won case, and reducing the penalty against the fourth.

Especially noteworthy is the fact that Jackson, against whom charges were dropped, was a member of Philadelphia's 14th Ward Democratic Committee, and was the party's credentialed poll watcher on election day.[47] *National Review's* Andy McCarthy noted: "Thanks to the dismissal, Jerry Jackson has gotten his poll-watcher credentials back. Next election season, he'll be right back in business."[48]

The Justice Department even demanded that the career attorneys involved refuse to answer subpoenas from the Civil Rights Commission. One of them was J. Christian Adams, who resigned from the Department after Perez's testimony. He later testified, and told the commission that Perez had lied.[49]

Obama's defenders have argued that this case is not a big deal. It would be more accurate to say that it should not have been a big enough deal that Obama appointees would pull strings to let thuggish, racist defendants off the hook when their disgraceful conduct was all over YouTube.

The fair administration of justice is government's primary and most important function. James Madison wrote that "[j]ustice is the end of government. It is the end of civil society. It ever has been, and ever will be pursued, until it be obtained, or until liberty be lost in the pursuit."[50]

It is hard to imagine that Madison had anything like the government's dogged pursuit of David Hamilton in mind. Equally, it is hard to imagine how the government's lenient treatment of the New Black Panthers was an in anyway a fair and disinterested act of law enforcement. And any comparison of the two cases suggests that if you have a political cause, which cause it is makes all the difference when you have a run-in with gangster government.

SUING ARIZONA

Some states just cannot get a break from the Obama administration. You could say that of South Carolina, where the Civil Rights Division of Obama's Justice Department has threatened legal action against the state's prison system. Their crime? After testing all incoming inmates for HIV, they keep the

HIV-positive inmates at a single facility, where they have separate housing and receive treatment. Infected prisoners do interact with the others during the day, but their housing arrangement makes it economical for the state to provide them with treatment. It has also prevented new infections—since the program was first implemented in 1998, state officials say, there has only been one new prisoner infection.[51]

Obama's Justice Department wants the infected prisoners to be dispersed among the general population. A DOJ letter to South Carolina officials notes that "inmates with HIV under the custody and control of the SCDC are housed exclusively at" two of the state's prisons, and that "as a result of this segregation, many inmates with HIV suffer disparate treatment."[52] Moreover, DOJ complains, "we found that inmates with HIV were restricted from jobs in the cafeteria and canteen."

The response from the South Carolina Department of Corrections, which came two months later, noted that the current system "has withstood a previous federal court challenge,... has protected non-HIV inmates from the transmission of the disease," and that "HIV-positive inmates have received far better medical care than if they were scattered across 28 facilities in every corner of the State."[53]

Josh Gelinas, a spokesman for the Department of Corrections, tells me that they have not received any further correspondence on the matter. It remains unclear whether the Obama administration will continue this battle in its war on common sense.

But if you want a state that Obama really treats as an enemy, it has to be Arizona. When its senators exercise their right to free speech and criticize the stimulus package, the Obama White House threatens to take the stimulus money and send it elsewhere. When Arizona enacts a new constitutional amendment guaranteeing workers secret ballots if they consider unionizing, the National Labor Relations Board threatens to sue the state. And after years of the federal government refusing either to enforce or liberalize its own immigration laws, it is now suing Arizona for taking action to protect its citizens from the deadly effects of an unguarded border.

Just how bad is it in Arizona? In 2007, the chief ranger of the Sonoran Desert National Monument in Arizona, about sixty miles from the Mexican border, actually asked the Bureau of Land Management to close the monument to the public.[54] Incidents of violence related to cross-border drug smuggling had made it unsafe for visitors. The Bureau of Land Management refused to go that far. Instead, it posted eleven signs, according to a report from the federal Government Accountability Office, "to warn the public against travel on portions of the monument because of potential encounters with armed criminals and smugglers' vehicles traveling at high rates of speed."[55]

So now we have national parks that are too dangerous to explore, but at least we have warning signs. We also have Border Patrol agents being gunned down, most recently in December 2010.[56]

You may not believe that Arizona's new immigration law, known as SB 1070, is the solution to this problem. But it was the product of years of frustration with a federal government unwilling to do anything about an immigration and smuggling problem at the border. No matter how many decent people there are among the illegal immigrant population (and there are many), unchecked illegal traffic across the border brings many unsavory characters—including human smugglers, drug traffickers, gang members, and, potentially, terrorists. The result is that Arizonans suffer the indignity of being told to stay away from national parks in their own state.

SB 1070 requires law enforcement to make "a reasonable attempt....to determine the immigration status" of people who are arrested or detained by state and local authorities for other alleged crimes. If they are discovered to be unlawfully present in the United States, they are to be transferred to federal authorities. The law sprang from an understandably strong and sincere feeling of necessity—not from the bitter, gun-clinging hatred of immigrants that President Obama once described.[57] It was intended to help the federal government do something it had always claimed it could not do without help. By offering up illegal immigrants who are arrested by state and local authorities, Arizona would be providing precisely the kind of help that the federal government has asked of states.

The law became popular, not only in Arizona but nationwide. Polls showed that 64 percent[58] of Arizonans approved, and 51 percent[59] of Americans wanted a similar law in their own state.

This put Obama in something of a bind. He was unwilling to push immigration reform with any sincerity, for obvious political reasons. But during the health care debate, he had swayed reluctant members of the Hispanic caucus to vote for Obamacare by reasserting his commitment to immigration reform in a series of meetings. He said he would "do everything in [his] power" to move an immigration bill in 2010.[60] Obama had already seen his numbers slide among Latino voters between January 2010 (from 69 percent) and May 2010 (to 57 percent).[61] As the *Washington Post* reported in July 2010, Obama had been banking on a long-term political strategy on immigration that he hoped would sew up the Hispanic vote in 2010 and beyond:[62]

> Obama invited a small group of influential Latino activists to the White House and reassured them that he is committed to reform. But to succeed, he said, they had to stop their public complaining about how slowly he was moving and instead direct their fire at Republicans.[63]

As it turns out, the Hispanic caucus was a cheap date. The only chance of passing reform has now vanished with the Republican takeover of the House of Representatives. So Obama got their votes on health care and then never took any substantive action on immigration reform while he still had a Democratic Congress with any reasonable chance of passing it.[64]

But he had to do something. So, unwilling to fulfill his promises to the Hispanic caucus, or let Arizona govern itself, or simply step up enforcement of current federal immigration laws, Obama killed two birds with one stone: he sued Arizona and defended our dysfunctional immigration status quo.

In July 2010, the Obama administration brought its complaint that "S.B. 1070 is preempted by federal law and therefore violates the Supremacy Clause of the United States Constitution."[65] Of course, Arizona had not passed an actual immigration law. SB 1070 did not create a process for naturalizing or deporting anyone—it simply directed Arizona law enforcement to cooperate with federal authorities. But it is interesting to see Obama invoke preemption when it suits him.

The Justice Department's court brief can be summed up in one sentence: "Immigration enforcement is our responsibility to shirk, not yours." The document lists the various agencies responsible for immigration policy and argues that they have "competing interests." If state and local law enforcement refer too many illegal immigrants to them, it will interfere "with the federal government's ability to administer and enforce the immigration laws in a manner consistent with the aforementioned concerns that are reflected in the INA [Immigration and Nationality Act]."[66]

Compare this to the testimony given last March before the House Committee on Homeland Security by Obama's director of Homeland Security and Justice, Richard Stana:

> ICE does not have the agents or the detention space that would be required to address all criminal activity committed by unauthorized aliens. Thus, state and local law enforcement officers play a critical role in protecting our homeland because, during the course of their daily duties, they may encounter foreign-national criminals and immigration violators who pose a threat to national security or public safety.[67]

In other words, we need your help to enforce immigration laws, but not *too much* help, because then there might be political problems.

The federal complaint against Arizona explains that immigration laws are selectively enforced by design:

> Assuring effective enforcement of the provisions against illegal migration and unlawful presence is a highly important interest, but it is not the singular goal of the federal immigration laws. The laws also take into account other uniquely national interests.... Congress vested substantial discretion in the President and the administering federal agencies to adjust the balance of these multiple interests as appropriate....

Non-citizen residents of the United States are already required by law to carry papers on their person at all times. So the lawsuit has only one purpose, and that is to prevent "too much" enforcement. This is not an Obama policy—it's been around for a long time—but Obama is the one going to court to defend it. President George W. Bush, at political cost to himself, at least advanced a reform plan. President Obama has acted out of political calculation, in gangster government fashion. He buys off the Hispanic caucus with empty promises, then punishes red-state Arizona for trying to fix a real problem.

"QUIS CUSTODIET IPSOS CUSTODES?"

If characters as unsavory as the New Black Panthers can get a break from Obama's Department of Justice, it only makes sense that actual friends of President Obama can do a bit better. That was certainly the case for Sacramento's Democrat Mayor Kevin Johnson. An unfortunate government watchdog made the mistake of looking too closely at his misuse of government funds and suddenly found himself out of the job.

It is undisputed that a president has power to fire inspectors general. But it is a very serious act. Inspectors general are supposed to be independent—this is what allows them to conduct investigations into federal agencies. If presidents fired them routinely, they could eliminate anyone who got too close to finding corruption or incompetence within their own administration. This is precisely why Congress passed the Inspectors General Reform Act of 2008 with broad bipartisan support.[68] Senator Barack Obama was even a co-sponsor. Among other things, it requires the president to inform Congress thirty days in advance of such a firing, and to provide a statement explaining the reasons for the firing.

When President Obama fired Gerald Walpin, the inspector general who oversaw the AmeriCorps program, he followed the letter of this law, but in a way that completely defeated its purpose. He placed Walpin on a thirty-day leave, during which time he had no authority, no duties, no access to his office or his staff or his office email, and at the end of which he was terminated. Obama provided Congress with an explanation so vague as to be completely meaningless: "It is vital that I have the fullest confidence in the appointees serving as Inspectors General. That is no longer the case with regard to this Inspector General."[69]

Corrupt and incompetent officials within the executive branch can now breathe a bit easier, both under Obama and future presidents. Obama has created a precedent that any inspector general can *effectively* be fired immediately, without any explanation from the president.

Walpin's mistake had been to discover evidence that Kevin Johnson, a former NBA star who around the time of his investigation was elected as Democratic mayor of Sacramento, had misused an $850,000 AmeriCorps grant. Johnson's St. HOPE program was an urban charity with a focus on education and community development.[70] Johnson described himself in a local television interview as a personal friend of President Obama. He had endorsed and donated to Obama early in the 2008 Democratic presidential primary, and he also served as an Obama campaign surrogate speaker at several locations during the 2008 election.[71]

My colleague Byron York pounced on this story as only he can, even when much of the major media seemed content to leave it alone. He cited Walpin's report on Johnson, which said Johnson "had failed to use the federal money they received for the purposes specified in the grant"—namely, to tutor students and develop buildings in the neighborhood where it operated. Instead, he had "used federally-funded AmeriCorps staff for, among other things, 'driving [Johnson] to personal appointments, washing his car, and running personal errands.'"[72] He had used them to help with a school board election. He had used them to perform functions that were part of St. HOPE's day-to-day functions, instead of for the purpose for which the grant had been given. He even temporarily converted St. HOPE employees into AmeriCorps employees so that he could pay them out the grant funds, without changing their responsibilities. Johnson, given the opportunity to contest these allegations during the investigative process, did not do so.

This was the typical kind of abuse that inspectors general find, but the target of this investigation was not typical.

Walpin recommended to the program's board of directors that Johnson's current grants be suspended, and that he be barred permanently from handling any future federal grants. The suspension was implemented in September 2008, right before Johnson was then elected mayor of Sacramento. Although there were fears that this meant the City of Sacramento would lose eligibility for federal grants unless he resigned, they were unfounded. Other city officials could have been appointed as guardians of federal money. But this still would have weakened Johnson and hurt his popularity.

Walpin had also referred the matter for criminal prosecution to the U.S. Attorney for the Eastern District of California, Lawrence Brown. Brown, a career prosecutor who had taken over from a departing Bush appointee, instead entered into settlement talks with Johnson, and on terms very favorable to Johnson. Brown wanted to let him pay back less than half of the grant he had misused over a ten year period, and he also offered to lift Johnson's suspension.

Walpin, objected—this would be like telling Johnson, We caught you misusing our money, but if you give some of it back we'll give you even more money. Walpin was subsequently "cut out of the settlement talks," and the AmeriCorps board accepted the weak settlement and the lifting of Johnson's suspension.[73]

Walpin's May 6, 2009 report to Americorps management, criticizing the settlement deal that they accepted, got a very frosty reception, particularly from Americorps' chairman, Alan Solomont, who had been a major Obama donor and bundler and would later be appointed ambassador to Spain. The reception was even frostier because Walpin declared his intention to forward the report to Congress, something he was allowed to do under the law that governs inspectors general. The report criticized the light treatment that Johnson was receiving: "The settlement…leaves the unmistakable impression that relief from a suspension can be bought. In addition, media pressures and political considerations both appear to have impacted the Corporation's decision here."

On May 20, after a heated meeting between Walpin and the AmeriCorps board (during which some board members believed that Walpin appeared "confused"), Solomont went straight to the White House to discuss his Walpin problem with then-White House counsel Greg Craig.

On June 10, 2009, Walpin received a telephone call from Norman Eisen, Obama's Special Counsel for Ethics and Government Reform. Eisen gave

Walpin two options: resign immediately or be terminated. Walpin, who had feared this might happen when he submitted his May 6 report, had contacted congressional staff in advance, which ensured that his firing would be investigated. Or so he thought—it turns out that only the Republican minority was even remotely interested.

So consider what happened. The board of the Corporation for National and Community Service, the organization that runs AmeriCorps, managed to get the White House to fire the independent watchdog charged with investigating it. What's more, the firing came after that watchdog had vociferously objected to apparent favoritism benefiting a friend of the president of the United States. Such an action would only be justified under extreme circumstances and a careful investigation. Or so one might think. As it turns out, the White House conducted an "investigation" that consisted of one telephone call to a board member—Stephen Goldsmith, the former Republican mayor of Indianapolis. Goldsmith said he supported Walpin's removal, but he later told congressional investigators that the decision to fire Walpin had already been made before he was asked. It didn't take much to fire a man investigating one of Obama's friends.

This less-than-rigorous investigation might have posed problems as the White House tried to justify its actions before Congress. So Eisen spoke briefly to two other AmeriCorps board members about what Walpin's "confused" behavior in the board meeting.

When he arrived on Capitol Hill, Eisen assured members of Congress that he had conducted an "extensive" review, which somehow had not included so much as a single interview of Walpin or any member of his inspector general staff.[74]

You can see that the fix was in. The White House cobbled together a rationale for the firing only after the fact. Gangster government managed to take a 2008 law intended to protect the independence of inspectors general, which Obama had co-sponsored, and bend it until it broke. And Walpin found out what happens when you try to hold Obama's friends to the letter of the law. You become an enemy.

Walpin didn't need the job. He had actually tried to retire in November 2008—relenting only when his staff begged him to stay—but he certainly did not want to be forced out by the Obama administration. After his firing, he went to court. The United States Court of Appeals for the District of Columbia finally ruled against him in January 2011, finding that because Walpin had been paid his salary during the 30-day period when he was forcibly put on leave, Obama had not broken the law.[75] Republican Senator Chuck Grassley of Iowa, a longtime champion of inspector generals' independence under presidents of both parties, released a statement, noting that Eisen's "one-hour ultimatum in order to force a resignation clearly would have side-stepped the legal notice requirement" in the law if "it had worked." Grassley went on: "It dilutes the independence of these government watchdogs if the only explanation necessary for their removal is something as vague as 'lost confidence.' That's bad news for accountability in government."

But for gangster government, accountability is not a high priority. Especially not when Obama's friends are involved.

CHAPTER EIGHT

RECOVERING FROM GANGSTER GOVERNMENT

If men were angels, no government would be necessary. If angels were to govern men, neither external nor internal controls on government would be necessary. In framing a government which is to be administered by men over men, the great difficulty lies in this: you must first enable the government to control the governed; and in the next place oblige it to control itself.

—*James Madison in Federalist No. 51.*

On December 21, 2010, the darkest day of the year, a federal power grab was afoot. Julius Genachowksi, President Obama's chairman of the Federal Communications Commission, was attempting to convince his colleagues to help President Obama fulfill a campaign promise. At issue was "net neutrality," a controversial scheme for government regulation of the Internet.

Net neutrality is an issue both obscure and complicated, but you might think of it as a legal framework for regulating the Internet in order to solve a problem that does not exist—of Internet Service Providers blocking legal online content and applications. The only significant support for net neutrality comes from left-wing groups that were originally funded by one set of corporations (content providers) to fight another set of corporations (Internet Service Providers).[1]

Yet Obama's FCC Chairman, Julius Genachowski, argued passionately in favor of net neutrality: "As we stand here now, the freedom and openness of the Internet is unprotected. No rules on the books to protect basic Internet values."[2]

Somehow, the Internet had been doing fine, but Genachowski's view carried the day, in a three to two vote on the panel. The result had been long expected, even though Genachowski had kept the precise language of his new rules under wraps until the night before the vote. The only surprise had been the FCC's decision to pursue this matter at all. For in April 2010, a federal appeals court had struck down the panel's first attempt to regulate the Internet.[3] In fact, the court had specifically ruled that the FCC lacks authority to interfere with the Internet. Congress had not given the FCC any new authority, yet here was Genachowski once again, acting as if he had the authority anyway.

Congress was not happy about the FCC's action, either. The incoming chairman of the House Energy and Commerce Committee, Republican Fred Upton of Michigan, had asked the panel to wait for Congress to act.

Genachowski did not heed these checks on his power. Gangster government seldom does. Meredith Baker, one of the FCC commissioners who voted against the measure, stated the situation quite well:

> We have two branches of government—Congress and the courts—expressing grave concerns with our agency becoming increasingly unmoored from our statutory authority. By seeking to regulate the Internet now, we exceed the authority Congress has given us, and justify those concerns.[4]

The media speculation afterward focused on whether—or how soon—the new rules would be struck down in court. Verizon has already sued to block them.[5] But why does that even have to happen? Why is Obama's administration so intent on claiming power it lacks?

"I want to know why, why it was so important that this Lone Ranger, Julius Genachowski, felt it was that important that the FCC gain this much power in one fell swoop, usurping Congressional authority," Republican Congressman Lee Terry of Nebraska, told NPR. "It's a power play that's almost unprecedented, even in Washington."[6]

POWER OF THE PRESIDENT

The situation in Washington in 2011 makes this bureaucratic story particularly important. The FCC's power grab serves as a reminder that even without a friendly Congress, President Obama still can and will enact more of his agenda, with varying degrees of destruction to Americans' freedom and property. The American people, and the new Congress they elected in 2010, have awakened to the problem of gangster government. But they will have to be more vigilant over the next two years if they want to prevent more damage.

Presidents are powerful, and they don't always need Congress on their side to get what they want. We saw in chapter 2 how Obama's auto czar, Steve Rattner, gloated about the near-total lack of congressional interference in the automotive bailout—a bailout that Congress had actually voted against when given a chance.

Congressional acquiescence to Obama—partly through institutional weakness and partly through partisan collusion—permitted a virtual government takeover of health care and a stimulus package which, to all appearances, was just a very large waste of money.

At least in those two cases, Congress actually gave its approval. But President Obama has found many other ways to use the machinery of the executive branch alone to help friends and political allies—especially in organized labor, the trial bar, and the environmental movement—in ways that do not create jobs or promote the general welfare.

Obama's allies now know that the favor factory on Capitol Hill has shut down. There will be no card-check bill for organized labor, no laws compelling states to let civil servants unionize, no must-pass bills with special tax breaks for trial lawyers tacked on, and no carbon cap-and-trade schemes. For the next two years, they will attempt to draw what they can from the White House. If further favors come, they will come in the form of favorable rulemaking, regulations, and executive orders.

Congressmen make a lot of important decisions, but many more are made each day by obscure bureaucrats in the federal office buildings scattered around Washington, D.C., and its suburbs. According to a 2005 government study, existing federal regulations at that time were placing a $1.1 trillion burden on the American economy each year, in addition to the burden of taxation.[7] And no administration has ever been as active in rule-making as Obama was in fiscal 2010.

James Gattuso and Diane Katz of the Heritage Foundation track new government regulations each year, compiling federal agencies' reports on their new "major rules"—rules that affect the economy by at least $100 million.[8] President Bush's most expensive regulatory year in terms of added burden was 2007, in which his administration added a net $14.7 billion to that annual regulatory burden. His most active regulatory year in terms of the number of major rules was 2008, in which his administration issued twenty-three.

In Obama's first full fiscal year as president, he has broken both records by a mile. He has promulgated forty-three major rules with an added net burden of $26.5 billion on the economy. The new regulations cover just about every-thing you can think of, from toy manufacturers (new testing requirements) to construction sites (added expenses for preventing water runoff). Both Obama figures are "far more than any other year for which records are available."

Like Obama's tax hikes and union set-asides, they have served as an "anti-stimulus" throughout Obama's term, and add another explanation for our economy's continued slump. As one industry representative told the *New York Times* in May 2010, "Dollars spent on compliance with cumbersome regula-tions are dollars not spent on hiring new employees."[9]

President Obama's January 2011 announcement that he was going to sift through the 150,000 pages of the Code of Federal Regulations, to eliminate a few old and bad regulations, will easily be offset and probably overwhelmed by the reams of new rules sure to come from Obamacare and the financial reform bill that passed in 2010.[10] Expect another record-breaking year in regulation.

Liberals are already suggesting ways for Obama to advance their agenda despite a Republican House majority. The Center for American Progress, a left-wing think tank, published a paper full of them in November 2010, titled "The Power of the President."[11] Obama has already turned the federal government into the world's largest automaker, private equity fund, benefits manager, and union organizer—now Sarah Rosen Wartell wants him to turn it into the world's largest landlord, too. Wartell writes that there are simply too many investors buying foreclosed houses, renovating them, and selling them. And it has to stop:

> To the extent these investors make repairs to the property to improve the chances of sale and increase their returns, the repairs are often largely cosmetic and can saddle unwary buyers with significant maintenance costs. Indeed, these kinds of investors have little regard for the long-term habitability of the homes they bought and sold.

If you're guessing that this problem requires a big government solution, then you read Wartell's mind. It's called "scattered site rentals," a whole new world of subsidies coming to a neighborhood near you.

> Currently, the Federal Housing Administration, Fannie Mae, and Freddie Mac are still taking on record numbers of REO (foreclosed properties)…. [W]ith effective government control of such large portfolios of REO housing at one time, we are at a unique moment when larger portfolios of geographically concentrated properties can be assembled creating efficiency and market value. Many of these properties will require some renovation to make them marketable, creating an important opportunity also to do energy efficiency retrofits, with savings recouped within an estimated three years of operation, making them more attractive to investors. Finally, the properties should be transferred to management entities for rental purposes, with stakes sold to private investors. Properties participating in these programs can be eligible for affordable housing subsidies or other incentive programs as well.

In other words, make way for a massive new government rental housing program—an excellent way to take advantage of a crisis and expand the size and power of government once again (while advancing the cause of "green" subsidies with "energy efficient retrofits"). And best of all, there's no need to involve the Congress in any of this. In order to circumvent elected lawmakers, the author recommends that President Obama direct the Treasury and the Department of Housing and Urban Development "to examine the availability of resources at FHA, Fannie Mae, and Freddie Mac and from existing appropriated funds…that can be used to finance pilot program implementation and evaluation."

ASSESSING THE DAMAGE

This and other ideas in the Center for American Progress report represent new and grand ways of going further down the path that voters rejected in November 2010. But perhaps it is a better idea to ask how America starts moving in the *right* direction.

After two years of watching unchecked executive power, economic management of private sector businesses by government officials with little or no business experience, the bullying of small lenders, and the ramming of an aggressive, unpopular left-wing agenda through Congress, the nation needs to heal. How does it recover from gangster government? The answer that involves the 2012 election is obvious, but what does the nation do in the meantime, and what does it do in the long run?

When it comes to Obama's big agenda items discussed in this book, there are some efforts afoot to undo them that give cause for hope. Obamacare has been successfully challenged in two federal courts as of this writing. Half of the states are now participating in legal challenges, and the health care reform law will surely end up in the same Supreme Court whose understanding of the Constitution Obama denigrated during his 2010 State of the Union Address.

If the law does not lose in court, the Congress has another trump card—the nation's purse strings. Under our Constitution, the government cannot spend a dime without congressional permission. The money needed to set up Obamacare's 159 bureaucracies, collect its taxes, and pay its subsidies would have to find substantial support from within a Republican House majority that unanimously voted against it on January 19, 2011. Congress routinely passes spending bills that state that "None of the funds in this bill may be made available for" certain purposes. This will be the first line of defense against Obamacare's development into a behemoth. With a properly written bill, the Congress can even prevent government officials from writing regulations.

Obamacare's most unpopular provisions—such as the one that forces small businesses to file IRS 1099 forms for every major purchase—can probably be repealed without too much resistance. Democrats would block or try to limit such an effort at their own peril.

But after that, it gets harder. Even if a Republican president is elected in 2012, it will still be a challenge to repeal Obamacare. Republicans probably will not have sixty votes in the Senate in 2013. If they do win a Senate majority and keep their House majority, they can use the reconciliation process to eliminate many of Obamacare's programs, and $921 billion in spending between 2014 and 2020. They cannot use that process to repeal its $770 billion in tax increases or its cuts to Medicare.[12]

The road to repealing Obamacare will not be an easy one, but at least there is a road. The same cannot be said for much of President Obama's other handiwork.

The property rights violated in the sham Chrysler bankruptcy obviously cannot be restored. The reputation of the Department of Justice is in tatters, and cannot be restored without a new president.

The stimulus money is nearly all gone, with perhaps $12 billion left, most of it dedicated to the high-speed rail projects. Newly elected Republican governors in Florida, Wisconsin, and Ohio have scrapped their white elephant projects, but their combined $3.6 billion share of the rail funds will merely be redistributed among thirteen other states.[13] Republican plans to rescind the money would require Obama's signature. Not only is he unlikely to sign such a bill, he is actually trying to quadruple down on this error. As this book went to press, the administration announced a $53 billion high-speed rail program over six years.[14]

THINKING ABOUT TOMORROW

The election of a new president in 2012 can arrest some of the damage Obama has inflicted, but it will not solve the long-term problem of gangster government. Our system had been weakened too far to bear the overreaching by a president versed in the Chicago Way. It's time we strengthen it against the gangster government of the future, whatever form it might take. No future administration of either party should be allowed to deem automakers "financial institutions" in order to steer funds to them (a decision made originally by George W. Bush), then use this questionable overreach (as Obama did) to justify ever greater and further overreaches, all in the name of getting a good deal for taxpayers. No future administration should be allowed to manipulate the bankruptcy process in order to obtain a predetermined outcome for a politically favored labor union or business—or even just to fulfill a president's ideological vision for an industrial or jobs policy.

No future presidential administration, without the consent of Congress, should be able to overturn seventy years of settled labor law, as Obama's National Mediation Board did in order to reward his friends. No future administration should be handed $1 trillion to blow on projects that are favored by the government, but have little or no value to the greater economy No future administration should be given as much power over health care as the last Congress has given this administration. .

Congress has been the victim and the facilitator of these massive expansions of executive power. Congress passed TARP and Obamacare and the stimulus package, giving Obama a blank check for his worst excesses. If gangster government is to be stopped, it will have to start with Congress reasserting its proper constitutional role. Here are few ideas that might help Congress regain its rightful stature.

Oversight. Single-party control of Washington weakens oversight—it is a built-in consequence of our partisan system. Each party goes easy on its own.

The 2009–2010 Congress was especially weak. House Oversight Chairman, Democrat Edolphus Towns of New York, gave new life to the image of a sleeping watchdog. When Obama became president, the number of information requests from the Oversight Committee suddenly plummeted—by 61 percent, according to an election year report by the committee's current chairman, Republican Congressman Darrell Issa of California. The number of hearings declined as well, and the hearings that were held often covered extremely low priority matters. A few samples:

- "The Restroom Gender Parity in Federal Buildings Act"
- "GPS: Can We Avoid a Gap in Service?"
- "Examining the Impact of Leafy Green Marketing Agreements"
- There was not a single hearing on the government's response to the Fort Hood or Christmas Day terror attacks. There were two soporific hearings on the mission of the National Archives.

This has changed for now, thanks to the incentive of partisanship. Chairman Issa is taking the screws to Obama's administration over the Freedom of Information Act, the Treasury's administration of TARP, regulatory obstacles to job creation, and a number of other important topics. This is a good thing.

As annoying as it might seem to have *your* party's president harassed by the other party's subpoenas and investigations, the absence of congressional scrutiny is far worse for everyone in the long run. It cedes greater Congressional power to the executive branch, empowering bureaucrats and making government less responsive to the public.

One solution would be to give more power to the minority on the oversight committee. It would require a very forward-thinking legislator to suggest such a thing, because it would involve a concession of power. But it would also provide an additional check on executive power—or the tyranny of the majority—if a substantial minority on the oversight committee could issue a subpoena.

Or why not go even further? In the United Kingdom and many British Commonwealth countries, the opposition party is often given the chairmanship of committees that oversee government spending. The same is true in Israel's parliament.[15] In 2005, *The Nation* published a favorable profile of liberal Democrat Congressman Henry Waxman of California, a dogged champion of presidential investigations right up until the moment President Obama was elected, at which point he decided he wanted to chair a different committee. But of the Israeli system, Waxman commented at that time, "It's an interesting idea."[16]

It *is* an interesting idea. Rather than continue a system that shifts abruptly from investigation of abuses of power to hearings on bathroom equality and leafy green marketing, congressional leaders could, through simple rule-changes or a collegial agreement, create a system in which presidents are always being overseen by members of the opposite party. Now is a perfect time to create such an arrangement, because the government is already divided and no one would perceive it as a power-grab.

Don't Leave the Details to the Devil. When the topic of earmarks comes up, members of Congress are quick to defend their constitutional prerogative. They, not the bureaucrats, should direct how money is spent, they say. The Constitution thus becomes an excuse for directing funds to bridges and museums in towns where they could use a few more votes in the next election.

Congressmen tend to be far less zealous about their constitutional powers when it comes to significant bills outside the appropriations process. The problem is that these bills are often much more important, as their effects can linger for decades.

When Congress passes a law, it has to leave some specifics to the executive. The Congress is not an expert body—even if you want it to pass a law requiring automotive safety standards, you probably don't want it deciding how many pounds of force your car's roof can withstand in a rollover accident. Congress may require that our soldiers be equipped with what they need, but they're not the ones to ask about the optimal kill radius of the standard-issue grenade.

Still, when Congress gets lazy, it leaves far too much leeway in the implementation of laws. The result is that vital policy decisions are made unilaterally by unelected bureaucrats. We saw several examples of how President Obama has exploited vague laws to help labor unions and trial lawyers. This is the risk that Congress takes when it leaves too much for future executives to interpret and decide.

In describing the financial reform bill he had drafted himself and shepherded through Congress, former Senator Chris Dodd, a Democrat from Connecticut, remarked: "No one will know until this is actually in place how it works."[17] No lawmaker from either party should ever be able to say such a thing. Nor should any bill pass for which it is true.

The best contemporary example of this is TARP, which basically allowed the Secretary of the Treasury to use $1.7 trillion in any way he saw fit. This is also true of Obamacare—your current health plan's survival will depend ultimately on decisions made by unelected regulators. In 2008, we saw the same danger in the Federal Reserve Act, originally enacted in 1913 and amended twenty years later. Central bankers used an almost forgotten provision of this law, which had long been gathering dust, to bail out AIG and Bear Stearns.

The 50-year-old Clean Air Act also gives an incredible amount of power to the executive—so much power that the Supreme Court decided in 2007 that its existing language justifies federal regulation of carbon dioxide, the gas we exhale with each breath, even if this was never specifically intended by Congress. This gave Obama a chance to threaten the Congress, in true gangster government style, with draconian regulations if it would not voluntarily subject all Americans to a cap-and-trade system. It is now giving him still more regulatory power to steer America's electricity generation in a direction that will be costly to consumers and harmful to businesses.

Experience shows that when Congress gives an inch, the executive takes several miles, whether it happens immediately or years down the road. Congress can override bureaucratic regulations under the Congressional Review Act, but this requires the president's signature and is therefore likely to fail whenever it is most needed. The lesson is for Congress to be very careful about the laws it writes today. You can never know who will be stretching their limits tomorrow.

Recess appointments. Although the historical evidence is unclear, it seems pretty safe to say that the modern use of the recess appointment bears little resemblance to its original purpose in the Constitution. Presidents are permitted to make temporary appointments without Senate approval, for a period that can last up to two years.

In the Federalist No. 67, Alexander Hamilton discusses this presidential power:

> The ordinary power of appointment is confined to the President and Senate *jointly*, and can therefore only be exercised during the

session of the Senate; but as it would have been improper to oblige this body to be continually in session for the appointment of officers and as vacancies might happen *in their recess*, which it might be necessary for the public service to fill without delay, the succeeding clause is evidently intended to authorize the President, *singly*, to make temporary appointments "during the recess of the Senate, by granting commissions which shall expire at the end of their next session.[18]

A 2008 Congressional Research Service report on the topic notes that the recess appointment probably had a sensible rationale at the time the Constitution was written, for "both Houses of Congress had relatively short sessions and long recesses between sessions during the early years of the Republic. In fact, until the beginning of the 20th century, Congress was, on average, in session less than half the year."[19] In modern times, when recesses rarely run longer than one month, the recess appointment serves no real purpose except to allow presidents of both parties to circumvent political controversy and take more power away from Congress. In 2007, during the Bush presidency, Senate Democrats highlighted the absurdity of this presidential power by holding daily one-minute sessions, for the sole purpose of avoiding a "recess," so that there could be no recess appointments.

President Obama's recess appointment of Craig Becker was typical of the way presidents abuse the power. But in another case, he added a new wrinkle to the recess appointment. With Donald Berwick, the administrator of the Centers for Medicare and Medicaid Services, he appears to have instead used it in order to avoid embarrassing confirmation hearings and help Democratic senators avoid an embarrassing vote. The Democrat-controlled Senate never held a single hearing on Berwick's nomination, possibly because his financial arrangements with his former non-profit group would have been questioned, and his extreme ideological views on health care would have been laid bare. As a result, a completely unaccountable nominee, not even subject to basic congressional scrutiny, will make vital decisions about the implementation of Obamacare. This unconfirmed official will affect millions of Americans' lives, health coverage, and health care. This is a clear case of gangster government exploiting loopholes to enhance its own power.

This is certainly not what the framers had in mind when they put the recess appointment into the Constitution. Rather than allow this kind of abuse to continue beyond the Obama presidency, Congress should consider amending the Constitution to abolish recess appointments, or at least to drastically limit their duration so that presidents will use them only in genuine emergencies.

Such an amendment would probably receive broad bipartisan support, especially if it takes effect at a future date, when no one knows yet which party will control the presidency. Even liberals objected when President Obama used a creative job title to avoid having to get Elizabeth Warren confirmed as head of the new Consumer Financial Protection Board. Even a hardened liberal like Democrat Senator Chris Dodd of Connecticut could see there was a problem: "You've got to have someone who has earned the respect and the support of the Senate," he said. "The confirmation process is very, very important. They still haven't answered that question, and it has to be answered."[20]

Understand what you're voting on. This is the only way to avoid another Obamacare. As obvious as this seems, recent experience suggests that it should not be taken for granted.

Even the admonition to "read the bill" is not enough when bills are thousands of pages long, and an innocuous instruction to alter a single word in existing law can cause billions of dollars to be spent or a previously permitted enterprise to become a crime.

The *proper* reading of legislation is extremely time-consuming. Members of Congress and senators have little choice but to rely on staffers to divide important bills up and comb through them, piece by piece, as they move through the committee process, and again when they come to the floor of each chamber. Transparency is the best answer to this problem, and it is an especially fitting virtue that Congress should practice, considering that it is the branch of government most accountable to the American people.

Unfortunately, transparency has been lacking in recent Congresses. Particularly under the recent Democratic majorities, leaders frequently bypassed the committee process altogether, sending *de novo* bills straight to the House floor. The 111ᵗʰ Congress passed so many massive and game-changing bills that its total lack of diligence in this matter became a serious problem. The most extreme example came in June 2009, when House Energy and Commerce Chairman, Democrat Henry Waxman of California, filed a 300-page amendment to his 1,000-page carbon emissions bill (known as "cap-and-trade") at three o'clock on the morning of the floor vote. This left legislators just a few hours to pore over hundreds of pages, refer the changes in the amendment back to the original bill, and then refer the changes in the bill back to the existing laws. No one can do that, and it's pretty safe to say that no one did. Responsible members of Congress can and should demand rules that increase transparency, do away with procedural shenanigans, and give members enough time to take their jobs seriously.

The 112ᵗʰ House of Representatives has already made a good start in this area, promising to post bills for seventy-two hours before they receive a floor vote. But it won't do much good if members of Congress fail to take advantage of it. Some Democrats in Congress claimed ignorance of some of the damaging provisions contained in Obamacare, such as its new (and non-health-related) tax filing requirements for small businesses.[21]

This implies that they failed to read a bill that had been unchanged for several months. A particularly alarming revelation came recently, when Democratic Senator Bill Nelson of Florida discussed the second court decision striking down Obamacare. When asked by ABC News whether he thought it would be ruled unconstitutional, he replied: "I think that's a possibility, but it's not a probability. We were very careful when we crafted this law. It is going to pass constitutional muster. There might be parts of it that might be struck down. But there is at the end of it what is called a severability clause, that says if parts are stuck down, that doesn't strike down the whole law."

From this, we at least know that know that Nelson was not "very careful." More than a year after he voted for Obamacare, he somehow had no clue that it does not, in fact, contain a severability clause. More astonishingly, he remained ignorant of this fact even though it came up in both court opinions that struck the law down, and was mentioned in several news reports.[22]

"IF YOU CAN KEEP IT"

John Adams wrote the Constitution of the Commonwealth of Massachusetts, which was adopted on June 15, 1780. Unlike the U.S. Constitution, Adams' document has its Bill of Rights at the beginning, instead of at the end. Its Article VII, which declares:

> Government is instituted for the common good, for the protection, safety, prosperity, and happiness of the people; and not for profit, honor, or private interest of any one man, family, or class of men....[23]

At various times in our history, this truth has been lived out in spectacular and exemplary ways. George Washington set a precedent for republican, civilian governance when he selflessly resigned his commission as commander-in-chief after the Revolutionary War, instead of staking a claim to power.

But more often, Adams' wisdom has been forgotten or disregarded. Even Adams, who wrote those fine words, would fail them miserably a few years later, when he became our nation's second president. His own "honor"—or more properly, his inability to accept strident criticism—overrode his concern for the common good when he signed the Sedition Act. That law forbade "false, scandalous, and malicious writing or writings against the government of the United States, or the President of the United States, with intent to... bring them...into contempt or disrepute."

Thankfully, this precise example is unlikely to repeat itself. But that doesn't mean our rulers in modern times place the common good ahead of profit, honor, or private interest. If even the author of that beautiful Article VII could succumb to the temptation to power, and to its abuse, we can only imagine how hard it is for other officials, no matter how pure their original intentions, to avoid doing the same.

Today, with a federal government and a presidency that are both far more powerful than they were in Adams' time, even much smaller abuses than his can pose much graver threats to Americans' freedom, prosperity, and happiness.

In the first two years of the Obama presidency, Adams' admonition was frequently violated. Private interests routinely superseded the common good. At the cost of billions to current and future taxpayers, stimulus money has been awarded to silly, politically correct projects designed to reshape the economy along the lines of someone's ideological vision, rather than to restore the economy.

Gangster government's dispensing of favors to labor unions took precedence over our bankruptcy laws, labor laws, and the interests of the taxpayers who foot the bill for the stimulus package. In the administration's so-called "Middle Class Task Force," taking care of unions took precedence over any serious government efforts to promote the *common* good. With its health care bill, read by so few but supported by so many in Congress, President Obama has stretched the constitutional limits of federal power beyond their breaking point. And by putting trial lawyers' well-being ahead of a truly efficient health care system, he has also cast serious doubts upon the purity of its intentions.

No administration that acts in this way serves America well. The Obama administration swept into power with promises that it would change a broken system of government. Instead, with his Chicago ways, Obama has exploited the system's brokenness, taken advantage of crisis after crisis, and worked zealously to help his friends and hurt his enemies.

It won't be easy to fix the damage. But happily the Obama presidency, with its profligate spending and power-grabs, has served as something of a wake-up call. Just two years after what seemed like the permanent death of conservatism, Americans—and not just those who count themselves part of the Tea Party movement—have rediscovered the serious problems posed by an oversized, pushy, and unresponsive federal government that seems to be putting private interests ahead of the common good. They have seen gangster government, and they have rejected it.

When Democrats were wiped out in the 2010 midterm, many liberal pundits chalked it up to a bad economy and high unemployment. So did Obama. But this explanation is both inadequate and unsupported by the facts.

After 2008, it wasn't just overly optimistic Democrats who were writing things like this:

An expanded map and an unmatchable organization in size and
scope will make Obama the most formidable incumbent in modern American history, making it impossible for any of his opponents to credibly go toe-to-toe. That reality will not be lost on the
GOP....Challenging Obama will seem like a fairly ill-advised
career move....Defeating him will require a set of circumstances
that simply will not exist in 2012.[24]

It seemed like the nation's fate—the permanent death of conservatism, and
the advent of the permanent Democratic majority—and a strong, solid coali-
tion in favor of big government, run by those who stand to gain from it.

Yet somehow, this isn't how things have developed at all.

We know from the 2010 exit polling that voters did not, and do not, blame
Barack Obama either for the economy or for the financial crisis, whose begin-
ning predated his inauguration. Nor is it enough to say, as Obama has, that
Americans were simply too impatient for positive results.

The election, the exit polls tell us, turned on the answer to one key question:

Which is closer to your view?

1. *Government should do more to solve problems*
2. *Government is doing too many things better left to businesses and
   individuals*

Those who said that government is doing too much went three-to-one for
Republicans. Those who said the opposite went three-to-one for Democrats.
And the ones who embraced limited, constitutional government outnum-
bered the others by eighteen points.

I believe the voters turned on Obama because they saw something they
didn't like: The big, heavy, pushy hand of big government, reaching out from
every shadow. They saw one overreach after another—the stimulus package,
the health care bill, the bailout of the automakers, the favoritism toward special interests. And they said No to gangster government.

In 1787, at the end of the Constitutional Convention, a woman asked Benjamin Franklin what sort of government the convention had produced. "A Republic," he famously replied, "if you can keep it."[25] There are hopeful signs today that we can.

ACKNOWLEDGMENTS

By the time you finish writing a book, you owe a lot of thanks to almost everyone you know—some of them for inspiration, some for direction, and some for simply putting up with you. In my case, there are many people who fall into each category, and I'd like to name just a few.

This book's alliterative title originated with Michael Barone, a columnist and colleague who will always have my admiration and gratitude. Without his encouragement, this could not have been written.

I especially want to thank my editors at the *Washington Examiner*, Mark Tapscott and Stephen Smith, for their support and for the freedom I needed to undertake this project. I also want to thank my other colleagues at the *Examiner*. Their work provided me with an excellent guide to President Obama's first two years.

I would like to thank everyone at Regnery, including Jeff Carneal, Marjorie Ross, and Mary Beth Baker. I would especially like to thank Harry Crocker. His suggestions began my work on this book, and his gentle prodding pushed me past the finish line. His wise editing has also spared the reader a great deal of dense and unnecessary prose.

I also want to thank Thomas Becket Adams for his help in my research, and Dr. Stephen Bird of the National Journalism Center. I thank my parents, who gave me two gifts that I will always treasure: the love of learning and the Catholic Faith. Finally, but most of all, I would like to thank my wife. She is my soulmate and the mother of my children. These last few months surely tested her patience to the limit, especially considering the uncanny alignment of my deadline with our anniversary. She handled it all with incredible grace. *"De ultimis finibus pretium eius."*

NOTES

CHAPTER ONE

1. *Plato, Reason & Persuasion: Three Dialogues by Plato*, trans. John Holbo and Belle Waring (Singapore: Pearson, 2009)

2. Patricia Cohen, "In Writings of Obama, a Philosophy Is Unearthed," *New York Times*, October 27, 2010; available at: http://www.nytimes.com/2010/10/28/books/28klopp.html (accessed January 18, 2011).

3. Lisa DePaulo, "$#!% Joe Biden Says," *GQ*, December 2010; available at: http://www.gq.com/news-politics/politics/201012/joe-biden-interview-vice-president-obama?printable=true (accessed January 18, 2011).

4. David Remnick, *The Bridge* (New York: Alfred A. Knopf, 2010), 274.

5. *Newsweek*'s Evan Thomas on MSNBC's *Hardball with Chris Matthews*, June 5, 2009.

6. David Jackson and Ray Long, "Obama knows his way around a ballot," *Chicago Tribune*, April 3, 2007; available at: http://www.chicagotribune.com/news/politics/obama/chi-070403obama-ballot-archive,0,5693903.story (accessed January 18, 2011).

7. Ryan Lizza, "Making It: How Chicago shaped Obama," *The New Yorker*, July 21, 2008; available at: http://www.newyorker.com/reporting/ 2008/07/21/080721fa_fact_lizza#ixzz1AZ8Sn9Tp (accessed January 18, 2011).

8. Ben Smith, "Obama brings a gun to a knife fight," *Politico*, June 14, 2008; available at: http://www.politico.com/blogs/bensmith/0608/Obama_brings_a_gun_to_a_knife_fight.html (accessed January 18, 2011).

9. Judy Marcus, "Spreading their wings Meigs," *Chicago Tribune*, July 29, 2001; available at: http://articles.chicagotribune.com/2001-07-29/travel/0107290042_1_young-eagles-tuskegee-airmen-black-fighter-pilots (accessed February 8, 2011).

10. John McCormick and Jon Hilkevitch, "Fate of 16 planes stranded at Meigs still up in the air," *Chicago Tribune*, April 2, 2003; available at: http://articles.chica-

gotribune.com/2003-04-02/news/0304020310_1_taxiway-planes-runway (accessed February 8, 2011).

11. The incident inspired new, more substantial fines to be set in place for others who might try to do the same, known as the Meigs Legacy provision.

12. Paul Merrion, "Meter runs on mayor's Meigs shutdown," *Chicago Business,* June 24, 2006; available to subscribers at: http://www.chicagobusiness.com/article/20060624/NEWS04/200021104/meter-runs-on-mayors-meigs-shutdown#axzz18oIrPQdb (accessed January 18, 2011).

13. Nancy Pelosi, speech to the 2010 Legislative Conference National Association of Counties, March 9, 2010.

14. Liam Ford, "The Meigs Field Controversy," *Chicago Tribune,* April 6, 2003; available at: http://articles.chicagotribune.com/2003-04-06/news/0304060355_1_nature-park-new-park-chicago-park-district/2 (accessed January 18, 2011).

15. Lynn Sweet and Fran Spielman, "Daley's Meigs Alibi Crumbles," *Chicago Sun-Times,* April 9, 2003.

16. "U.S. Transportation Secretary Ray LaHood Announces Funding Commitment for New O'Hare South Air Traffic Control Tower," U.S. Department of Transportation, November 15, 2010; available at: http://www.dot.gov/affairs/2010/dot20010.html (accessed February 8, 2011).

17. Michael Barone, "White House puts UAW ahead of property rights," *Washington Examiner,* May 5, 2009; available at: http://washingtonexaminer.com/politics/2009/05/white-house-puts-uaw-ahead-property-rights (accessed January 18, 2011).

18. John Kass, "Black Ministers Praise Daley Name," *Chicago Tribune,* February 9, 1995; available at: http://articles.chicagotribune.com/1995-02-09/news/9502090103_1_joseph-gardner-black-church-mayor-richard-daley (accessed January 18, 2011).

19. Thomas J. Gradel, Dick Simpson, and Andris Zimelis, "Curing Corruption in Illinois: Anti-Corruption," Report Number 1, February 3, 2009, University of Illinois at Chicago Department of Political Science; available at: http://www.uic.edu/depts/pols/ChicagoPolitics/Anti-corruptionReport.pdf (accessed January 19, 2011).

20. Editorial, "How about Clout U.?" *Chicago Tribune,* June 21, 2009.

21. John Kass, "Duff indictments a story you can sink your teeth into," *Chicago Tribune,* September 28, 2003.

22. *Northern District of Illinois, Eastern Division, United States of America v. Robert Sorich, Ill.* (2005)

23. Matt O'Connor and Ray Gibson, "Duff told mom to lie, U.S. says," *Chicago Tribune,* November 23, 2004.

24. Tim Novak, "File: Daley's son's secret deal," *Chicago Sun-Times,* December 14, 2007.

25. Todd Lightly and Dan Mihalopoulos, "Sewer firm tied to Mayor Richard Daley's son folds," *Chicago Tribune,* April 24, 2008.

26. "Daley's Son's Business Partner Indicted for Mail Fraud," FOX News, January 7, 2011; available at: http://www.myfoxchicago.com/dpp/news/metro/mayor-daley-patrick-anthony-duffy-business-partner-indicted-20110107 (accessed January 19, 2011).

27. Tim Novak, "Mayor's nephew cashing in," *Chicago Sun-Times*, September 23, 2007.

28. Fran Spielman, Chris Fusco, and Tim Novak, "Lease with Daley nephew sparks aldermanic crackdown," *Chicago Sun-Times*, June 24, 2009.

29. My FOX Chicago, "Feds probe Daley city pension deals," May 29, 2009; available at: http://www.myfoxchicago.com/dpp/news/politics/feds_probe_Daley_city_pension_Deals (accessed January 19, 2011).

30. John O'Connor, "Emil Jones' wife received $70,000 raise," Associated Press, April 10, 2007.

31. Carol Marin, "Feeling conflicted? Jones says no," *Chicago Sun-Times*, May 6, 2007.

32. Ibid.

33. Jonathan Alter, *The Promise* (New York: Simon & Schuster, 2010), 80.

34. United States v. Rod Blagojevich and Robert Blagojevich, 08 CR 888 (2010), "Government's Evidentiary Proffer Supporting the Admissibility of Co-Conspirator Statements"; available at: http://capitolfax.com/08888santiagoproffer.pdf (accessed January 19, 2011).

35. Tim Novak, "How reform-minded City Hall critic became a cozy insider: Foe of Daley I, now ally of Daley II, caught in glare of unwanted spotlight," *Chicago Sun-Times*, November 11, 2007.

36. Jodi S. Cohen, Stacy St. Clair and Tara Malone, "Clout goes to college," *Chicago Tribune*, May 29, 2009; available at: http://www.chicagotribune.com/news/watchdog/college/chi-070529u-of-i-clout,0,5173000.story (accessed January 15, 2011).

37. *United States v. Rod Blagojevich and Robert Blagojevich.*

38. Associated Press, "Rezko owes Vegas $800,000 gambling debts," May 29, 2008.

39. David Fredosso, "Mr. Ethics," National Review Online, August 26, 2008; available at: http://www.nationalreview.com/articles/225437/mr-ethics/david-fredosso (accessed February 8, 2011).

40. While still in office: "Free loans for Jones," *Chicago Sun-Times*, May 22, 2008. Today: Records available at Elections.Il.gov.

41. David Mendell, *Obama: From Promise to Power* (New York: Amistad, 2007) 206.

42. Rick Pearson, "Jones: 'Doubting Thomas not Uncle Tom,'" *Chicago Tribune* Clout Street blog, August 25, 2008; available at: http://newsblogs.chicagotribune.com/clout_st/2008/08/jones-doubting.html (accessed January 19, 2011).

43. John McCormick, "Obama calls Emil Jones on ethics bill," *Chicago Tribune* The Swamp blog, September 17, 2008; available at: http://www.swamppolitics.com/news/politics/blog/2008/09/obama_calls_emil_jones_on_ethi.html (accessed January 19, 2011).

44. From Spielman, "Obama endorses Daley," *Chicago Sun-Times*, January 22, 2007.

45. Lynn Sweet, "Sweet scoop: Obama, after initial refusal, releases all earmark requests. Read them here. UPDATES," *Chicago Sun-Times*, March 13, 2008; available at: http://blogs.suntimes.com/sweet/2008/03/sweet_scoop_obama_after_ initia.html (accessed February 8, 2011).

46. Barack Obama, *The Audacity of Hope* (NY: Crown, 2006), 354–55.

47. Chuck Neubauer and Tom Hamburger, "Obama donor received state grant: His letter on behalf of a table tennis company preceded the funding," *Los Angeles Times*, April 27, 2008; available at: http://www.latimes.com/news/printedition/ front/la-na-killerspin27apr27,0,1814779,full.story (accessed January 19, 2011).

48. Ibid.

49. Eric Lichtblau, "Across From White House, Coffee With Lobbyists," *New York Times*, June 24, 2010; available at: http://www.nytimes.com/2010/06/25/us/ politics/25caribou.html (accessed February 8, 2011).

50. Editorial, "Wind Jammers at the White House," *Wall Street Journal*, November 12, 2010; available at: http://online.wsj.com/article/SB10001424052748704635 704575604502103371986.html (accessed January 19, 2011).

51. Vice Presidential economic advisor Jared Bernstein, quoted in Jonathan Alter, *The Promise.*

52. Steven Rattner, *Overhaul: An Insider's Account of the Obama Administration's Emergency Rescue of the Auto Industry* (Houghton Mifflin Harcourt: New York, 2010), 149–50.

53. "Obama's Fifth News Conference," transcript at the *New York Times*, July 22, 2009; available at: http://www.nytimes.com/2009/07/22/us/politics/22obama. transcript.html?pagewanted=11 (accessed February 8, 2011).

54. Glenn Thrush, "Berry: Obama said 'big difference' between '10 and '94 is 'me,'" *Politico*, January 25, 2010; available at: www.politico.com/blogs/glennthrush/ 0110/ Berry_Obama_said_big_difference_between_10_and_94_is_me.html (accessed February 8, 2011).

55. Alter, *The Promise*, 129.

56. David Espo, "Obama assails GOP on clouded final campaign push," Associated Press, October 25, 2010.

57. The White House, "Remarks by the President at a Rally for State Senator Creigh Deeds," August 6, 2009.

58. *Plato, Reason & Persuasion: Three Dialogues by Plato*, 332d.

59. Ashley Southall, "Obama Vows to Push Immigrations Changes," *New York Times* The Caucus, October 25, 2010; available at: http://thecaucus.blogs.nytimes. com/2010/10/25/in-appeal-to-hispanics-obama-promises-to-push-immigra- tion-reform/ (accessed January 19, 2011).

CHAPTER TWO

1. "How GM IPO Proves the Tea Party Wrong," *Newsweek* The Street, November 17, 2010; available at: http://www.newsweek.com/2010/11/17/how-gm-ipo-proves-the-tea-party-wrong.html (accessed January 20, 2011).

2. As *Forbes'* Dan Ikenson put it: "Did anyone really think that a chosen company so coddled and insulated from market realities couldn't turn a short-run profit? Yes, even GM, under those favorable conditions should have been expected to turn a profit this year," in "GM: A Successful IPO Does Not A Justifiable Bailout Make," *Forbes* Business in the Beltway, November 18, 2010; available at: http://blogs.forbes.com/beltway/2010/11/18/gm-a-successful-ipo-does-not-a-justifi-able-bailout-make/?partner=contextstory (accessed January 21, 2011).

3. Steven Rattner, *Overhaul*, 185.

4. Ibid., 85.

5. Ibid., 86.

6. Ibid.

7. Ibid., 29.

8. Ibid., 87.

9. Ibid., 79.

10. Ibid., 183

11. Ibid., 76.

12. Ibid., 27.

13. Joe Benton, "GM Spens $17 Million Per Year on Viagra," ConsumerAffairs.com, April 18, 2006; available at: http://www.consumeraffairs.com/news04/2006/04/gm_viagra.html (accessed January 20, 2011). Referenced in Rattner, 153.

14. Rattner, 202.

15. The union's official name is The International Union, United Automobile, Aerospace and Agricultural Implement Workers of America.

16. Chelsea Emery, "U.S. business bankruptcies rise 38 pct in 2009," Reuters, January 5, 2010; available at: http://www.reuters.com/article/idUSN059048720100105 (accessed January 21, 2011).

17. Tim Higgins, "UAW Strikes Chrysler: Workers move to picket lines," Freep.com, October 10, 2007; available at: http://www.freep.com/apps/pbcs.dll/article?AID=/20071010/BUSINESS01/71010030/UAW-STRIKES-CHRYSLER-Workers-move-to-picket-lines&template=fullarticle (accessed January 20, 2011).

18. Rattner, *Overhaul*, 120.

19. Ibid., 300.

20. Department of Labor, 2008 and 2009 LM-2 disclosure forms for AFL-CIO Auto Workers. Filed March 30, 2009 and March 29, 2010, respectively.

21. GM Annual Report, 2010 and United States Bankruptcy Court, Southern District of New York, In re Chapter 11, Chrysler LLC Case no. 9. Executed April 30, 2009.

22. Roger Kerson, "UAW agreements a model for labor law reform," UAW, March/April 2007; available at: http://uaw.org/node?page=46 (accessed January 20, 2011).

23. This is the figure the Department of Labor gives for Ford's September 2007 collective bargaining agreement, which is listed at http://www.dol.gov/olms/regs/compliance/cba/Cba_FaGo.htm (accessed January 10, 2011). However, the UAW reported at earlier that year that it only had 58,000 workers at Ford. Available at http://www.uaw.org/node/287 (accessed February 4, 2011).

24. "The UAW: Who we are," available at: http://www.uaw.org/node/908 (accessed January 20, 2011).

25. Department of Labor, 2009 LM-2 disclosure form for UAW AFL-CIO Auto Workers, filed March 29, 2010.

26. Rattner, *Overhaul*, 227.

27. Michael de la Merced, "Judge OKs plan to sell Chevy, other GM assets to US-backed firm," *New York Times*, July 6, 2009.

28. Patrice Hill, "GM's union recovering after stock sale," *Washington Times*, November 20, 2010.

29. Congressional Oversight Panel, "An Update on TARP Support for the Domestic Automotive Industry," January 13, 2011.

30. Daimler Chrysler Media Briefing Book: 2007 Labor Talks, 37; available at: http://chryslerlabortalks07.com/Media_Briefing_Book.pdf (accessed January 21, 2011).

31. Editorial, "Delphi salaried retirees right to cry foul," *Dayton Daily News*, October 14, 2010.

32. "Was politics behind the government's decision to preserve the UAW's pensions?" *Washington Post*, September 18, 2010; available at: http://www.washingtonpost.com/wp-dyn/content/article/2010/09/17/AR2010091706617.html (accessed January 21, 2011).

33. Ibid., 225.

34. Ibid., 231.

35. Timothy P. Carney, "The Big Business of Big Labor," *Washington Examiner*, May 7, 2009; available at: http://washingtonexaminer.com/op-eds/2009/05/big-business-big-labor#ixzz17AHsPTn9 (accessed January 21, 2011).

36. Rattner, *Overhaul*, 183.

37. Ibid., 301–4.

38. Michael Corkery and Michael Rothfeld, "Suit Seeking Wall Street Ban Spoils Ex-Car Czar's Big Day," *Wall Street Journal*, November 19, 2010; available at: http://online.wsj.com/article/SB10001424052748704104104575622500156880416.html (accessed January 21, 2011).

39. Courtney Comstock, "Rattner Settles With Cuomo For $10 Million—And He's Only Banned For 5 Years," *Business Insider*, December 30, 2010; available at:

http://www.businessinsider.com/breaking-rattner-settles-with-cuomo-for-10-million-2010-12#ixzz1AMK5deAj (accessed January 21, 2011).

40. Gerald F. Sieb, "In Crisis, Opportunity for Obama," *Wall Street Journal*, November 21, 2008; available at: http://online.wsj.com/article/SB122721278056345271.html (accessed January 21, 2011).

41. Rattner, *Overhaul*, 214–17.

42. Ibid.

43. Public Law 110-343, sec. 3.

44. "Bush says sacrificed free-market principles to save economy," Agence France-Presse, December 16, 2008.

45. Rattner, *Overhaul*, 158.

46. Ibid., 237–38.

47. Ibid., 210.

48. Neil King, Jr., and Jeffrey McCracken, "U.S. Pushed Fiat Deal on Chrysler: Internal Emails Reveal Resentment; Court Upholds Pact," *The Wall Street Journal*, June 6, 2009.

49. Public Law 111-5, sec. 1221. Incidentally, the presence of this provision also indicates that the outcome of majority union ownership had been predetermined from at least February 12, 2009. This provision had not been contained in the original version of HR 1, which was filed on January 26, 2009.

50. Rattner, *Overhaul*, 214–17.

51. Randall Smith and Sharon Terlep, "GM Could Be Free of Taxes for Years," *Wall Street Journal*, November 3, 2010; available at: http://online.wsj.com/article/SB10001424052748704462704575590642149103202.html (accessed January 21, 2011).

52. Randall Smith and Sharon Terlep, "Tax Breaks for Bailout Recipients Stir Up Debate," *Wall Street Journal*, December 3, 2010; available at: http://online.wsj.com/article/SB10001424052748704377004575651134154809918.html (accessed January 21, 2011).

53. Rattner, *Overhaul*, 251.

54. Reproduced in Frédéric Bastiat, *Essays on Political Economy* (London: Provost and Co., 4 ed.), 50–54.

55. Dan Ikenson, "GM: A Successful IPO Does Not A Justifiable Bailout Make," *Forbes* Business in The Beltway.

56. Michael Barone, "White House puts UAW ahead of property rights," *Washington Examiner,* May 5, 2009. Available at http://washingtonexaminer.com/politics/2009/05/white-house-puts-uaw-ahead-property-rights#ixzz1DFEW4SF0 (accessed Feb. 6, 2011).

57. Mark J. Roe and David Skeel, "Assessing the Chrysler Bankruptcy," *Michigan Law Review*, Vol. 108, pp. 727, 2010; 753. Available at SSRN: http://ssrn.com/abstract=1426530 (accessed February 8, 2011).

58. Rattner, *Overhaul*, 149.

59. Ibid., 149–50.

60. Ibid., 180

61. The White House, "Remarks by the President on the Auto Industry," April 30, 2009; available at: http://www.whitehouse.gov/the-press-office/remarks-president-auto-industry (accessed January 21, 2011).

62. Ron Bloom, "If I ran the zoo," *Democratic Left*, Fall 2006 issue. Bloom's piece was based on a speech he gave at the Steel Success Strategies XXI conference in New York City in June 2006; available at: http://www.scribd.com/doc/39028634/Democratic-Socialists-of-America-Fall-2006

63. Rattner, *Overhaul*, 179–80.

64. Sven Gustafson, "Experts hope for quick GM turnaround," MLive.com, June 2, 2009; available at: http://www.mlive.com/businessreview/oakland/index.ssf/2009/06/experts_hope_for_quick_gm_turn.html (accessed February 8, 2011).

65. Mark J. Roe, and David A. Skeel, "Assessing the Chrysler Bankruptcy."

66. The case is *Northern Pacific Railway Co. v. Boyd*, 228 U.S. 482 (1913).

67. Chrysler LLC, *et al.*, Debtors, Declaration of Robert Manzo in United States Bankruptcy Court, Southern District of New York, http://www.bankruptcylitigationblog.com/uploads/file/manzo%20decl.pdf (accessed February 8, 2011).

68. Mark J. Roe and David A. Skeel, "Assessing the Chrysler Bankruptcy."

69. Luca Ciferri, "Fiat's Marchionne says he won't walk away from Chrysler deal," AutoWeek.com, June 9, 2009; available at: http://www.autoweek.com/article/20090609/carnews/906099997 (accessed February 8, 2011).

70. "Fiat plays double or quits with Chrysler," *The Economist*, November 25, 2010; available at: http://www.economist.com/node/17575017 (accessed February 8, 2011).

71. Objection to Chrysler Sale Motion, May 4, 2009; available at: http://www.scribd.com/doc/14952818/Objection-to-Chrysler-Sale-Motion (accessed February 8, 2011).

72. Rattner, *Overhaul*, 181.

73. Zachery Kouwe, "The Lenders Obama Decided to Blame," *New York Times*, April 30, 2009; available at: http://www.nytimes.com/2009/05/01/business/01hedge.html (accessed January 21, 2011).

74. May 1, 2010. The audio of the interview is available at http://www.760wjr.com/article.asp?id=1301727&spid=6525 (accessed January 21, 2011).

75. Chrysler Debtholders' Motion to File Under Seal, May 5, 2009; available at: http://www.scribd.com/doc/14990220/Chrysler-Debtholders-Motion-to-File-Under-Seal (accessed February 8, 2011).

76. Bill Frezza, "Obama to Secured Creditors: Drop Dead," Real Clear Markets, May 4, 2009; available at: http://www.realclearmarkets.com/articles/2009/05/obama_to_secured_creditors_dro.html (accessed January 21, 2011).

77. Zachery Kouwe, "The Lenders Obama Decided to Blame," *New York Times*.

78. "Obama Says He Has 'No Intention' of Running General Motors," FOX News, March 30, 2009; available at: http://www.foxnews.com/politics/2009/03/30/obama-says-intention-running-general-motors/ (accessed February 8, 2011).

79. Rattner, *Overhaul*, 203.

80. Ibid., 235.

81. Rattner, *Overhaul*, 194.

82. Mark Tapscott, "Furor grows over partisan car dealer closings," *Washington Examiner*, Beltway Confidential blog, May 26, 2009; available at: http://washingtonexaminer.com/blogs/beltway-confidential/2009/05/furor-grows-over-partisan-car-dealer-closings (accessed January 21, 2011).

83. Andrew Grossman, "Bailouts, Abusive Bankruptcies, And the Rule of Law," The Heritage Foundation, May 22, 2009; available at: http://www.heritage.org/research/testimony/bailouts-abusive-bankruptcies-and-the-rule-of-law (accessed January 21, 2011).

84. Rattner, *Overhaul*, 54.

85. Alter, *The Promise*, 182–83.

86. Warren Brown, "The Station Wagon Stealthily Returns," *Washington Post*, August 29, 2004; available at: http://www.washingtonpost.com/wp-dyn/content/article/2004/08/29/AR2005032405083.html (accessed January 21, 2011).

87. *Wall Street Journal* Market Data Center. Up-to-date monthly statistics on auto sales are available online at http://online.wsj.com/mdc/public/page/2_3022-autosales.html (accessed January 21, 2011).

88. "GM Orion Assembly workers to picket UAW over two-tier wage structure," *Detroit News*, October 9, 2010.

89. Angela Greiling Keane and Jeff Green, "Obama Bolsters U.S. Hybrid Automobile Sales in Waning Consumer Market," *Bloomberg News*, November 23, 2010; available at: http://www.bloomberg.com/news/2010-11-23/obama-bolsters-u-s-hybrid-auto-sales-in-waning-consumer-market.html (accessed January 21, 2011).

90. In all it distributed $238,000 to 86 House incumbents running for re-election and 16 sitting senators, slightly favoring the GOP.

91. Ed Whitacre, "The GM Bailout: Paid Back in Full," *Wall Street Journal*, April 21, 2010; available at: http://online.wsj.com/article/SB10001424052702303491304575188473069446344.html (accessed January 21, 2011).

92. Shikha Dalmia, "Still Government Motors," *Forbes*, April 23, 2010; available at: http://www.forbes.com/2010/04/23/general-motors-economy-bailout-opinions-columnists-shikha-dalmia_print.html (accessed January 21, 2011).

93. "Energy official: GM, Chrysler retooling loans on track," *Detroit News*, September 23, 2010. Taxpayers got a break in late January 2011, when GM dropped its application.

94. Available online at http://www.treasury.gov/press-center/press-releases/Pages/tg650.aspx (accessed January 21, 2011).

95. "Obama Administration Awards First Three Auto Loans for Advanced Technologies to Ford Motor Company, Nissan Motors and Tesla Motors," Energy.gov, June 23, 2009; available at: http://www.energy.gov/news/7544.htm (accessed February 8, 2011).

96. Department of Energy Press release, August 27, 2009; available at: http://www1. eere.energy.gov/recovery/pdfs/battery_awardee_list.pdf (accessed January 21, 2011).

97. "Ex-Im Bank Approves $250 Million in Export Financing for 211,000 Ford Motor Company Vehicles," Export-Import Bank of the United States Office of Communications, August 5, 2010; available at: http://www.exim.gov/pressrelease. cfm/428E02A0-DFB9-2BC0-36C4F6788D7222B0/ (accessed January 21, 2011).

98. Justin Hyde, "Ford, BMW, Toyota Took Secret Government Money," Jalopnik, December 2, 2010; available at: http://jalopnik.com/5704575/ford-bmw-toyota-took-secret-government-money (accessed January 21, 2011).

99. The figure for Chrysler is for a $31 billion bailout to save 38,500 American jobs and does not include possible job losses at subsidiaries. The figure for GM is for a $49.5 billion bailout to save 77,000 U.S. jobs. This figure, taken from GM's 2009 annual report, does not include all subsidiaries, but it does include 11,000 employees of Nexteer, a Delphi operation acquired by GM.

CHAPTER THREE

1. Donnie Johnston, "Make newspapers required reading," Fredericksburg.com, December 17, 2010; available at: http://fredericksburg.com/News/ FLS/2010/122010/12172010/595007 (accessed January 21, 2011).

2. Commonwealth of Virginia v. Kathleen Sebelius, 3:10CV188-HEH.

3. George Stephanopoulos, "Obama: Mandate is Not a Tax," ABC News, September 20, 2009; available at: http://blogs.abcnews.com/george/2009/09/obama-mandate-is-not-a-tax.html (accessed January 21, 2011).

4. Washington Post-ABC News Poll, http://www.washingtonpost.com/wp-srv/ politics/polls/postpoll_062209.html (accessed January 21, 2011). This finding squares almost perfectly with the 83 percent in a more rigorous but less recent study by the Kaiser Family Foundation.

5. Mary Lu Carnevale, "Obama: 'If You Like Your Doctor, You Can Keep Your Doctor,'" Wall Street Journal, June 15, 2010; available at: http://blogs.wsj.com/washwire/2009/06/15/obama-if-you-like-your-doctor-you-can-keep-your-doctor/ (accessed January 21, 2011).

6. Department of Health and Human Services, "Keeping the Health Plan You Have: The Affordable Care Act and 'Grandfathered' Health Plans," June 14, 2010; available at: http://www.healthcare.gov/news/factsheets/keeping_the_health_plan_ you_have_grandfathered.html (accessed January 21, 2011).

7.   David Hogberg and Sean Higgins, "Keep Your Health Plan Under Overhaul? Probably Not, Gov't Analysis Concludes," *Investors Business Daily*, June 11, 2010; available at: http://www.investors.com/NewsAndAnalysis/Article/537208/201006111932/Keep-Your-Health-Plan-Under-Overhaul-Probably-Not-Govt-Analysis-Concludes.aspx (accessed January 21, 2011).

8.   Kerry Picket, "Pelosi: 'Will do what is necessary' to pass health care bill," *Washington Times*, March 16, 2010; available at: http://www.washingtontimes.com/weblogs/watercooler/2010/mar/16/pelosi-admits-will-do-what-necessary-pass-health-c/ (accessed January 21, 2011).

9.   "Additional Information on CBO's Preliminary Analysis of H.R. 2," Congressional Budget Office Director's Blog, January 7, 2011; available at: http://cboblog.cbo.gov/?p=1759 (accessed February 8, 2011).

10.   Letter from Douglas Elmendorf to The Honorable Evan Bayh, November 30, 2009; available at: http://www.cbo.gov/ftpdocs/107xx/doc10781/11-30-Premiums.pdf (accessed February 8, 2011).

11.   Public Law 148, Sec. 1411

12.   Kim Dixon, "IRS could tap refunds for health insurance penalties," Reuters, April 5, 2010; available at: http://www.reuters.com/article/2010/04/05/tax-health-idUSN0517093120100405 (accessed January 21, 2011).

13.   National Federation of Independent Business, "The Free-Rider Provision: A One-Page Primer"; available at: http://www.nfib.com/Portals/0/PDF/AllUsers/Free%20Rider%20Provision.pdf (accessed January 21, 2011).

14.   Department of Health and Human Services, "Approved Applications for Waiver of the Annual Limits Requirements of the PHS Act Section 2711 as of December 3, 2010"; available at: http://www.hhs.gov/ociio/regulations/approved_applications_for_waiver.html (accessed January 21, 2011).

15.   Public Law 111-148, Sec. 1513.

16.   "Where are the jobs? For many companies, overseas," Associated Press, December 28, 2010; available at: http://www.google.com/hostednews/ap/article/ALeqM5iFY0R9agrMVljqtaB6ccsILSKd3Q?docId=771fbe245e624cbd95ab5a49122dd701 (accessed January 21, 2011).

17.   Ricardo Alonso-Zaldivar, "Fact Check: Tax cut math doesn't add up for some," Associated Press, May 20, 2010.

18.   Public Law 111-148, 238.

19.   "Just the Facts: Small Business Healthcare Tax Credit," NFIB; available at: http://www.nfib.com/press-media/press-media-item?cmsid=52099 (accessed February 8, 2011).

20.   David Leonhardt, "After the Great Recession," *The New York Times Magazine*, April 28, 2009; available at: http://www.nytimes.com/2009/05/03/magazine/03Obama-t.html (accessed January 21, 2011).

21.   American Medical Association, "Major Medicare savings under health reform legislation," April 7, 2010; available at: http://www.ama-assn.org/ama1/pub/

upload/mm/399/hsr-medicare-savings-under-reform.pdf (accessed January 21, 2011).

22. The memo is available on *Politico's* website at http://www.politico.com/pdf/ PPM130_oact_memorandum_on_financial_impact_of_ppaca_as_enacted.pdf (accessed February 4, 2011).

23. CBO Director's Blog, "Correction Regarding the Longer-Term Effects of the Manager's Amendment to the Patient Protection and Affordable Care Act," Congressional Budget Office, Director's Blog, December 20, 2009; available at: http://cboblog.cbo.gov/?p=447 (accessed January 21, 2011).

24. David Olmos, "Mayo Clinic in Arizona to Stop Treating Some Medicare Patients," *Bloomberg News*, December, 31, 2009; available at: http://www.bloomberg.com/ apps/news?pid=newsarchive&sid=aHoYSI84VdL0 (accessed January 21, 2011).

25. Katherine Harmon, "Government panel recommends fewer and later mammograms, no self-exams," *Scientific American*, November 17, 2009; available at: http://www.scientificamerican.com/blog/post.cfm?id=government-panel-recommends-fewer-a-2009-11-17 (accessed January 21, 2011).

26. John S. Hoff, "Implementing Obamacare: A New Exercise in Old-Fashioned Central Planning," Heritage Foundation Backgrounder, September 10, 2010; available at: http://www.heritage.org/Research/Reports/2010/09/Implementing-Obamacare-A-New-Exercise-in-Old-Fashioned-Central-Planning (accessed January 21, 2011).

27. Associated Press, "Drug industry helping Obama overhaul health care," August 8, 2009.

28. Timothy Noah, "Obama's Biggest Health Reform Blunder: How Big Pharma's Billy Tauzin conned the White House out of $76 billion," *Slate*, August 6, 2009; available at: http://www.slate.com/id/2224621/ (accessed January 21, 2011).

29. David Kirkpatrick, "White House Affirms Deal on Drug Cost," *New York Times*, August 5, 2009; available at: http://www.nytimes.com/2009/08/06/health/ policy/06insure.html (accessed February 8, 2011).

30. David Freddoso, "Big Drugmakers' secret D.C. meeting," *Washington Examiner*, July 22, 2009; available at: http://washingtonexaminer.com/blogs/beltway-confidential/2009/07/updated-big-drugmakers-secret-dc-meeting (accessed January 21, 2011).

31. Duff Wilson, "Drug Makers Raise Prices in Face of Health Care Reform," *New York Times*, November 15, 2009; available at; http://www.nytimes. com/2009/11/16/business/16drugprices.html (accessed January 21, 2011).

32. Footage of the CNBC interview is available online at http://www.cnbc.com/id/ 15840232?video=1051746993&play=1 (accessed January 21, 2011).

33. Obama's ad is available on YouTube at http://www.youtube.com/ watch?v=NCRO0g9CfAw (accessed January 21, 2011).

34. Eight video clips of Obama making this promise are available online at http:// www.breitbart.tv/the-c-span-lie-did-obama-really-promise-televised-health-care-negotiations/ (accessed February 8, 2011).

35. Public Law 111-148, Sec. 2701.

36. Tarren Bragdon, "A Series of Unfortunate Events: Dirigo—Maine's 'Public Option'—is a costly failure," *Crisis to Cure*, Issue 3, June 30, 2009.

37. Michael F. Cannon, "ObamaCare's 'Medical Loss Ratio' Regs Encourage Fraud, Unnecessary Medical Services," Cato.com, November 23, 2010; available at: http://www.cato-at-liberty.org/obamacares-medical-loss-ratio-regs-encourage-fraud-unnecessary-medical-services/ (accessed January 21, 2011).

38. Jane Orient, M.D., "'ObamaCare:' What's in it," *Journal of American Physicians and Surgeons*, Vol. 15, no. 3, Fall 2010.

39. "Budgetary Treatment of Proposals to Regulate Medical Loss Ratios," Congressional Budget Office, December 13, 2009; available at: https://www.cbo.gov/ftpdocs/107xx/doc10731/MLR_and_budgetary_treatment.pdf (accessed February 8, 2011).

40. Public Law 111-152, Sec. 1406.

41. CQ Transcriptions, "Transcript of Obama Prime-Time News Conference," July 22, 2009.

42. "One Health Insurance Company Turned a Profit, But Not a Record," *St. Petersburg Times*, PolitiFact.com, July 22, 2009; available at: http://www.politifact.com/truth-o-meter/statements/2009/jul/23/barack-obama/health-insurance-company-turned-profit-not-rec/ (accessed February 8, 2011).

43. *Fortune* 500: 2010 Industry: Pharmaceuticals; available at: http://money.cnn.com/magazines/fortune/fortune500/2010/industries/21/index.html (accessed January 21, 2011).

44. *Fortune* 500: 2010 Industry: Health Insurance and Managed Care; available at: http://money.cnn.com/magazines/fortune/fortune500/2010/industries/223/index.html (accessed January 21, 2011).

45. CNBC, "If Buffett were president: Ask Warren," March 1, 2010; transcript available at: http://www.cnbc.com/id/35643967/If_Buffett_Were_President_Ask_Warren_Transcript_Part_3 (accessed January 21, 2011).

46. Gary Cohn and Darrell Preston, "AARP's Stealth Fees Often Sting Seniors with Costlier Insurance," Bloomberg, December 4, 2008; available at: http://www.bloomberg.com/apps/news?pid=newsarchive&refer=&sid=a4OkPQIPF6Kg (accessed February 8, 2011).

47. Year 2008 IRS Form 990 for AARP

48. Ibid.

49. 110 Congress, H.R. 3162.

50. David Whelan, "ObamaCare Snuffs Out A Publicly-Traded Hospital Company," *Forbes*, September 14, 2010; available at: http://blogs.forbes.com/david-whelan/2010/09/14/obamacare-snuffs-out-a-publicly-traded- hospital-company/ (accessed February 8, 2011).

51. Susan Ferrechio, "Big payoffs to senators on health bill stoke public anger," *Washington Examiner*, December 23, 2009.

52. Carrie Budoff Brown, "White House scores key labor deal," *Politico*, January 14, 2010; available at: http://www.politico.com/news/stories/0110/31527.html (accessed February 8, 2011).

53. ABC *World News Tonight*, January 25, 2010.

54. CBS *Evening News*, January 27, 2010.

55. Alter, *The Promise*, 129.

56. Brad Todd and Mike Shields, "How the NRCC won in 2010," *Politico*, November 30, 2010; available at: http://dyn.politico.com/printstory.cfm?uuid=9AE34D9B-E4A8-7A90-750150BDED1931FB (accessed February 8, 2011).

57. Duke Helfand, "Blue Shield of California seeks rate hikes of as much as 59% for individuals," *Los Angeles Times*, January 5, 2011; available at: http://www.latimes.com/health/healthcare/la-fi-insure-rates-20110106,0,1904183,print.story (accessed February 8, 2011).

58. Shaya Tayfee Mohajer, "Blue Shield submits to rate hike delay in Calif.," *Washington Post*, February 1, 2011; available at: http://www.washingtonpost.com/wp-dyn/content/article/2011/02/01/AR2011020104999.html (accessed February 8, 2011).

59. Matthew Sturdevant, "State OKs Anthem Rate Hikes, Some More Than 20 Percent," Courant.com, September 17, 2010; available at: http://articles.courant.com/2010-09-17/business/hc-anthem-rate-hike-0918-20100917_1_large-group-and-middle-market-plans-small-group-hmo-plans-federal-health-reform (accessed February 8, 2011).

60. Michael Barone, "Gangster government stifles criticism of Obamacare," *Washington Examiner*, September 10, 2010; available at: http://www.washingtonexaminer.com/politics/Gangster-government-stifles- criticism-of-Obamacare-811664-102642044.html (accessed January 21, 2011).

61. Janet Adamy, "U.S. Rebukes Health Insurers," *Wall Street Journal*, September 10, 2010; available at: http://online.wsj.com/article/SB10001424052748704644404575482213099258430.html (accessed January 21, 2011).

62. Citigroup Industry Overview: "If You Think Nature Is a Friend, Then You Sure Don't Need an Enemy," November 22, 2010; available at: https://www.citigroup-geo.com/pdf/SNA67995.pdf (accessed November 30, 2010).

63. Article previously available at: http://www.washingtonexaminer.com/politics/Democrats-threaten-companies-hit-hard-by-health-care-bill-89347127.html

64. *Wall Street Journal* editorial.

65. The Prowler, "Obama in Rude Denial," *American Spectator*, March 29, 2010; available at: http://spectator.org/archives/2010/03/29/obama-in-rude-denial/print (accessed January 21, 2011).

66. Ibid.

67. Jon Ward, "States fear that five words in Obama health law will open door to lawsuits," *Daily Caller*, April 2, 2010.

68. Donald Berwick, "A Transatlantic View of the NHS at 60," *NHS Live: Wembley: July 1, 2008.*

69. "Donald Berwick on Redistributing Wealth," May 12, 2010; video available at: http://www.youtube.com/watch?v=r2Kevz_9lsw&feature=player_embedded (accessed January 21, 2011).

70. Byron York, "In special deal, charity gives rationing advocate Berwick health coverage for life," *Washington Examiner* Beltway Confidential, July 14, 2010; available at: http://washingtonexaminer.com/blogs/beltway-confidential/special-deal-charity-gives-rationing-advocate-berwick-health-coverage-life#ixzz19wlMQw5V (accessed January 21, 2011).

71. Timothy P. Carney, "Obama skirts Congress to appoint lobbying lawyer," *Washington Examiner* Politics, January 2, 2011; available at: http://washingtonexaminer.com/politics/2011/01 obamas-skirts-congress-appoint-lobbying-lawyer#ixzz19zmHSGFn (accessed January 21, 2011).

72. Benjamin Domenech, *Consumer Power Report #248*, Heartland Institute, November 19, 2010.

CHAPTER FOUR

1. Lawrence B. Lindsey, "Did the Stimulus Stimulate?" The Weekly Standard, Vol. 15, No. 45, August 16, 2010; available at: http://www.weeklystandard.com/print/articles/did-stimulus-stimulate (accessed January 26, 2011).

2. *This Week with George Stephanopoulos*, transcript of July 12, 2009; available at: http://abcnews.go.com/ThisWeek/Politics/story?id=8063029&page=1 (accessed January 26, 2011).

3. Mary Lu Carnevale and Jonathan Weisman, "Obama to GOP: 'I Won,'" *Wall Street Journal*, January 23, 2009; available at: http://blogs.wsj.com/washwire/2009/01/23/obama-to-gop-i-won/ (accessed January 26, 2011).

4. City of Chicago website: "O'Hare Modernization"; available at: http://www.cityofchicago.org/city/en/depts/doa/provdrs/omp.html (accessed January 26, 2011).

5. Department of Transportation press release: "U.S. Transportation Secretary Ray LaHood Announces Funding Commitment for New O'Hare South Air Traffic Control Tower," November 15, 2010; available at: http://www.dot.gov/affairs/2010/dot20010.html (accessed January 26, 2011).

6. Carol D. Leonnig, "LaHood Sponsored Millions in Earmarks," *Washington Post*, January 14, 2009; available at: http://www.washingtonpost.com/wp-dyn/content/article/2009/01/13/AR2009011302860.html (accessed January 26, 2011).

7. Quoted in Carol Leonnig, "LaHood Sponsored Millions in Earmarks," Washington Post, January 14, 2009; available at: http://www.washingtonpost.com/wp-dyn/content/article/2009/01/13/AR2009011302860.html (accessed February 14, 2011).

8. Jill Zuckman, "By pouring money into relief, GOP leaders risk backlash over deficit," *Chicago Tribune*, September 13, 2005.

9.   Citizens Against Government Waste, "Rep. Ray LaHood is October Porker of the Month," October 5, 2005; available at: http://www.cagw.org/newsroom/porker-of-the-month/2005/rep-ray-lahood-is-october.html (accessed January 26, 2011).

10.   Farm Services Agencies website, http://www.apfo.usda.gov/FSA/webapp?area=about&subject=landing&topic=sao (accessed January 26, 2011).

11.   George Will, "Ray LaHood, Transformed," *Newsweek*, May 16, 2009; available at: http://www.newsweek.com/2009/05/15/ray-lahood-transformed.html (accessed January 26, 2011).

12.   "Secretary of Transportation Ray LaHood Delivers Remarks at The National Press Club on Stimulus Spending on Roads and Infrastructure," CQ Transcriptions, May 21, 2009. Cited in Terence P. Jeffrey, *Control Freaks: 7 Ways Liberals Plan to Ruin Your Life* (Regnery: Washington, 2009).

13.   Eric Bland, "Gov't evaluating cell phone blocking tech in cars," November 16, 2010; available at: http://www.msnbc.msn.com/id/40418794/ns/technology_and_science-wireless/ (accessed January 26, 2011).

14.   The full letter is available from ABC News at http://a.abcnews.go.com/images/Politics/AZ_ARRA.pdf (accessed Nov. 1, 2010).

15.   Jonathan Martin, "The White House Strikes back," *Politico*, July 16, 2009; available at: http://www.politico.com/news/stories/0709/25003.html (accessed January 26, 2011).

16.   Alter, *The Promise*, 160.

17.   Bureau of Labor Statistics, "Employment, Hours, and Earnings from the Current Employment Statistics survey"; available at BLS.gov.

18.   President Obama, "Economic Town Hall," Elkhart, Indiana, February 9, 2009. Text is available from the *Indianapolis Star* at http://www.indystar.com/article/20090209/NEWS05/90209041/Read-text-Obama-s-speech (accessed January 22, 2011).

19.   Government Printing Office, "Budget of the United States Government: Historical Tables Fiscal Year 2010"; available at: http://www.gpoaccess.gov/usbudget/fy10/hist.html (accessed January 26, 2011).

20.   Peter Baker, "The Education of a President," *The New York Times Magazine*, October 12, 2010; available at: http://www.nytimes.com/2010/10/17/magazine/17obama-t.html (accessed January 26, 2011).

21.   *The Promise*, xiv.

22.   *Washington Post*-ABC News Poll, http://www.washingtonpost.com/wp-srv/politics/polls/postpoll_10052010.html (accessed January 26, 2011).

23.   Transcript, CNN's "State of the Union," January 24, 2010.

24.   Transcript, *FOX News Sunday*, January 24, 2010.

25.   Transcript, NBC's *Meet the Press*, January 24, 2010.

26.   Rick Klein, "$18M Being Spent to Redesign Recovery.gov Website," ABC News blog The Note; available at: http://blogs.abcnews.com/thenote/2009/07/18m-being-spent-to-redesign-recoverygov-web-site.html (accessed August 8, 2010).

27. "Persistent Errors in Stimulus Job Count," CBS News, November 4, 2009; available at: http://www.cbsnews.com/stories/2009/11/04/politics/main5523044.shtml (accessed January 26, 2011).

28. Michael Cooper and Ron Nixon, "Reports Show Conflicting Number of Jobs Attributed to Stimulus Money," *New York Times*, November 4, 2009; available at: http://www.nytimes.com/2009/11/05/us/05stimulus.html?_r=1 (accessed January 26, 2011).

29. Read more: Melissa Santos, "Fewer local jobs saved by federal stimulus than reported," *The News Tribune*, October 31, 2009; available at: http://www.thenewstribune.com/2009/10/31/v-printerfriendly/936585/fewer-local-jobs-saved-by-federal.html#ixzz1B4v0BadK (accessed January 26, 2011).

30. David Freddoso, "Obama has a banana in his ear," *Washington Examiner*, February 4, 2010; available at: http://washingtonexaminer.com/node/123076#ixzz1AhUZ539W (accessed January 26, 2011).

31. Jay Fitzgerald, "Stimulus saves hacks: 70% of Mass. jobs paid by feds in public sector," *Boston Herald*, February 2, 2010; available at: http://www.bostonherald.com/business/general/view/20100202stimulus_saves_hacks_70_of_mass_jobs_paid_by_feds_in_public_sector/srvc=home&position=1 (accessed January 26, 2011).

32. State of New Hampshire, Office of Economic Stimulus, Governor John H. Lynch and the Honorable Executive Council, American Recovery and Reinvestment Act, Progress Report—Data through September 30, 2009; available at: http://www.scribd.com/doc/21383273/Jobs-Contracts-Approved-093009 (accessed January 27, 2011).

33. Louise Radnofsky, "Stimulus-Jobs Tally in Doubt," *Wall Street Journal*, November 20, 2009; available at: http://online.wsj.com/article/SB125867486730556589.html (accessed January 26, 2011).

34. "Statement by Vice President Biden on Congressional Budget Office Report on Recovery Act Employment Impact," December 1, 2009; available at: http://www.whitehouse.gov/the-press-office/statement-vice-president-biden-congressional-budget-office-report-recovery-act-empl (accessed January 26, 2011).

35. For an example, see CBO's August 2010 report at http://www.cbo.gov/ftpdocs/117xx/doc11706/08-24-ARRA.pdf (accessed January 26, 2011).

36. "CBO Director Elmendorf on Stimulus Law and the Economy," C-SPAN.org, March 8, 2010; available at: http://www.c-span.org/Events/CBO-Director-Elmendorf-on-Stimulus-Law-and-the-Economy/17329-1/ (accessed January 26, 2011).

37. Peter Suderman, "Heckuva Job-Creation Estimate," Reason.com, March 26, 2010; available at: http://reason.com/blog/2010/03/26/heckuva-job-creation-estimate (accessed January 26, 2011).

38. Lawrence B. Lindsey, "Did the Stimulus Stimulate?" *The Weekly Standard*, August 16, 2010; available at: http://www.weeklystandard.com/articles/did-stimulus-stimulate (accessed January 26, 2011).

39. Brody Mullins and John McKinnon, "Campaign's big spender," *Wall Street Journal*, October 22, 2010; available at: http://online.wsj.com/article/SB1000142405 270230333950457556648176179028.html (accessed January 26, 2011).

40. John F. Cogan and John B. Taylor, "The Obama Stimulus Impact? Zero," *Wall Street Journal*, December 10, 2010; available at: http://online.wsj.com/article/SB1 0001424052748704679204575646603792267296.html (accessed January 26, 2011).

41. Christina Romer and Jared Bernstein, "The Job Impact of the American Recovery and Reinvestment Plan," January 9, 2009; available at: http://otrans.3cdn. net/45593e8ecbd339d074_l3m6bt1te.pdf (February 14, 2011).

42. Lawrence B. Lindsey, "Did the Stimulus Stimulate?" The Weekly Standard, August 16, 2010; available at: http://www.weeklystandard.com/articles/did-stimulus-stimulate (accessed February 14, 2011).

43. Daniel J. Wilson, "Fiscal Spending Jobs Multipliers: Evidence from the 2009 Recovery and Reinvestment Act," working paper 2010-17; available at: http:// www.frbsf.org/publications/economics/papers/2010/wp10-17bk.pdf (accessed February 14, 2011).

44. President Obama, "Economic Town Hall," Elkhart, Indiana, February 9, 2009. Text is available from the *Indianapolis Star* at http://www.indystar.com/article/20090209/NEWS05/90209041/Read-text-Obama-s-speech (accessed January 22, 2011).

45. Robert Hendin, "Obama Hits Ohio," CBS News Political Hotsheet, January 16, 2009; available at: http://www.cbsnews.com/8301-503544_162-4727659-503544. html (accessed January 26, 2011).

46. "Study of the effect on employment of public aid to renewable energy sources," Universidad Rey Juan Carlos; available at: http://www.juanandmariana.org

47. Abhishek Shah, "Spain may renege on guaranteed electricity rates under Feed in Tariff Law for Renewable Energy," April 30, 2010; available at: http://greenworld-investor.com/2010/04/30/spain-may-renege-on-guaranteed-electricity-rates-under-feed-in-tariff-law-for-renewable-energy/ (accessed January 26, 2011).

48. Ben Sills, "Spain's Solar Deals on Edge of Bankruptcy as Subsidies Founder," *Bloomberg Markets Magazine*, October 18, 2010; available at: http://www.bloomberg.com/news/2010-10-18/spanish-solar-projects-on-brink-of-bankruptcy-as-subsidy-policies-founder.html (accessed January 26, 2011).

49. "Study of the effect on employment of public aid to renewable energy sources," Universidad Rey Juan Carlos; available at: http://www.juandemariana.org/ pdf/090327-employment-public-aid-renewable.pdf (accessed January 26, 2011).

50. Giles Tremlett, "Scandal sullies Spain's clean energy," *Guardian*, March 22, 2009; available at: http://www.guardian.co.uk/world/2009/mar/22/la-muela-renewables-spain-corruption (accessed January 26, 2011).

51. Angel Gonzalez and Keith Johnson, "Spain's Solar-Powered Collapse Dims Subsidy Model," *Wall Street Journal*, September 8, 2009; available at: http://online. wsj.com/article/SB125193815050081615.html (accessed January 26, 2011).

52. Steve Johnson, "Investors may walk after Spain's solar cut," *Financial Times*, January 9, 2011.

53. David Roman and Juan Montes, "Spain Confirms 30% Cut To Solar Power Subsidies," *The Wall Street Journal*, December 23, 2010.

54. "Study of the effect on employment of public aid to renewable energy sources," Universidad Rey Juan Carlos.

55. "El ministro Ángel Gabilondo pidió al rector de la Rey Juan Carlos que se desvincurlara del informe español célèbre en EEUU por sus críticas a las renovables," *ECD Política*, September 24, 2009; available at: http://www.elconfidencialdigital.com/Articulo.aspx?IdObjeto=22226 (accessed January 26, 2011).

56. Cristina Blas, "España admite que la economía verde que vendió a Obama es una ruina," *La Gaceta* (Spain), May 21, 2010.

57. Press Briefing by Press Secretary Robert Gibbs, April 14, 2009; transcript available at: http://www.whitehouse.gov/the_press_office/Briefing-by-White-House-Press-Secretary-Robert-Gibbs-4-14-09/ (accessed January 26, 2011).

58. News Conference by the President, July 23, 2009; transcript available at: http://www.whitehouse.gov/the_press_office/News-Conference-by-the-President-July-22-2009/ (accessed January 26, 2011).

59. Sean Higgins, "DOE E-Mails To Wind Energy Lobbyists Cast Cloud Over Green Jobs Proposals," *Investor's Business Daily*, March 10, 2010; available at: http://www.investors.com/NewsAndAnalysis/Article/526944/201003102006/DOE-E-Mails-To-Wind-Energy-Lobbyists-Cast-Cloud-Over-Green-Jobs-Proposals.aspx (accessed January 26, 2011).

60. Eric Lantz and Suzanne Tegen, "NREL Response to the Report *Study of the Effects on Employment of Public Aid to Renewable Enerfy Sources* from King Juan Carlos University (Spain)," National Renewable Energy Laboratory, August 2009; available at: http://www.nrel.gov/docs/fy09osti/46261.pdf (accessed January 26, 2011).

61. George F. Will, "Tilting at Green Windmills," *Washington Post*, June 25, 2009; available at: http://www.washingtonpost.com/wp-dyn/content/article/2009/06/24/AR2009062403012.html (accessed January 26, 2011).

62. "DOE LPO Finalizes Deal on the World's Largest Wind Project to Date," U.S. Department of Energy, December 17, 2010; available at: http://lpo.energy.gov/?p=1955 (accessed January 26, 2011).

63. "DOE LPO Finalizes Deal on the World's Largest Wind Project to Date," U.S. Department of Energy, December 17, 2010.

64. Nichola Groom, "Analysis: Solar stocks face another tough year in 2011," Reuters, January 12, 2011; available at: http://www.reuters.com/article/idUS-TRE70B6GV20110112 (accessed January 26, 2011).

65. Council of Economic Advisers, "The Economic Impact of the American Recover and Reinvestment Act of 2009: Fifth Quarterly Report"; available at: http://www.whitehouse.gov/sites/default/files/cea_5th_arra_report.pdf (accessed January 26, 2011). Although they did not break out co-investment in that report, they

had done so in the July 2010 quarterly report, attributing a multiplier of 2.32 to private co-investment in the category of "Clean Energy." That earlier report is available at http://www.whitehouse.gov/blog/2010/07/14/cea-releases-fourth-quarterly-report-economic-impact-recovery-act (accessed January 26, 2011).

66. Portions of this section are based on part of my column, "Obama's big green gamble," *Washington Examiner*, July 14, 2010; available at: http://washingtonexaminer.com/node/65146 (accessed January 26, 2011).

67. Todd Woody, "Solar-Panel Maker to Close a Factory and Delay Expansion," *New York Times*, November 3, 2010; available at: http://www.nytimes.com/2010/11/03/business/energy-environment/03solar.html (accessed January 26, 2011).

68. Jim McTague, "Our Tough-Luck President," *Barrons*, July 10, 2010; available at http://online.barrons.com/article/SB50001424052970203296004575352982133405348.html (accessed January 10, 2011).

69. U.S. Securities and Exchange Commission, Form S-1 for Solyndra, Inc; March 16, 2010.

70. OpenSecrets.org

71. "$1M Of Stimulus Will Go To Bike Parking," KPTV.com; available at: http://www.kptv.com/traffic/18889128/detail.html (accessed February 9, 2011).

72. Paul Conner, "Obama's weatherization program makes little economic sense for taxpayers," *The Daily Caller*, June 8, 2010; available at: http://dailycaller.com/2010/06/08/obamas-weatherization-program-makes-no-economic-sense-and-little-environmental-impact (accessed February 9, 2011).

73. Speech transcript, "Obama, Biden, LaHood Deliver Remarks on High-Speed Rail," April 16, 2009; available at: http://projects.washingtonpost.com/obama-speeches/speech/4/ (accessed February 9, 2011).

74. Rich Connell and Dan Weikel, "Some fear California's high-speed rail won't deliver on early promises," *Los Angeles Times*, February 28, 2010.

75. Source: U.S. Census Bureau.

76. *HSR in America*, America 2050. Annual flights between California hubs are listed on page 29. Available online at: http://www.america2050.org/pdf/HSR-in-America-Complete.pdf (accessed January 2, 2011).

77. Wendell Cox and Robert Poole, "The Tampa to Orlando High-Speed Rail Project," Florida Taxpayer Risk Assessment, The Reason Foundation, January 6, 2011.

78. "Fact Sheet: High Speen Intercity Passenger Rail Program: Tampa – Orlando – Miami," WhiteHouse.gov, January 28, 2010; available at: http://www.whitehouse.gov/the-press-office/fact-sheet-high-speed-intercity-passenger-rail-program-tampa-orlando-miami

79. *HSR in America*, America 2050. 33. Available online at: http://www.america2050.org/pdf/HSR-in-America-Complete.pdf (accessed January 2, 2011).

80. David Warner, "U.S. plans to inject $53 billion into passenger rail," Reuters, February 8, 2011; available at MSNBC.com, http://www.msnbc.msn.com/id/41021318/ns/business/ (accessed February 9, 2011).

81.   Randal O'Toole, "High-Speed Rail The Wrong Road for America," Cato Institi-
        tute, *Policy Analysis*, No. 625, October 31, 2008; available at: http://www.cato.org/
        pubs/pas/pa-625.pdf (accessed February 9, 2011).

82.   "Remarks by Vice President Joseph Biden and Secretary of Energy Steven Chu
        on the impact of the Recovery Act investments in innovation, science and tech-
        nology," Eisenhower Executive Office Building, August 24, 2010; available at:
        http://www.whitehouse.gov/the-press-office/2010/08/24/vice-president-biden-
        releases-report-recovery-act-impact-innovation (accessed January 26, 2011).

83.   Source: Energy Information Administration, "Table 10.1 Renewable Energy
        Production and Consumption by Primary Energy Source, 1949-2009"; available
        at EIA.gov. It is worth noting that the entire increase in renewable energy con-
        sumption and production during that period was the result of ethanol mandates,
        with growth in biofuels far exceeding the market gains of wind and solar power
        combined.

84.   Brent Lang, "Obama: Lobbyist Requests Will Be Posted Online," CBS News,
        March 20, 2009; available at: http://www.cbsnews.com/8301-503544_162-
        4879616-503544.html?tag=contentMain;contentBody (accessed January 26,
        2011).

85.   American Recovery and Reinvestment Act of 2009, Sec. 1604.

86.   "Recovery Summer: A Casino, Aquarium, Zoo, Golf Course and Swimming
        Pool?" House Oversight Committee Republican staff, September 24, 2010; avail-
        able at: http://oversight.house.gov/index.php?option=com_content&task=vie
        w&id=968&Itemid=29 (accessed January 26, 2011).

87.   Jonathan Karl and Gregory Simmons, "Signs of the Stimulus," ABC News, July
        14, 2010; available at: http://abcnews.go.com/Politics/signs-stimulus/
        story?id=11163180 (accessed January 26, 2011).

88.   Letter from Transportation Inspector General Calvin Scovel to Representative
        Darrell Issa, Republican, California, August 17, 2010; available at: http://over-
        sight.house.gov/images/stories/Letters/20100817DoTIGStimulusSignGuidanc
        eResponse.pdf (accessed January 26, 2011). News reports on stimulus signs
        included Jonathan Karl, "Signs of Progress or Stimulus Spending Outrage? Crit-
        ics Are Angry Over How Stimulus Funds Are Spent," ABCNews, July 10, 2009.
        Local news reports on the costs of stimulus signs include Michelle Breidenbach,
        "Highway signs identifying federal stimulus projects cost thousands of dollars
        each," *Syracuse Post-Standard*, July 5, 2009.

89.   Jonathan Karl, "Signs of Progress or Stimulus Spending Outrage? Critics Are
        Angry Over How Stimulus Funds Are Spent," ABC News, July 10, 2009; available
        at: http://abcnews.go.com/Politics/story?id=8026587&page=1 (accessed January
        26, 2011).

90.   Angela Couloumbis, "Rendell paying consultant $100,000 to publicize federal
        stimulus," *Philadelphia Inquirer*, March 19, 2009. Read more: "Rendell paying
        consultant $100,000 to publicize federal stimulus," Post-Gazette.com, January

26, 2011; available at: http://www.post-gazette.com/pg/09078/956788-454. stm#ixzz1B8qsraus (accessed January 26, 2011).

91. Sebastian Jones and Michael Grabell, "PR Firm Behind Propaganda Videos Wins Stimulus Contract," *ProPublica*, March 30, 2010; available at: http://www.pro-publica.org/article/pr-firm-behind-propaganda-videos-wins-stimulus-contract (accessed January 26, 2011).

92. Alexander Bolton, "Mark Penn's two firms awarded millions from stimulus for public relations work," *The Hill*, December 2, 2009; available at: http://thehill. com/homenews/administration/71353-mark-penn-got-6-million-from-stim-ulus (accessed January 26, 2011).

93. Starr Penny, "Joe Biden: 'We Have to Go Spend Money to Keep From Going Bankrupt," CNSNews.com, July 16, 2009; available at: http://www.cnsnews.com/news/article/51162 (accessed February 9, 2011).

94. Blair Kamin, "Stimulus dollars turn federal buildings green," *Chicago Tribune*, January 31, 2011.

95. Project description is available from Northwestern University at http://www. research.northwestern.edu/stimulus/hammond.html (accessed February 9, 2011).

96. Whitney Ray, "A Tunnel for Turtles to Cross the Highway," WJHG (Panama City, Florida); video available at: http://www.wjhg.com/news/headlines/48278457. html (accessed January 1, 2011).

97. Edwin Mora, "U.S. Will Pay $2.6 Million to Train Chinese Prostitutes to Drink Responsibly on the Job," CNSNews.com, May 11, 2009; available at: http://www. cnsnews.com/node/47976 (accessed February 14, 2011).

98. "Free BlackBerries for smokers," CNN Newsroom, February 12, 2010; video available at: http://www.cnn.com/video/?/video/tech/2010/02/11/levs.free. blackberries.smokers.cnn (accessed February 9, 2011).

99. Michael Grabell, "Tine Airports Take Off With Stimulus," *ProPublica*, July 13, 2009; available at: http://www.propublica.org/article/tiny-airports-take-off-with-stimulus-713 (accessed January 26, 2011).

100. Abbie Boudreau and Jessi Joseph, "Stimulus-funded Florida bridge draws criti-cism," CNN.com, May 4, 2009; available at: http://articles.cnn.com/2009-05-04/us/florida.bridge.stimulus_1_new-bridge-palm-city-bridge-indian-street-bridge?_s=PM:US (accessed December 15, 2010).

101. "Stimulus Money Used To Fix Unused Hillsborough Bridge," WMUR.com; available at: http://www.wmur.com/r/24608274/detail.html (accessed December 31, 2010).

102. "Moving New Hampshire Forward," TRIP, June 2010; available at: http://www. tripnet.org/New_Hampshire_Report_June_2010.pdf (accessed January 26, 2011).

103. "GOP Senator Slams 100 Stimulus Projects," Associated Press, June 16, 2009; available at: http://www.cbsnews.com/stories/2009/06/16/politics/main5091416. shtml?source=related_story (accessed January 10, 2011).

104. Oklahoma City News9 report, "New Boynton Sidewalk Makes List of Top Wasteful Stimulus Projects," April 12, 2010. The news report can be viewed online at: http://www.news9.com/global/story.asp?s=12298407 (accessed January 27, 2011).

105. Kim Fundingsland, "Refuge center dedicated," *Minot Daily News*, September 3, 2010. For an amusing story about a visit to the visitors' center, see Rob Port, "North Dakota's New $6.1 Million, Stimulus-Funded Visitor's Center Is Only Open When You're At Work," Say Anything Blog; available at: http://sayanything-blog.com/entry/north-dakotas-new-6-million-stimulus-funded-visitors-center-is-only-open-bankers-hours/ (accessed January 27, 2011).

106. Steve Bennish, "Large recycling bins offered to more Dayton neighborhoods," *Dayton Daily ews*, June 18, 2010; available at: http://www.daytondailynews.com/news/dayton-news/large-recycling-bins-offered-to-more-dayton-neighbor-hoods-768463.html (accessed January 27, 2011).

107. "Dancing stimulus project has critics," WCNC.com, July 6, 2010; available at: http://www.wcnc.com/news/local/Dancing-Stimulus-Project-Has-Crit-ics-97677354.html (accessed January 27, 2011).

108. Michelle Breidenbach, "Stimulus funding for Syracuse University sex study questioned," *Syracuse Post-Standard*," August 24, 2009; available at: http://www.syracuse.com/news/index.ssf/2009/08/stimulus_funding_for_syracuse.html (accessed December 31, 2010).

109. Project summary is available at http://www.recovery.gov/Transparency/RecipientReportedData/pages/RecipientProjectSummary508.aspx?AwardIdSur=8352&AwardType=Grants (accessed January 27, 2011).

110. Project summary is available at http://www.recovery.gov/Transparency/RecipientReportedData/Pages/RecipientProjectSummary508.aspx?AwardIDSUR=13677&AwardType=Grants (accessed January 27, 2011).

111. Drew Griffin and Kathleen Johnston, "Feds plan to spend millions on remote Montana border posts," CNN, September 18, 2009; available at: http://www.cnn.com/2009/US/09/17/border.security/index.html#cnnSTCText (accessed January 27, 2011).

112. Drew Griffin and Kathleen Johnston, "Feds plan to spend millions on remote Montana border posts," CNN.

113. Eileen Sullivan and Matt Apuzzo, "Report: Stimulus money not reaching most needy border checkpoints," Associated Press, August 26, 2009.

114. Matt Apuzzo, "AP Impact: Secret process benefits pet projects," Associated Press, August 26, 2009.

115. "Tester: Browning business expects to create 40-50 jobs with new port contract," Jon Tester, Senate.gov, April 26, 2010; available at: http://tester.senate.gov/Newsroom/pr_042610_ports.cfm (accessed January 27, 2011).

116. Matt Gouras, "Government takes steps to close border post," Associated Press, September 28, 2010.

117. "Tester: Dept. of Homeland Security begins process of closing Port of Whitetail," Jon Tester, Senate.gov, September 28, 2010; available at: http://tester.senate.gov/Newsroom/pr_092810_whitetail.cfm (accessed January 27, 2011).

118. Lori Montgomery, "National debt to be higher than White House forecast, CBO says," *Washington Post*, March 6, 2010; available at: http://www.washingtonpost.com/wp-dyn/content/article/2010/03/05/AR2010030502974.html (accessed January 27, 2011).

119. "The Long-Term Budget Outlook," CBO, June 2010; available at: http://www.cbo.gov/doc.cfm?index=11579 (accessed January 27, 2011).

CHAPTER FIVE

1. "Richard Foster for President," *Wall Street Journal* Review & Outlook, August 8, 2010; available at: http://online.wsj.com/article/SB10001424052748703309704575413263344491010.html?mod=WSJ_Opinion_LEADTop (accessed February 3, 2011).

2. Michael Cembalest, "Obama's Business Blind Spot," *Forbes*, November 24, 2009; available at: http://www.forbes.com/2009/11/24/michael-cembalest-obama-business-beltway-cabinet.html (accessed February 3, 2011).

3. House Committee on Ways & Means, "Democrats Have Increased Taxes by $670 Billion and Counting…" April 14, 2010; available at: http://republicans.waysandmeans.house.gov/UploadedFiles/DemTaxIncreases1.pdf (accessed February 3, 2011).

4. "Remarks of Senator Barack Obama: Town Hall on the Economy," MyBarackObama.com, August 2, 2008; available at: http://www.barackobama.com/2008/08/02/remarks_of_senator_barack_obam_102.php (accessed February 3, 2011).

5. "Obama calls for Congress to face health care challenge," CNN, September 9, 2009; available at: http://articles.cnn.com/2009-09-09/politics/obama.speech_1_health-care-health-insurance-large-businesses-and-individuals?_s=PM:POLITICS (accessed February 3, 2011).

6. Jonathan Martin, "'They talk about me like a dog,'" *Politico*, September 6, 2010; available at: http://www.politico.com/news/stories/0910/41816.html (accessed February 3, 2011).

7. Press Release, "Use of Project Labor Agreements for Federal Construction Projects," The White House, February 6, 2009; available at: http://www.whitehouse.gov/the-press-office/executive-order-use-project-labor-agreements-federal-construction-projects (accessed February 3, 2011).

8. "Annual Report of the White House Task Force on the Middle Class Task Force, February 2010"; available at: http://www.whitehouse.gov/sites/default/files/microsites/100226-annual-report-middle-class.pdf (accessed February 3, 2011).

9. Data available at: http://www.bls.gov/news.release/union2.t04.htm (accessed February 3, 2011).

10. David G. Tuerck, "Why Project Labor Agreements Are Not in the Public Interest," *Cato Journal*; available at: http://www.cato.org/pubs/journal/cj30n1/cj30n1-3.pdf (accessed February 3, 2011).

11. Mark Hemingway, "Mandatory PLAs put tax dollars into union coffers," *Washington Examiner*, December 5, 2010; available at: http://washingtonexaminer.com/opinion/columnists/2010/12/mark-hemingway-mandatory-plas-put-tax-dollars-union-coffers#ixzz1BEPQbZeg (accessed February 3, 2011).

12. David Mendell, *Obama: From Promise to Power* (New York: Amistad, 2008), 207.

13. Peter Nicholas, "Obama's curiously close labor friendship," *Los Angeles Times*, June 28, 2009; available at: http://articles.latimes.com/2009/jun/28/nation/na-stern28 (accessed February 3, 2011).

14. "Obama earns SEIU backing," UnionLeader.com, February 16, 2008; available at: http://www.unionleader.com/article.aspx?headline=Obama+earns+SEIU+backing&articleId=755c2c05-0817-42f1-977b-e22d2849584a (accessed February 3, 2011).

15. MSNBC transcript, "Democratic Presidential Candidates Participate in a Candidates' Forum Hosted by the AFL-CIO," August 7, 2007; available at: http://www.msnbc.msn.com/id/20180486/ns/msnbc_tv-hardball_with_chris_matthews/ (accessed February 3, 2011).

16. Mark Hemingway, "Union chief doesn't deserve a presidential medal," *Washington Examiner*, November 22, 2010; available at: http://washingtonexaminer.com/opinion/columnists/2010/11/mark-hemingway-union-chief-doesnt-deserve-presidential-medal (accessed February 3, 2011).

17. Department of Labor LM-2 report of the AFL-CIO, filed September 28, 2009.

18. *The Audacity of Hope*, 119.

19. See, for example, http://www.disabilityrightsca.org/advocacy/v.l.-v-Wagner/Complaint.pdf, and http://www.cft.org/uploads/takingaction/docs/cftsuit.pdf (accessed February 3, 2011).

20. Eric Bailey and Patrick McGreevey, "California begins printing IOUs," *Los Angeles Times*, July 3, 2009; available at: http://articles.latimes.com/2009/jul/03/local/me-iou-budget3 (accessed February 3, 2011).

21. President's Economic Recovery Advisory Board, Anna Burger, http://www.whitehouse.gov/administration/eop/perab/members/burger (accessed February 3, 2011).

22. Jake Sherman, "W.H. aide failed to disclose payout," *Politico*, June 28, 2010; available at: http://dyn.politico.com/printstory.cfm?uuid=7F9A27C4-18FE-70B2-A829E3E7519889BC (accessed February 3, 2011).

23. "FEC to Collect $775,000 Civil Penalty From America Coming Together," FEC.gov, August 29, 2007; available at: http://www.fec.gov/press/press2007/20070829act.shtml (accessed February 3, 2011).

24. Michael Beebe, "Nurse Presses Complaint Against Ervolino," *Buffalo News*, June 19, 1995.

25. Craig Becker, "Democracy in the Workplace: Union Representation Elections and Federal Labor Law," 77 *Minnesota Law Review* 495 (February 1993); available at: http://www.hrpolicy.org/downloads/2009/77%20Minn%20%20L%20%20 Rev%20%20495%20%281992-1993%29.pdf (accessed February 3, 2011).

26. Craig Becker, "Elections Without Democracy," *New Labor Review*, Fall/Winter 1998.

27. "First 100 Days: Broken Promises," *National Journal*, April 29, 2009.

28. Becker participated in rulings and decisions in at least 17 cases involving the SEIU:
    - *Northern Health Facilities, Inc. d/b/a Mountain City Nursing and Rehabilitation Center and SEIU Healthcare Pennsylvania*, December 3, 2010.
    - *Laro Service Systems, Inc. and Local 32BJ, Service Employees International Union*, November 22, 2010.
    - Gateway Care Center and 1199 SEIU Healthcare Workers East, New Jersey Region, November 19, 2010.
    - *Monmouth Care Center and SEIU 1199 New Jersey Health Care Union*, November 17, 2010.
    - *Mildord Manor Nursing and Rehabilitation Center and SEIU 1199 New Jersey Health Care Union*, November 17, 2010.
    - *Pinebrook Nursing Home and Rehabilitation Center and SEIU 1199 New Jersey Health Care Union*, November 17, 2010.
    - *Wayneview Care Center and Victoria Health Care Center and SEIU 1199, New Jersey Health Care Union*, November 18, 2010.
    - *75 Putnam Pike Operations, LLC, d/b/a Greenville Skilled Nursing and Rehabilitation Center*, November 10, 2010.
    - *Watkins Security Agency of D.C., Inc.*, October 28, 2010.
    - *Pavilions at Forrestal Nursing & Rehabilitation Center*, October 22, 2010.
    - *Laurel Bay Health & Rehabilitation Center*, October 15, 2010.
    - *Lutheran Homes of Michigan, Inc. d/b/a Lutheran Home of*, October 6, 2010.
    - *Regency Grande Nursing & Rehabilitation Center*, August 23, 2010.
    - *Transcare New York, Inc.*, July 29, 2010.
    - *Service Employees International Union, Nurses Alliance, Local 121RN (Pomona Valley Hospital Medical Center) and Carole Jean Badertscher*, June 8, 2010.
    - *St. Barnabas Hospital and Committee of Interns and Residents, Local 1957, SEIU, Petitioner*, June 3, 2010.

    One case: In *Altercare of Wadsworth Center for Rehabilitation and Nursing Care, Inc.*, August 19, 2010, Becker was part of a unanimous panel throwing out charges filed by the SEIU Local 1199.

29. Ed O'Keefe, "Obama nominee for GPO chief accepted, repaid improper payments," *Federal Eye*, July 15, 2010; available at: http://voices.washingtonpost.com/ federal-eye/2010/07/obama_nominee_accepted_repaid.html (accessed February 9, 2011).

30. Dan Morain and Evelyn Larrubia, "Hilda Solis' belief in unions runs deep," *Los Angeles Times*, January 9, 2009; available at: http://articles.latimes.com/2009/ jan/09/local/me-solis9 (accessed February 9, 2011).

31. See, for example, House of Representatives, "Budget Cuts Harm Women and Children," March 29, 2006; The Negative Effects of Social Security Privatization on Women," January 25, 2005; "Medicaid Cuts and Their Impact on Women," October 19, 2005; "Budget Impact on Women," May 17, 2006.

32. Greg Sargent, "Labor Leaders Hail Obama's Pick For Labor Secretary," TPM ElectionCentral, December 18, 2008; available at: http://tpmelectioncentral. talkingpointsmemo.com/2008/12/andy_stern_on_obamas_labor_sec.php (accessed February 3, 2011).

33. Husband's tax problems: http://voices.washingtonpost.com/44/2009/02/05/ solis_senate_session_canceled.html (accessed February 3, 2011); and Union front group: "Republicans want Labor nominee to stop lobbying for 'card check' bill," *Los Angeles Times*, February 5, 2009; available at: http://articles.latimes.com/2009/ feb/05/nation/na-solis5 (accessed February 3, 2011).

34. "U.S. Department of Labor Strategic Plan, Fiscal Years 2011-2016," emphasis in original; available at: http://www.dol.gov/_sec/stratplan/StrategicPlan.pdf (accessed February 3, 2011).

35. Kris Maher, "Labor wants Obama to take on big fight," The Wall Street Journal, November 6, 2008.

36. BLS Data cited in Dickens, William, and Leonard, Jonathan, "Accounting for the Decline in Union Membership, 1950-1980," *Industrial and Labor Relations Review*, Vol. 38, no. 3 (April, 1985), 323–34.

37. Economic News Release, Bureau of Labor Statistics; available at: http://www. bls.gov/news.release/union2.t01.htm (accessed February 3, 2011).

38. Historical data from BLS.gov.

39. Source: Bureau of Labor Statistics, assumes dues of $7 per week.

40. Source: Bureau of Labor Statistics. Sixty percent of non-union workers are below age forty-five.

41. Peter Cohan, "Boeing union woes persist as it opens 787 facility in South Carolina," *Daily Finance*, October 29, 2009; available at: http://www.dailyfinance.com/ story/boeing-opens-787-facility-in-south-carolina-as-struggle-with- uni/19214693/ (accessed February 3, 2011).

42. "Introduction to Multiemployer Plans," Pension Benefit Guaranty Corporation, http://www.pbgc.gov/prac/multiemployer/introduction-to-multiemployer- plans.html (accessed February 3, 2011).

43. United States General Accounting Office, "Private Pensions: Multiemployer Plans Face Short- and Long-Term Challenges," March 2004; available at: http://www.gao.gov/new.items/d04423.pdf (accessed February 3, 2011).

44. United States Department of Labor, "Critical, Endangered and WRERA Status Notices," http://www.dol.gov/ebsa/criticalstatusnotices.html (accessed February 3, 2011).

45. See, for example, Testimony of Randy G. DeFrehn before the Health, Education, Labor and Pensions Committee, http://www.nccmp.org/submissions/pdfs/HELP/6_7_05.pdf (accessed February 3, 2011).

46. United States General Accounting Office, "Private Pensions: Multiemployer Plans Face Short- and Long-Term Challenges," March 2004.

47. Pension Benefit Guaranty Corporation, 2006 Annual Report, http://www.pbgc.gov/Documents/2006_annual_report.pdf (accessed February 3, 2011).

48. The Communications Workers of America and the International Typographical Union

49. "Notice of Critical Status For CWA/ITU Negotiated Pension Plan," http://www.dol.gov/ebsa/pdf/notice042610004.pdf (accessed February 3, 2011).

50. "CWA/ITU Negotiated Pension Plan Notice of Plan Changes and Reductions in Adjustable Benefits under the Rehabilitation Plan/Summary of Material Modiciations," http://www.cwa-itunegotiate.qwestoffice.net/noticeofchgs42010.pdf (accessed February 3, 2011).

51. IRS form 5500, CWA/ITU Negotiated Pension Plan 2009, filed September 9, 2010.

52. Message to Participants, April 28, 2010, http://www.cwa-itunegotiate.qwestoffice.net/message42810.pdf (accessed February 3, 2011).

53. Mark Hemingway, "Will November be the death knell of labor unions?" *Washington Examiner*, October 16, 2010; available at: http://www.washingtonexaminer.com/opinion/columns/Will-November-be-the-death-knell- for-big-labor-unions_-1246982-105141124.html (accessed February 3, 2011).

54. Mark Hemingway, "Unions are desperate for a tax-paid pension bailout," *Washington Examiner*, October 17, 2010; available at: http://www.washingtonexaminer.com/opinion/columns/Unions-are-desperate-for-a-tax-paid-pension-bailout-1254773-105211749.html#ixzz12v5TLjJe (accessed February 3, 2011).

55. Sam Hananel, "Rule Change Favors Unions At Airlines, Railroads," Associated Press, May 10, 2010; available at: http://www.breitbart.com/article.php?id=D9FK0UP80&show_article=1 (accessed February 3, 2011).

56. Kelly Yamanouchi, "Delta flight attendants to union: No thanks," *Atlanta Journal-Constitution*, November 3, 2010; available at: http://www.ajc.com/business/delta-flight-attendants-to-716123.html (accessed February 3, 2011).

57. Wayne Risher, "Machinists lose bid to represent Delta Air Lines ground workers," *The Commercial Appeal*, November 18, 2010; available at: http://www.commer-

cialappeal.com/news/2010/nov/18/second-union-loses-bid-represent-delta-air-lines-w/ (accessed February 3, 2011).

58. *Dana Corporation and International Union, United Automobile, Aerospace, and Agricultural–CIO and Gary L. Smeltzer, Jr. and Joseph Montague and Kenneth A. Gray,* December 6, 2010; NLRB Member Brian Hayes dissenting.

59. "Collective Bargaining Rights Finally a Reality at TSA," AFGE, February 4, 2011; available at: http://afge.org/index.cfm?Page=PressReleases&PressReleaseID=1245&from=home (accessed February 9, 2011).

60. Jeanne Meserve and Mike M. Ahlers, "TSA clears way for airport screeners to seek broader union rights," CNN, February 4, 2011; available at: http://www.cnn.com/2011/TRAVEL/02/04/tsa.collective.bargaining/ (accessed February 9, 2011).

61. Mike M. Ahlers and Jeanne Meserve, "TSA shuts door on private airport screening program," CNN, January 29, 2011; available at: http://articles.cnn.com/2011-01-29/travel/tsa.private_1_tsa-government-screeners-screening-program?_s=PM:TRAVEL (accessed February 9, 2011).

62. "DoL Rescinds T-1 Reporting Requirement for Union Trusts," PlanSponsor, December 1, 2010; available at: http://www.plansponsor.com/DoL_Rescinds_T1_Reporting_Requirement_for_Union_Trusts.aspx (accessed February 3, 2011).

63. James Sherk, "Congress Should Block Union Transparency Rollback," the Heritage Foundation, December 16, 2010; available at: http://www.heritage.org/research/reports/2010/12/congress-should-block-union-transparency-rollback (accessed February 3, 2011).

64. Data available at: http://www.theworddoctors.com/docs/Benchmark%20Study%20of%20Union%20Employee%20Election%20Year%20Attitudes.pdf (accessed February 3, 2011).

65. Fred Lucas, "Three SEIU Locals—Including Chicago Chapter—Waived From Obamacare Requirement," CNSNews.com, January 24, 2011; available at: http://cnsnews.com/news/article/seiu-locals-including-chicago-chapter-wa (accessed February 3, 2011).

66. Statistics on the labor force come from the Bureau of Labor Statistics: http://www.bls.gov/news.release/union2.t03.htm (accessed February 3, 2011).

67. "White House Announces Middle Class Task Force," *Wall Street Journal,* January 30, 2009; available at: http://blogs.wsj.com/washwire/2009/01/30/white-house-announces-middle-class-task-force/ (accessed February 3, 2011).

68. "Annual Report of the White House Task Force on the Middle Class Task Force," February 2010; available at: http://www.whitehouse.gov/sites/default/files/microsites/100226-annual-report-middle-class.pdf (accessed February 3, 2011).

69. Claire Suddath, "Obama's Middle-Class Task Force Has No Middle Class," *Time,* March 4, 2009; available at: http://www.time.com/time/politics/article/0,8599,1882913,00.html (accessed February 3, 2011)

70. Department of Labor, form LM-2 for 2009.

71. "Annual Report of the White House Task Force on the Middle Class Task Force," February 2010; available at: http://www.whitehouse.gov/sites/default/files/ microsites/100226-annual-report-middle-class.pdf (accessed February 3, 2011).

72. Center for Union Facts, "When Voting Isn't Private: The Union Campaign, Against Secret Ballot Elections"; available at: http://www.unionfacts.com/down-loads/report.cardCheck.pdf (accessed February 3, 2011).

73. TED: The Editor's Desk, "Independent contractors in 2005," Bureau of Labor Statistics, July 29, 2005; available at: http://www.bls.gov/opub/ted/2005/jul/wk4/ art05.htm (accessed February 3, 2011).

74. Andrew Biggs, "Truth in Accounting: Calculating the market value of unfunded obligations in state and local government pensions," The Free Enterprise Nation; available at: http://www.thefreeenterprisenation.org/FENI/media/Docs-Edito-rial/FEN%20-%20Truth%20in%20Accounting%20by%20Andrew%20Biggs. pdf (accessed February 3, 2011).

75. Evan Hapler, "U.S. threatens to rescind stimulus money over wage cuts," *Los Angeles Times*, May 8, 2009; available at: http://articles.latimes.com/2009/may/08/ local/me-health-cuts8 (accessed February 3, 2011).

76. Evan Helpler, "SEIU may be linked to ultimatum on withholding stimulus funds," *Los Angeles Times*, May 11, 2009; available at: http://articles.latimes. com/2009/may/11/local/me-cal-healthcare11 (accessed February 3, 2011).

77. Capitol Weekly Staff, "Feds okay pay cuts for healthcare workers," *Capitol Weekly*, May 21, 2009; available at: http://www.capitolweekly.net/article.php?_c=xzshu 7zy3a9ck9&xid=xzsf2zufvrp2a9&done=.xzshu7zy3arck9 (accessed February 3, 2011).

78. Dennis Cauchon, "Federal pay ahead of private industry," *USA Today*, March 8, 2010; available at: http://www.usatoday.com/news/nation/2010-03-04-federal-pay_N.htm (accessed February 3, 2011). For a look at federal employees in one local region numbers, see Danielle Cervantes, "Federal paychecks top private in county," *San Diego Union-Tribune*, December 17, 2010; available at: http://www. union-trib.com/news/2010/dec/17/federal-paychecks-top-private/ (accessed February 3, 2011).

79. Tad DeHaven, "Federal Employees Continue to Prosper," *Cato@Liberty*, August 10, 2010; available at: http://www.cato-at-liberty.org/federal-employees-con-tinue-to-prosper/ (accessed February 3, 2011).

80. Stephen Losey, "Federal pay freeze plan wouldn't stop raises," FederalTimes.com, December 6, 2010; available at: http://www.federaltimes.com/article/20101206/ BENEFITS01/12060301/1001 (accessed February 3, 2011).

81. Data on federal separations by category are available on the website of the White House Office of Personnel Management.

82. Historical data on layoffs and discharges of federal and private employees is available from the Bureau of Labor statistics at BLS.gov.

83. Executive Order 13522, Federal Register, December 14, 2009; available at: http:// edocket.access.gpo.gov/2009/pdf/E9-29781.pdf (accessed February 3, 2011).

84.   Memorandum for Heads of Executive Departments/Agencies and Labor-Management Forums, United States Office of Personnel Management, http://www.lmrcouncil.gov/meetings/handouts/Predecisional_letter_LMF.pdf (accessed February 3, 2011).

CHAPTER SIX

1.   Wendy Davis, "Edwards's career tied to jury award debate," *Boston Globe*, September 15, 2003.

2.   See, for example, Matt Blunt, "How Missouri Cut Junk Lawsuits," *Wall Street Journal*, September 22, 2009; available at: http://online.wsj.com/article/SB1000 1424052970204488304574426823146241800.html (accessed December 1, 2010).

3.   Mike Lillis, "Trial lawyers tout new report on cost of medical malpractice," *The Hill*, September 7, 2010; available at: http://thehill.com/blogs/healthwatch/health-reform-implementation/117479-trial-lawyers-tout-new-report-on-cost-of-medical-malpractice (accessed February 3, 2011).

4.   Center for Medicare and Medicaid Services, National Health Expenditures data; available at: https://www.cms.gov/NationalHealthExpendData/downloads/tables.pdf (accessed February 3, 2011).

5.   Note that the report predicts a half-point reduction from the excise tax alone, and then another half-point reduction from all other provisions. The excise tax was eliminated from the bill for years prior to 2018. Available at http://www.whitehouse.gov/sites/default/files/microsites/091213-economic-case-health-care-reform.pdf (accessed January 10, 2011).

6.   Although Kerry's presidential website is now offline, his campaign's statement on the matter remains available online at http://vote-ma.org/PoliticianIssue.aspx?State=MA&Id=MAKerryJohnF&Issue=BUSMedicalInsurance (accessed February 4, 2011).

7.   Lisa Wangsness, "Biden Gaffes Leave Democrats With Mixed Emotions," *Boston Globe*, October 1, 2008; available at: http://www.boston.com/news/nation/washington/articles/2008/10/01/biden_gaffes_leave_democrats_with_mixed_emotions/ (accessed February 3, 2011).

8.   Mark Tapscott, "Dean says Obamacare authors don't want to challenge trial lawyers," *Washington Examiner*, August 25, 2009; available at: http://washington-examiner.com/blogs/beltway-confidential/2009/08/dean-says-obamacare-authors-dont-want-challenge-trial-lawyers#ixzz1C3uXfQER (accessed February 3, 2011).

9.   Aaron Sharockman, "Former Florida Gov. Charlie Crist takes job with Morgan & Morgan law firm," *St. Petersburg Times*, January 8, 2011; available at: http://www.tampabay.com/news/politics/stateroundup/former-florida-gov-charlie-crist-takes-job-with-morgan-amp-morgan-law-firm/1144262 (accessed February 9, 2011).

10. "Trial Lawyer Bonanza," *Wall Street Journal*, January 9, 2009; available at: http://online.wsj.com/article/SB123146294351966567.html (accessed February 3, 2011).

11. Adam Liptak and Steven Greenhouse, "Supreme Court Agrees to Hear Wal-Mart Appeal," *New York Times*, December 6, 2010; available at: http://www.nytimes.com/2010/12/07/business/07bizcourt.html (accessed February 3, 2011).

12. This section is based in part on Author, "Will the Obama administration give trial lawyers a $1.6 billion tax break?" *Washington Examiner* Beltway Confidential blog; available at: http://washingtonexaminer.com/blogs/beltway-confidential/will-obama-administration-give-trial-lawyers-16-billion-tax-break (accessed January 1, 2011).

13. "Remarks by the President on Wall Street Reform in Quincy, Illinois," April 28, 2010; available at http://www.whitehouse.gov/the-press-office/remarks-president-wall-street-reform-quincy-illinois (accessed January 10, 2011).

14. "Weekly Address: President Obama: GOP Leadership Standing up for Outsourcing and Special Interests, Instead of American Workers," The White House, September 25, 2010; available at: http://www.whitehouse.gov/the-press-office/2010/09/25/weekly-address-president-obama-gop-leadership-standing-outsourcing-and-s (accessed February 9, 2011).

15. George F. Will, "Linda McMahon vs. Richard Blumenthal: Connecticut's wrestling match," *Washington Post*, October 27, 2010; available at: http://www.washingtonpost.com/wp-dyn/content/article/2010/10/27/AR2010102705973.html (accessed February 9, 2011).

16. John O'Brien, "Sources: Trial lawyers expect tax break from Treasury Department," LegalNewsline.com, July 13, 2010; available at: http://www.legalnewsline.com/news/227944-sources-trial-lawyers-expect-tax-break-from-treasury-department (accessed February 9, 2011).

17. The letter is available online at http://republicans.waysandmeans.house.gov/UploadedFiles/Camp_Grassley_Letter_to_Geithner_7-22-10.PDF (accessed January 25, 2011).

18. "Proposed tax break for lawyers would worsen liability mess," amednews.com, October 4, 2010; available at: http://www.ama-assn.org/amednews/2010/10/04/edsa1004.htm (accessed February 9, 2011).

19. 552 U.S. 312 (2008).

20. Michael Cembalest, "Obama's Business Blind Spot," *Forbes*, November 24, 2009; available at: http://www.forbes.com/2009/11/24/michael-cembalest-obama-business-beltway-cabinet.html (accessed February 3, 2011).

21. The 4 Circuit took this position in an unpublished decision on jury instructions, in *Philson v. Goldsboro Milling Co.* (1998). The 5 Circuit held that plaintiffs must prove a likelihood of injury to competition in *Wheeler v. Pilgrim's Pride Corp.*, 591 F. 3d 355 (2009). The 6 Circuit did the same in *Terry v. Tyson Farms* (2010); The 7 Circuit in *Pac. Trading Co. v. Wilson & Co.*, 547 F.2d 367, 369-70 (1976). The 8 Circuit in *Jackson v. Swift Eckrich, Inc.*, 53 F.3d 1452, 1458 (1995); the 9

Circuit in *DeJong Packing Co. v. USDA*, 618 F.2d 1329 (1980); the 10 Circuit in *Been v. OK Industries, Inc.*, 495 F. 3d 1217 (2007); and the 11 Circuit in *Pickett v. Tyson Fresh Meats*, Inc., 420 F. 3d 1272 (2005).

22. *Federal Register*, Vol. 75, No. 119, June 22, 2010. 35338.

23. House Agriculture Committee on Livestock, Dairy and Poultry, hearing of July 20, 2010. Full testimony is available at: http://democrats.agriculture.house.gov/testimony/111/111-56.pdf (accessed February 3, 2011).

24. Letter from Congress to the Honorable Tom Vilsack, October 1, 2010; available at: http://www.meatami.com/ht/a/GetDocumentAction/i/63222 (accessed February 3, 2011).

25. Federal contributions from OpenSecrets.org. State contributions from RICampaignFinance.com.

26. Editorial, "Mr. Lead Paint buys a federal judgeship," *Washington Examiner*, June 30, 2010; available at: http://washingtonexaminer.com/opinion/mr-lead-paint-buys-federal-judgeship#ixzz1C5AiMfmY (accessed February 3, 2011).

27. *State of Rhode Island v. Lead Industries Association, Inc., et al.*, No. 2004-63-M.P., http://www.courts.ri.gov/supreme/pdf-files/04-63_7-2-08.pdf (accessed February 3, 2011).

28. Jef Feeley, "Ohio Drops Lawsuits Over Lead Paint Against Sherwin-Williams," Bloomberg, February 7, 2009; available at: http://www.bloomberg.com/apps/news?sid=abd9EfwRuP6k&pid=newsarchive (accessed February 3, 2011).

CHAPTER SEVEN

1. Stanley Kurtz, "Stripping Away the Mask," NRO, October 25, 2008; available at: http://www.nationalreview.com/corner/172644/stripping-away-mask/stanley-kurtz (accessed February 3, 2011).

2. Jim Vandehei and Mike Allen, "Obama strategy: Marginalize most powerful critics," *Politico*, October 21, 2009; available at: http://www.politico.com/news/stories/1009/28532.html (accessed February 3, 2011).

3. Saul Alinsky, *Rules for Radicals*, (Vintage, 1989) 130. (Originally Published by Random House, 1971).

4. Michael Scherer, "Calling 'Em Out: The White House Takes on the Press," *Time*, October 8, 2009; available at: http://www.time.com/time/politics/article/0,8599,1929058,00.html (accessed February 3, 2011).

5. CNN, *State of the Union*, Oct. 11, 2009.

6. ABC's *This Week*, October 18, 2009.

7. Michael Scherer, "Calling 'Em Out," *Time*, October 8, 2009.

8. "White House Urges Other Networks to Disregard Fox News," FOX News, October 19, 2009; available at: http://www.foxnews.com/politics/2009/10/19/white-house-urges-networks-disregard-fox-news#ixzz1CsZX09Hj (accessed February 3, 2011).

9. FOX News, *The O'Reilly Factor*, September 18, 2009.

10. David Mendell, *Obama: From Promise to Power* (New York: Amistad, 2007), 7.

11. David Horowitz, "I'm a uniter, not a divider," Salon.com, May 6, 1999; available at: http://www.salon.com/news/feature/1999/05/06/bush (accessed February 9, 2011).

12. Sarah Pulliam Bailey, "Obama: 'They cling to guns or religion,'" *Christianity Today*, April 13, 2008; available at: http://blog.christianitytoday.com/ctliveblog/archives/2008/04/obama_they_clin.html (accessed February 3, 2011).

13. Scott Helman, "Obama keeps pressure on McCain," *Boston Globe*, September 17, 2008; available at: http://www.boston.com/news/politics/politicalintelligence/2008/09/obama_keeps_the.html (accessed February 9, 2011).

14. "Obama Tells Republicans to 'Sit in Back,'" FOX News, October 25, 2010; available at: http://www.foxnews.com/politics/2010/10/25/obama-tells-republicans-sit/ (accessed February 9, 2011).

15. Peter Ferrara, "Obama's Shut-Up-America Speech," National Review Online, August 10, 2009; available at: http://www.nationalreview.com/critical-condition/48518/obamas-shut-america-speech/peter-ferrara (accessed February 9, 2011).

16. Michelle McPhee and Sara Just, "Obama: Police Acted 'Stupidly' in Gates Case," ABC News, July 22, 2009; available at: http://abcnews.go.com/US/story?id=8148986&page=1 (accessed February 3, 2011).

17. Barack Obama, *The Audacity of Hope*, 59.

18. Michael Scherer, "Team Obama's Petty Limbauch Strategy," *Time* Swampland blog, March 4, 2009; available at: http://swampland.blogs.time.com/2009/03/04/team-obamas-petty-limbaugh-strategy/#ixzz1DBbHiezJ (accessed February 9, 2011).

19. "Shutting Up Business," *Wall Street Journal* Review & Outlook, October 10, 2010; available at: http://online.wsj.com/article/SB10001424052748703735804575536370151720874.html (accessed February 9, 2011).

20. Jonathan Martin, "Rush Job: Inside Dems' Limbaugh plan," *Politico*, March 4, 2009; available at: http://www.politico.com/news/stories/0309/19596.html (accessed February 9, 2011).

21. "Remarks by the President in state of the Union Address," WhiteHouse.gov, January 27, 2010; available at: http://www.whitehouse.gov/the-press-office/remarks-president-state-union-address (accessed February 9, 2011).

22. Bradley A. Smith, "President Wrong on *Citizens United* Case," NRO, January 27, 2010; available at: http://www.nationalreview.com/corner/193894/president-wrong-i-citizens-united-i-case/bradley-smith (accessed February 3, 2011).

23. Carol E. Lee, "Obama: Rove meddling in Illinois Senate race," *Politico*, October 7, 2010; available at: http://www.politico.com/news/stories/1010/43307.html (accessed February 9, 2011).

24. Peter Baker, "Obama Ratchets Up Tone Against G.O.P.," *New York Times*, October 10, 2010; available at: http://www.nytimes.com/2010/10/11/us/politics/11obama.html (accessed February 9, 2011).

25. Eric Lichtblau, "Topic of Foreign Money in U.S. Races Hits Hustings," New York Times, October 8, 2010; available at: http://www.nytimes.com/2010/10/09/us/politics/09donate.html (accessed February 15, 2011).

26. "Dem Claim on Foreign Money Lacks Evidence," CBS News, October 12, 2010; available at: http://www.cbsnews.com/stories/2010/10/12/politics/main6950387.shtml (accessed February 9, 2011).

27. "Axelrod to US Chamber: What Are You Hiding That You Don't Want the American People to See?" ABC News, October 11, 2010; available at: http://blogs.abcnews.com/politicalpunch/2010/10/axelrod-to-us-chamber-what-are-you-hiding-that-you-dont-want-the-american-people-to-see.html (accesed February 3, 2011).

28. Americans United for Change, IRS Form 990, 2008.

29. Michael Isikoff, "Obama's Lobbyist Connection," Newsweek, May 24, 2008; available at: http://www.newsweek.com/2008/05/24/obama-s-lobbyist-connection.html (accessed February 3, 2011).

30. Siobhan Hughes, "Oil Chiefs Leave Meeting with Interior 'Disappointed'" Dow Jones Newswires for the Wall Street Journal, June 29, 2010.

31. Seahawk's press release, which specifically blames the moratorium for forcing the company's sale, can be found at http://www.kten.com/Global/story.asp?S=14015821 (accessed February 15, 2011).

32. Department of the Interior, "Increased Safety Measures for Energy Development on the Outer Continental Shelf," May 27, 2010.

33. Statement: "The Primary Recommendation in the May 27, 2010 report, 'INCREASED SAFETY MEASURES FOR ENERGY DEVELOPMENT ON THE OUTER CONTINENTAL SHELF' Given by Secretary Salazar to The President Misrepresents our Position," June 9, 2010; available from E&E Newsire at: http://www.eenews.net/assets/2010/06/09/document_pm_03.pdf (accessed January 20, 2011).

34. "Report says White House editing of Gulf safety report favored drilling ban," Associated Press, November 10, 2010; available at: http://www.cleveland.com/nation/index.ssf/2010/11/report_says_white_house_editin.html (accessed February 9, 2011).

35. Hornbeck v. Salazar, United States District Court, Eastern District of Louisiana, No. 2:10-cv-01663-MLCF-JCW, Section "F;" Feb. 2, 2011.

36. Jason Riley, "Lawsuit filed against Louisville abortion protester," Courier-Journal.com, December 22, 2010.

37. Ibid.

38. Ibid.

39. The report is still available at: http://www.fas.org/irp/eprint/rightwing.pdf (accessed February 9, 2011).

40. Holder v. Hamilton, complaint against David Hamilton.

41. Obama, The Audacity of Hope, 177–78.

42. State of Illinois, 92nd General Assembly, Regular Session Senate Transcript, March. 30, 2001, 85; available at: http://www.ilga.gov/senate/transcripts/strans92/ST033001.pdf (accessed January 30, 2011)

43. Transcript: "'This is your victory,' says Obama," *CNN Politics*; available at: http://edition.cnn.com/2008/POLITICS/11/04/obama.transcript (accessed February 3, 2011).

44. *"Race Neutral Enforcement of the Law? DOJ and the New Black Panther Party Litigation," November 25, 2010; available at:* www.usccr.gov/NBPH/CommissionInterimReport_11-23-2010.pdf *(accessed February 3, 2011).*

45. The emails are available at Judicial Watch's website: http://www.judicialwatch.org/files/documents/2010/doj-nbpp-docs-11022010.pdf (accessed February 3, 2011).

46. *Official court order, available at:* www.usccr.gov/NBPH/MotionforDefaultJudgmentreKingSamirShabazz.pdf *(accessed February 3, 2011).*

47. John Fund, "Holder's Black Panther Stonewall," *Wall Street Journal*, August 20, 2009; available at: http://online.wsj.com/article/SB10001424052970203550604574361071968458430.html#mod=article-outset-box (accessed February 3, 2011).

48. Andrew C. McCarthy, *How the Obama Administration Has Politicized Justice* (New York: Encounter Books, 2010), 40–41.

49. "Top Justice Dept. Official Lied Under Oath About Dismissal of New Black Panther Case, Ex-DOJ Lawyer Says," FOXNews.com, July 1, 2010; available at: http://www.foxnews.com/politics/2010/07/01/justice-dept-official-lied-oath-dismissal-new-black-panther-case-ex-doj-lawyer/ (accessed February 3, 2011).

50. James Madison, Federalist No. 51, cited in William J. Bennett, *The Spirit of America: Our Sacred Honor* (New York: Simon and Schuster, 1997), 319.

51. J. Christian Adams, "J. Christian Adams: Justice Department's Civil Rights Division is out of control," *Washington Examiner*, August 9, 2010; available at: http://washingtonexaminer.com/node/470196 (accessed February 9, 2011).

52. Letter of William F. Lynch to David Tatarsky, June 22, 2010.

53. Letter from David Tatarsky, General Counsel, SCDC to William F. Lynch Esq., Department of Justice, Disability Rights Section, August 20, 2010.

54. Edwin Mora, "BLM Spurned Chief Ranger's Recommendation to Close National Monument Near Mexican Border for Safety Reasons," CNSNews.com, December 21, 2010; available at: http://www.cnsnews.com/news/article/interior-dept-kept-federal-lands-open-de (accessed February 3, 2011).

55. "*GAO-11-177 Border Security*," http://www.gao.gov/new.items/d11177.pdf (accessed February 3, 2011).

56. Steve Stout, "Border Agent Killed in Shootout with 'Bandits,'" KPHO.com, December 15, 2010.

57. SB 1070 Revised (HB 2162), text available from the *Tucson Sentinel* at http://www.tucsonsentinel.com/files/pdf/hb2162.pdf (accessed February 3, 2011).

58. Anne Ryman, "Some Arizonans waiting to pick sides regarding state's new immigration law," *Arizona Republic*, January 8, 2011; available at: http://www.azcentral.com/arizonarepublic/news/articles/2010/04/30/20100430arizona-immigration-law-moderates.html (accessed February 3, 2011).

59. Jeffrey M. Jones, "More Americans Favor Than Oppose Arizona Immigration Law," *Gallup*, April 29, 2010; available at: http://www.gallup.com/poll/127598/americans-favor-oppose-arizona-immigration-law.aspx (accessed February 3, 2011).

60. "Obama backs Senate Immigration Reform Plan," CBS News, March 18, 2010; available at: http://www.cbsnews.com/stories/2010/03/18/politics/main6312915.shtml (accessed February 9, 2011).

61. Lydia Saad, "Hispanics' Approval of Obama Drops in 2010," *Gallup*, June 7, 2010; available at: http://www.gallup.com/poll/139379/hispanics-approval-obama-drops-2010.aspx (accessed February 3, 2011).

62. Michael Shear, "Republican immigration position likely to alienate Latinos, Democrats say," *Washington Post*, July 20, 2010; available at: http://www.washingtonpost.com/wp-dyn/content/article/2010/07/19/AR2010071905351.html (accessed February 3, 2011).

63. Michael Shear, "Republican immigration position likely to alienate Latinos, Democrats say," *Washington Post*, July 20, 2010; available at: http://www.washingtonpost.com/wp-dyn/content/article/2010/07/19/AR2010071905351.html (accessed February 3, 2011).

64. All Obama ever delivered was a futile, lame-duck vote in the Senate on the DREAM Act, which would have applied to very few immigrants. It provided a path to citizenship for certain illegal immigrants who entered the United States as children, if they attended college or served in the military.

65. United States v. Arizona, 2010, available at http://www.scribd.com/doc/33972991/U-S-v-A-Z-Complaint

66. Ibid.

67. "Immigration Enforcement: Controls over Program Authorizing State and Local Enforcement of Federal Immigration Laws Should Be Strengthened," *GAO, U.S. Government Accountability Office*, March 4, 2009; available at: http://www.gao.gov/products/GAO-09-381T (accessed February 3, 2011).

68. Public Law 110-409.

69. Byron York, "What's behind Obama's sudden attempt to fire the AmeriCorps inspector general?" *Washington Examiner* Beltway Confidential blog, June 10, 2009; available at: http://washingtonexaminer.com/blogs/beltway-confidential/2009/06/whats-behind-obamas-sudden-attempt-fire-americorps-inspector-gener (accessed February 9, 2011).

70. Byron York, "Gerald Walpin loses appeal; court guts protections for agency watchdogs," *Washington Examiner*, January 4, 2011; available at: http://washingtonexaminer.com/blogs/beltway-confidential/2011/01/gerald-walpin-loses-appeal-court-guts-protections-agency-watchdog (accessed February 3, 2011).

71. Donations recorded at OpenSecrets.org. Johnson discussed his relationship with Obama ("I'm friends with Barack") in an interview with Sacramento News10, October 30, 2008; available at: http://www.youtube.com/watch?v=1KHEZg9pS E8&feature=player_embedded (accessed January 30, 2011).

72. Byron York, "Gerald Walpin speaks: The inside story of the AmeriCorps firing," *Washington Examiner,* June 13, 2009; available at: http://washington examiner.com/blogs/beltway-confidential/2009/06/gerald-walpin-speaks-inside-story-americorps-firing#ixzz1CuJKlYq3 (accessed February 3, 2011).

73. Ibid.

74. "Issa/Grassley Report On Walpin Firing, 10/29/09"; available at: http://www.scribd.com/doc/22824710/Issa-Grassley-Report-On-Walpin-Firing-10-20-09 (accessed February 9, 2011).

75. *Gerald Walpin Appellant v. Corporation for National and Community Services et al.,* http://www.cadc.uscourts.gov/internet/opinions.nsf/AE086493A0FC15488 5257814005A907D/$file/10-5221-1286007.pdf (accessed February 9, 2011).

CHAPTER EIGHT

1. John Fund, "The Net Neutrality Coup," *The Wall Street Journal,* December 21, 2010; available at: http://online.wsj.com/article/SB10001424052748703886904 576031512110086694.html (accessed February 9, 2011).

2. Jim Puzzanghera, "FCC approves net neutrality regulations," *Los Angeles Times,* December 21, 2010.

3. William McQuillen and Todd Shields, "Comcast Wins in Case on FCC Net Neutrality Powers," *Bloomberg Businessweek,* April 6, 2010; available at: http://www.businessweek.com/news/2010-04-06/comcast-wins-in-case-on-fcc-net-neutrality-powers-update6-.html (accessed January 27, 2011).

4. FCC, "Remarks of Commissioner Meredith Attwell Baker," December 9, 2010; available at: http://www.fcc.gov/Daily_Releases/Daily_Business/2010/db1209/DOC-303457A1.txt (accessed January 1, 2011).

5. Edward Wyatt, "Verizon Sues F.C.C. to Overturn Order on Blocking Web Sites," *The New York Times,* January 20, 2011; available at: http://www.nytimes.com/2011/01/21/business/media/21fcc.html (accessed January 29, 2011).

6. Joel Rose, "Critics: 'Net Neutrality' Rules Full Of Loopholes," NPR, December 22, 2010; available at: http://www.npr.org/2010/12/22/132250803/Critics-Net-Neutrality-Rules-Full-Of-Loopholes (accessed January 27, 2011).

7. W. Mark Crain, "The Impact of Regulatory Costs on Small Firms," Small Business Administration, Office of Advocacy, September 2005; available at: www.sba.gov/ADVO/research/rs264tot.pdf (accessed January 27, 2011).

8. "Red Tape Rising: Obama's Torrent of New Regulation," Heritage Foundation, October 26, 2010; available at: http://www.heritage.org/Research/Reports/2010/10/Red-Tape-Rising-Obamas-Torrent-of-New-Regulation (accessed January 27, 2011).

9. Eric Lipton, "With Obama, Regulations Are Back in Fashion," *New York Times*, May 12, 2010; available at: http://www.nytimes.com/2010/05/13/us/politics/13rules.html?pagewanted=1 (accessed January 27, 2011).

10. Jared A. Favole, "Health Care, Financial Reform Skirt Obama Review," *Wall Street Journal*, January 18, 2011; available at: http://online.wsj.com/article/SB1000142 4052748703954004576090301539476490.html (accessed January 27, 2011).

11. Center for American Progress Staff and Senior Fellows, "The Power of the President," Center for American Progress, November 2010; available at: http://www.americanprogress.org/issues/2010/11/pdf/executive_orders.pdf (accessed January 27, 2011).

12. Philip Klein, "Frm Parliamentarian Says Major Parts of HC Law Could Be Repealed Via Reconciliation," *American Spectator*, May 6, 2010; available at: http://spectator.org/blog/2010/05/06/frm-parliamentarian-says-major (accessed January 27, 2011).

13. Alex Keefe, "Illinois to get Ohio, Wisconsin high-speed rail money," WBEZ.com, December 9, 2010; available at: http://www.wbez.org/story/news/transportation/illinois-get-ohio-wisconsin-high-speed-rail-money (accessed January 27, 2011).

14. David Warner, "U.S. plans to inject $53 billion into passenger rail," Reuters, February 8, 2011; available at MSNBC.com: http://www.msnbc.msn.com/id/41021318/ns/business/ (accessed February 9, 2011).

15. "Parliamentary Oversight for Government Accountability," World Bank Institute, 2006; available at: http://siteresources.worldbank.org/WBI/Resources/ParliamentaryOversightforGovernmentAccountability.pdf (accessed January 27, 2011).

16. David Corn, "Waxman: democrats' Eliot Ness: His headline-grabbing investigations are enough to give the GOP heartburn," *The Nation*, February 14, 2005.

17. David Cho, Jia Lynn Yang, and Brady Dennis, "Lawmakers guide Dodd-Frank bill for Wall Street reform into homestretch," *Washington Post*, June 26, 2010; available at: http://www.washingtonpost.com/wp-dyn/content/article/2010/06/25/AR2010062500675.html (accessed January 27, 2011).

18. Alexander Hamilton, Federalist No. 67.

19. Henry B. Hogue, "Recess Appointments: Frequently Asked Questions," CRS Report for Congress, March 12, 2008; available at: http://www.senate.gov/reference/resources/pdf/RS21308.pdf (accessed January 27, 2011).

20. Brady Dennis, "Capitol Hill divided on Obama plan to bypass approval for Elizabeth Warren," *Washington Post*, September 17, 2010; available at: http://www.washingtonpost.com/wp-dyn/content/article/2010/09/16 AR2010091607085.html (accessed January 27, 2011).

21. See, for example, former Representative Phil Hare, Democrat, Illinois, Doug Wilson, "Hare hears from skeptics as he explains health care reform to Quincy crowd," Whig.com, April 1, 2010; available at: http://www.whig.com/story/news/hare-in-quincy-040210 (accessed January 27, 2011).

22. "Sen. Bill Nelson: 'Possibility but not Probability' Health Care Law is Unconstitutional," ABC News *The Note*; February 3, 2011; available at: http://blogs.abc-news.com/thenote/2011/02 sen-bill-nelson-possibility-but-not-probability-health-care-law-is-unconstitutional.html (accessed February 9, 2011).

23. Constitution of the Commonwealth of Massachusetts, Article VII, Adopted June 15, 1780.

24. Loewe, 86–87, 101.

25. James McHenry, *The Records of the Federal Convention of 1787*, ed. Max Farrand, vol. 3, appendix A, (1911, reprinted 1934), 85. Cited in *Respectfully Quoted: A Dictionary of Quotations Requested from the Congressional Research Service*. ed. Suzy Platt, Washington D.C.: Library of Congress, 1989; Bartleby.com, 2003. www.bartleby.com/73/ (accessed January 27, 2011).

INDEX

112th Congress, 131, 202

A

AARP, 66, 70

abortion, 73, 163, 171–75

Adams Capital Management, 44

Adams, J. Christian, 179

Adams, John, 2, 203–4

AFL–CIO (see: Association of Flight Attendants)

Agency for Healthcare Research and Quality (AHRQ), 57

AIG, 34, 199

Almanac of American Politics, The, 6

Alter, Jonathan, 47, 88

America Coming Together, 123

American Association for Justice (AAJ), 145, 147–51

American Bar Association, 153

American Hospital Association, 71

American Wind Energy Association (AWEA), 101

AmeriCorps, 184–86

Arizona, 28, 63, 81–82, 85, 179–84

ASK Public Strategies, 168

Association of Flight Attendants, 24, 121–23, 132

AT&T, 76

Atlanta Journal-Constitution, 47

Audacity of Hope, The, 12, 122, 174–75

Avastin, 63–64

Axelrod, David, 6, 89, 161, 167–68

B

Baker, Meredith, 190

Barone, Michael, ix, 6

Bastiat, Frédéric, 32, 51

Baucus, Max, 71, 113

Bear Stearns, 142, 199

Becker, Craig, 123–24, 132, 134, 200

Belshe, Kim, 138

Berry, John, 139

Berwick, Donald, 78–80, 200

Biden, Joe, 2, 94, 96, 105, 108–10, 121, 141, 144, 167

Big Labor, 117–40

Big Three Automakers, 48

Blackwell, Robert, 12

Blagojevich, Patti, 9

Blagojevich, Rod, 3, 4, 8–10

Bloom, Ron, vii, 6, 30, 34, 36

Boarman, William, 124, 129

Boehner, John, 164

Boeing, 76, 127

Border Patrol, 181

Boston Globe, 141, 144

Boston Herald, 94

Braley, Bruce, 149

Brewer, Jan, 82–85

Bristol–Myers Squibb, 69

Brown, Lawrence, 186

Browner, Carol, 47, 170

Bureau of Labor Statistics (BLS), 137, 180

Bureau of Land Management, 180–81

Burger, Anna, 122, 136

Burke, Edmund, 155

Burson–Marsteller, 110

Bush, George W., 80, 115, 119, 150, 162, 184, 196, 200

    administration of, viii, 18, 167, 186

    automaker bailouts, 28

    free market and, 29

    stimulus package of, 90

C

Caithness Energy, LLC, 102

Calzada, Gabriel, 100

Cambridge, 100, 163

Cantor, Eric, 85

Carney, Tim, 24, 80, 101

Case against Barack Obama, The, viii, 158, 174

Casey, Bob, 131

Cash for Clunkers, 32

Cembalest, Michael, 151

Center for American Progress, 101, 192, 194

Centers for Disease Control (CDC), 57

Chao, Elaine, 133

Chicago, 3–9, 11, 83, 110, 121, 155, 158, 196, 204

Chicago Park District, 3

Chicago Sun-Times, 8

Chicago Tribune, 7, 83, 120

Chrysler, 17–18, 20–21, 23, 28–31, 33, 35, 37–40, 42–48, 50–51, 54, 195

Citigroup, 35

Citizens Against Government Waste, 84

Citizens United, 164

Clean Air Act, 199

Clinton, Hillary, 11, 43, 110, 121

CNS News, 135

Coburn, Tom, 109

Code of Federal Regulations, 192

Cogan, John, 96

Communications Workers of America, 124, 129

Congress, 4–5, 13, 26–28, 31–32, 45–46, 48, 55, 57, 60, 66, 71–72, 75, 77, 82–83, 85, 87, 89, 91, 95, 117, 124–25, 131, 134, 140, 145, 147–48, 152–53, 182–84, 186– 87, 190–91, 194–96, 198–202, 204

Congressional Budget Office (CBO), 58, 62, 68, 77, 91, 94

Congressional Review Act, 199

Constitution, 15, 20, 26, 47, 51, 54–56, 182, 194, 198–201, 203

Constitutional Convention of 1787, 206

Consumer Financial Protection Board, 201

Consumers Organized for Reliable Electricity (CORE), 168

Cornusker Kickback, 72–73

Corporate Average Fuel Economy (CAFE), 47, 49

Credit Suisse, 66

Crist, Charlie, 145

Cuccinelli, Ken, 54–55
Cuomo, Andrew, 27

D
Daley, Patrick, 7
Daley, Richard, 3–5, 7–8, 11–12, 83
Dalmia, Shikha, 49
Dana Corporation, 132
"Dance Draw" project, 112
Davis, Allison, 8–9
death panel (see also: Independent Payment Advisory Board), 63
Delphi, 19, 21, 23, 37
Democratic Left, 36
Department of Health and Human Services, 57
Department of Homeland Security, 4, 113–14
Department of Justice (DOJ), 13, 172–73, 178, 184, 195
Detroit, 30, 43, 45, 47–48
Detroit News, 48
Dodd, Chris, 71, 198, 201
drug industry, 66, 69
Duckworth, Tammy, 161–62
Duff, James, 7
Dunn, Anita, 160
DV Urban Realty, 8

E
Edgar, Jim, 3
electric vehicles, 50, 109
Elmendorf, Mark, 62, 95
Emanuel, Rahm, 6, 9, 28, 51, 72, 76, 82, 85, 161
Employee Free Choice Act (EFCA), 121, 130
EMW Women's Surgical Center, 171, 173
Ervolino, Frank, 123
Executive Order 13522, 139

Export-Import Bank of the United States, 50, 119

F
Federal Aviation Administration (FAA), 4
Federal Communications Commission (FCC), 189–90
Federal Election Commission (FEC), 105, 123, 165
Federal Reserve Act, 199
Federal Reserve Bank, 51, 97
Federation of American Hospitals, 71
Financial Accounting Standards Board, 129–30
First Amendment, 74, 171, 175
Fitzgerald, Pete, 4
Fleischer, Aaron, 173
Flynn, Diana, 178
Food and Drug Administration (FDA), 63, 150
Forbes, 33, 49, 151
Ford, 18, 21, 47, 50–51
Foster, Richard, 62, 117
Founding Fathers, 12
FOX Business Network, 73
FOX News, 15, 160–62, 164
FOX News Sunday, 161
Franklin, Benjamin, 206
Freedom of Access to Clinic Entrances Act of 1994 (FACE), 175
Freedom of Information Act, 140, 197
Frezza, Bill, 44

G
gangster government
    enemies of, 157–88
    friends of, 15, 117–40, 141–56
    Michael Barone and, 6, 44

recovering from, 189–208

taxpayers and, 21–22, 24, 26, 31–32, 37, 48, 60, 108, 115, 119, 126, 131, 138, 142–43, 204

victims of, 33, 37, 115

Garrett, Scott, 85–87

Gaspard, Patrick, 123

Gates, Bill, 36

Gates, Henry Louis, 100

Gattuso, James, 192

Genachowksi, Julius, 189–90

General Electric, 26, 102

General Electric Energy Financial Services, 102

General Motors (GM), 17, 19, 45–46
    bailout of, 25, 33, 49
    common stock, 17, 22–23
    as financial institution, 29
    as "government motors," 49–50
    initial public offering (IPO), 17, 22, 25
    viability plans, 18–19

Gettelfinger, Ron, 22

Giannoulias, Alexi, 165

Gibbs, Robert, 85, 89, 100, 157, 161

GMPAC, 48

Goldman Sachs, 35–36

Government Accountability Office, 110, 128, 181

Government Printing Office (GPO), 124, 129

Grain Inspection, Packers and Stockyard Administration (GIPSA), 152–53

Great Recession, 87

Gregoire, Chris, 93

Grossman, Andrew, 46

H

Hamilton, Alexander, 199

Hamilton, David, 171–75, 179

Health Affairs, 141–42

Health Savings Accounts (HSAs), 60

Hemingway, Mark, 93, 131

Heritage Foundation, 46, 64, 192

Hevesi, Alan, 27

high-speed rail, 90, 103, 105–8, 195

Hill, Christopher, 176

Hired Truck program, 7

Hirsch, Sam, 178

Hoffman, Zach, 59

Hoglander, Harry, 132

Honda, 23, 48

House Agriculture Subcommittee, 152

House Energy and Commerce Committee, 66, 76, 190, 202

House Labor Committee, 134

House Oversight Committee, 196–97

Hudson, Henry, 53–55

Hurricane Katrina, 83

I

IBM, 26

Ikenson, Dan, 33

illegal immigration, 181, 183

Independent Payment Advisory Board (see also: death panel), 63, 123

Internal Revenue Service (IRS), 31, 58, 78, 125, 129, 148, 195

Internet regulation, 189–90

Investor's Business Daily, 101

Iowa Trial Lawyers' Association, 149, 153

Isikoff, Michael, 168

Issa, Darrell, 196

J

Jackson, Jerry, 176, 179
Jarrett, Valerie, 2, 6, 76, 89
Jeszeck, Charles, 128–29
John Deere, 76
Johnson & Johnson, 69
Johnson, Kevin, 184–85
Jones, Emil III, 8
Jones, Jr., Emil, 8–10, 120
JP Morgan, 35, 151
JP Morgan Chase, 43

K

Kansas Trial Lawyers' Association, 143
Kass, John, 7
Katz, Diane, 192
Kennedy, Robert F., 177
Ketchum, Inc., 110
King George, 55
King Juan Carlos University, 100
Kline, John, 134
Koch family, 15, 164
Kouwe, Zachery, 44
Kozinski, Alex, 146
Kurtz, Stanley, 158–60
Kyl, John, 81–82, 84–85

L

Lafayette Building, 119
LaHood, Ray, 83–87
Lauria, Tom, 37, 39–41, 43–44
Lilly Ledbetter Fair Pay Act, 145–46
Lindsey, Bruce, 97

Lindsey, Lawrence, 81, 96
Lipsen, Linda, 151
Louisville *Courier-Journal*, 172
Lukovich, Mike, 47

M

Madison, James, 2, 53, 179, 189
Majestic Weaving, 133
Making Work Pay, 95
Marchionne, Sergio, 39
Marin, Carol, 9
Mayo organization, 63
McBee, Steven, 105
McCain, John, 121, 169, 177
McCarthy, Andy, 179
McConnell, Jack, 153–55
medical malpractice, 70, 118, 142–43, 155
Medicare, 62–63, 66, 70–71, 75–76, 78, 110, 117, 163, 195, 200
Medicare Advantage, 62, 70–71
Medicare Prescription Drug program, 75, 110
Mendell, David, 120, 162, 164
Merck, 69
Merrill C. Meigs Field, 3
Middle Class Task Force, 137, 204
Monk, Lon, 9–10
Morning Joe, 84
Motley Rice, 154–55
Mourdock, Richard, 39, 41–43
MSNBC, 84

N

Nation, The, 197
National Institutes of Health (NIH), 57

National Labor Relations Board, 123–24, 132, 134, 180

National Mediation Board, 131–32, 196

National Rail Act, 131–32

National Renewable Energy Laboratory, 101

National Review, 158, 165, 179

Nelson, Ben, 72–73

Nelson, Bill, 71, 202

net neutrality, 189

New Black Panthers, 179, 184

    voter intimidation case, 176–77

New York Times, vii, 1, 43–44, 80, 88, 167, 192

New York Times Magazine, The, 60, 88

Newsweek, 168

Nissan, 18

Nixon, Richard, 15

No Child Left Behind Act, 110

NPR, 190

O

O'Hare International Airport, 4, 83

Obama, Barack

    2010 State of the Union address, 164, 194

    administration of, vii–viii, 6, 24, 34, 39, 42, 46, 49, 56, 58, 64, 70, 76–77, 81, 83, 87, 89, 91, 94, 96, 100–1, 103, 121, 134, 138–39, 151, 161–64, 172, 179–80, 182, 188, 204

    bailouts and, 13, 21, 28, 45

    Cash for Clunkers and, 32

    Chrysler and, vii, 13, 28, 45–47

    failure of, 117

    federal debt and, 115

    General Motors and, 13, 20, 24, 45–46, 49, 51

    health care and, 53–80, 81, 117–18, 135–36, 143, 145, 166, 182, 192, 194–96, 199–202

    helping friends, 117–56

    labor unions and, 58, 70, 118, 119, 198, 204

    lobbyists and, 13

    Middle Class Task Force and, 137, 204

    private sector and, viii, 12, 14, 139

    punishing enemies, 15, 69, 157–88

    recess appointments and, 13, 80, 200–1

    Richard Daley and, 3–5, 7–8, 11–12, 83

    shovel-ready projects and, 88

    Spain and, 98–102

    stimulus package of, 21, 34, 82, 87, 91, 106, 108–10, 115, 117–18, 138, 166, 180, 191, 196, 205

    as state senator, 3, 12, 174

    Tony Rezko and, 3, 9–10

    transparency and, 13, 74, 126, 133

    trial lawyers and, 70, 118, 141, 143, 149, 151–52, 155, 191, 198, 204

    UAW and, 20

    unions and, 20, 24, 34

    voters and, 14, 90, 114, 149, 160, 164, 205

Obamacare (See also: Patient Protection and Affordable Care Act), 53–80, 81, 118, 135–36, 143, 145, 166, 182, 192, 194–96, 199–202

Overhaul, 18, 45

P

partial-birth abortion, 163

Patient Protection and Affordable Care Act (see also: Obamacare), 54

Paulson, Hank, 28

Pearce, Mark, 123

Pelosi, Nancy, 57, 73, 77

Pension Benefit Guaranty Corporation, 24, 128

Perella Weinberg, 43, 44

Perelli, Thomas, 178

Perez, Thomas, 178

Perlmutter, Deana, 105

Perlmutter, Ed, 105

PhRMA, 64–67

Plato, 1, 15

Politico, 73, 85, 160, 164

porkulus (see also: stimulus package), 81

"The Power of the President", 192

PriceWaterhouseCoopers, 104

project labor agreement (PLA), 119, 136

Promise, The, 85

Puchala, Linda, 132

Q

Quadrangle, 27

R

Radical-in-Chief, 159

Railway Labor Act, 131

Rattner, Steve

    bailout and, 26, 27, 28, 45–47

    as car czar, 6, 17, 25, 27, 30, 32, 34, 35, 191

    Overhaul, 18–22, 24, 26, 29, 30, 37, 42

    settlements, 27

Reason, 49

recess appointments, 13, 80, 199–201

Recovery Act, 90, 94, 95, 97, 104, 105, 108

Recovery.gov, 91, 93, 94

Reid, Harry, 73

Rendell, Ed, 110

Republic, The, 15

Rezko, Antoin ("Tony"), 3, 9, 10, 211

RFID chips, 112

Rivera, Dennis, 122

Roe v. Wade, 174

Rosenberg, Milt, 158

Rove, Karl, 164–66

Ryan, George, 4

S

Schwarzenegger, Arnold, 138

Scobey checkpoint, 114

Scott, David, 152

Sebelius, Kathleen, 74, 143

Sedition Act, 203

Shabazz, "King" Samir, 176

Shadegg, John, 28

Shepherds Flat wind farm, 102, 103

Smartronix, 91

Smith, Adam, 12

Smith, Bradley, 165

Solis, Hilda, 124, 125, 133

Solyndra, 104, 105

Sonoran Desert National Monument, 180

Sorich, Robert, 7

St. HOPE, 185

Stana, Richard, 183

Stanford University, 96

Steelworkers' Union, 36

Stephanopoulos, George, 55, 81, 161

Sterling, John, 8

Stern, Andy, 120, 121, 136

stimulus package (see also: porkulus), 13, 21, 34, 57, 73, 81–83, 87–97, 103, 104, 106, 108–110, 112, 115, 117, 118, 138, 166, 180, 191, 196, 204, 205

stimulus waste, 109

Stupak, Bart, 73

Sullivan, John, 123

Summers, Larry, 102

Sweeney, John, 122

T

Tauzin, Billy, 66

Taylor, John, 96

Tea Party, 17, 62, 204

Terry, Lee, 190

Tester, Jon, 113

This Week with George Stephanopoulos, 81, 161

Thrasymachus, 1

Towns, Edolphus, 196

Toyota, 23, 46, 48

Transportation Security Administration (TSA), 133

Troubled Asset Relief Program (TARP), 26, 28, 29, 32, 34, 35, 43, 44, 87, 196, 197, 199

Trumka, Richard, 121

U

United Auto Workers (UAW), vii, 6, 13, 17–51, 126, 132
    rubber rooms and, 18–23

United States Commission on Civil Rights, 178

University of Chicago, viii, 11

University of North Carolina–Charlotte, 112

UPS, 26, 129

V

Valero, 76

Vanecko, Robert, 7

Verizon, 76, 190

Veterans Administration, 119

Viagra, 19

Vilsack, Tom, 153

Voss, Gerie, 150

W

Wagoner, Rick, 18, 30

Wall Street, 27, 34, 35, 44, 45, 49, 75, 147

Wall Street Journal, 13, 28, 30, 49, 75, 96, 146

Wallace, Chris, 161

WalMart, 26, 146, 147

Walpin, Gerald, 184

Warren, Elizabeth, 201

Wartell, Sarah Rosen, 192

Washington Examiner, vii, viii, ix, 24, 101, 145, 153, 207

Washington Post, 24, 45, 56, 83, 88, 182

Washington Tax Group, 105

Washington, George, 203

Waxman, Henry, 76, 197, 202

Weekly Standard, 81, 96, 97

WGN Radio, 157, 158

Whitacre, Ed, 30, 49

White House Council of Economic Advisers (CEA), 103, 143

White House Task Force on the Middle Class, 136

White, Maureen, 27

Whitehouse, Sheldon, 154

Whitetail checkpoint, 114

Will, George, 84, 101

Willard Hotel, 64

Woodhouse, Brad, 167

Y

York, Byron, 79, 185